WITHDRAWN
HARVARD LIBRARY
WITHDRAWN

GOODNESS AND NATURE

MARTINUS NIJHOFF PHILOSOPHY LIBRARY
VOLUME 22

For a complete list of volumes in this series see final page of the volume.

Goodness and Nature
A Defence of Ethical Naturalism

by

Peter Simpson
Catholic University of America

1987 **MARTINUS NIJHOFF PUBLISHERS**
a member of the KLUWER ACADEMIC PUBLISHERS GROUP
DORDRECHT / BOSTON / LANCASTER

Distributors

for the United States and Canada: Kluwer Academic Publishers, P.O. Box 358, Accord Station, Hingham, MA 02018-0358, USA
for the UK and Ireland: Kluwer Academic Publishers, MTP Press Limited, Falcon House, Queen Square, Lancaster LA1 1RN, UK
for all other countries: Kluwer Academic Publishers Group, Distribution Center, P.O. Box 322, 3300 AH Dordrecht, The Netherlands

Library of Congress Cataloging in Publication Data

Simpson, Peter, 1951-
   Goodness and nature.

   (Martinus Nijhoff philosophy library ; v. 22)
   Bibliography: p.
   Includes index.
   1. Ethics, Evolutionary. 2. Naturalistic fallacy.
3. Naturalism. I. Title. II. Series.
BJ1311.S55 1987   171'.2   86-33180
ISBN 90-247-3477-0

ISBN 90-247-3477-0

Copyright

© 1987 by Martinus Nijhoff Publishers, Dordrecht.

All rights reserved. No part of this publication may be reproduced, stored in a retrieval system, or transmitted in any form or by any means, mechanical, photocopying, recording, or otherwise, without the prior written permission of the publishers,
Martinus Nijhoff Publishers, P.O. Box 163, 3300 AD Dordrecht,
The Netherlands.

PRINTED IN THE NETHERLANDS

To My Parents
Sine Quibus Non

Contents

Acknowledgements xi

Citations and Abbreviations xiii

Introduction 1
   Aims and Procedure of the Book 1
   Contemporary Moral Philosophy 4

PART ONE: THE NATURALISTIC FALLACY

Chapter 1: Moore: Goodness as Indefinable 11
   The Naturalistic Fallacy 11
   Idea of Goodness 13
   Idea of Nature 28
   Ethics and Metaethics 30

Chapter 2: Stevenson: Goodness as Emotive . . . 35
   The Rejection of Moore's Cognitivism 35
   Cognition and Attitudes 40
   Nature of Cognition 47
   Attitude to Science 50

Chapter 3: Hare: Goodness as Prescriptive 57
   The Contrast with Emotivism 57
   Description and Evaluation 59
   Imperatives and Choice 64
   Freedom and Reason 77
   Summary 81

Chapter 4: Critics of Non-Naturalism 83
   The Non-Naturalist Ought 83
   The Non-Naturalist Good 86
   Foot's Cognitive Good 91
   The Naturalism of Lovibond and Lee 98
   Warnock's Cognitive Hobbesian Good 104

Chapter 5: Historical Origins 108
   Review 108
   The Modern Vision of 'Realism' 110
   The 'Realist' Transformation of Good 116
   Kantian Autonomous Morality 121
   Summary 129

PART TWO: THE DEFENCE OF NATURALISM

Chapter 6: Good and Being 135
   Preliminaries 135
   The Idea of Being 139
   The Idea of Good 148
   Natural Desire and Evil 155
   Contrast with Non-Naturalism 163

Chapter 7: Nature and the Science of Nature . . . 167
   The Study of the Natural 167
   Natural Philosophy 168
   Modern Mathematical Science 181
   Merits of Each 190

Chapter 8: Willing and Thinking 194
   The Question Posed 194
   The Idea of Will and of the Willed Good 196
   Good and Action, or the 'Is' and the 'Ought' . . 209
   The Will and Freedom 218

Chapter 9: Virtue and Wisdom 229
   The Need to Ask about the Good Life 229
   Nature as a Guide to the Good Life 232

The Universal Life	239
The Ascent towards the Highest	252
Postscript	261
Some Concluding Remarks	261
MacIntyre on Aristotle	263
Finnis and Grisez on Aquinas	266
Bibliography	271
Index	275

Acknowledgements

Many people have assisted me in the writing of this book. First and foremost of these is Harry Lesser. For many years, both during and after my time as a graduate student at the University of Manchester in England, he was my principal philosophical mentor as well as a friend, and regularly displayed the qualities and discharged the duties of both. His generous encouragement and patient criticism as my doctoral advisor first enabled me to articulate my inchoate ideas into a coherent and ordered form. Without him it would have been impossible to complete the first stages through which this work went as quickly or as well. I would also like to thank Professor S.R.L. Clark who, as doctoral examiner, subjected the results of those first stages to some searching criticisms. I have reworked substantial parts of the last few chapters as a response to what he then said. His own writings, I found, were a particular stimulus to that end.

In a more general way I would like to thank the many friends who sustained and supported me over the years while this work was in preparation. Those in Manchester where I spent three years as a doctoral student; those in University College Dublin where I spent two years as a young philosophy lecturer; and finally those in Washington where I have currently made my home. Without any of them, this work would either not have been completed, or not completed as well and with as much expedition.

Some of the material in this book is already due to appear elsewhere. Chapter 5 contains material to be published under the heading of 'Autonomous Morality and the Idea of the

Noble' in *Interpretation*, vol.14, 2-3, 1986. Chapters 6 and 8 contain material to be published under the title of 'St. Thomas on the Naturalistic Fallacy' in a forthcoming issue of the *Thomist*. Chapters 7 and 9 contain material to be published under the heading of 'Politics and Human Nature' in *The American Journal of Jurisprudence*, December 1986. I am grateful to the editors of each of these journals for permission to use this material again.

Finally I must express a special note of thanks to my friend Pamela Fenty. She kindly proof-read the whole manuscript, and offered innumerable editorial suggestions which saved me from many stylistic as well as material deficiencies.

To the extent this book has value, all these friends and critics must share in the credit. The faults and imperfections that remain are my own responsibility.

This book is, however, not dedicated to any of these friends and critics, but to my parents. Without their unfailing support and guidance, moral, spiritual and financial, over many years, very little at all would have been possible. To them the due of thanks can be acknowledged, but never fully paid.

Washington, D.C.
September, 1986.

Citations and abbreviations

In citing modern works I have followed the convention of giving the year of publication and the page number in that order. Which book is being referred to will be found in the bibliography under the relevant author's name. Sometimes I have not given the year but only the page number. I have done this particularly in the earlier chapters when one book by one author was the main object of attention. I have only done it elsewhere when it will be obvious from the context which book is being referred to. In citing pre-modern works, I have given the title or some readily intelligible abbreviation, and then the page number of the edition referred to in the bibliography, or the number of the relevant sections or parts into which the book is standardly divided. Abbreviations that may not be readily intelligible are listed here.

Aristotle
- *APo*　　Analytica Posteriora
- *de An*　De Anima
- *EE*　　 Ethica Eudemia
- *EN*　　 Ethica Nicomachea
- *MM*　　Magna Moralia
- *Metaph* Metaphysica
- *PA*　　 De Partibus Animalium
- *Ph*　　 Physica
- *Po*　　 Poetica
- *Pol*　　Politica
- *SE*　　 Sophistici Elenchi

Aspasius
  ENC   In Ethica Nicomachea Commentaria

Avicenna
  M   Metaphysica

Kant
  AA   The Prussian Academy Edition of the Complete Works (Akademieausgabe)
  B   The Second Edition of the First Critique

Thomas Aquinas
  CE   Commentary on Aristotle's Nicomachean Ethics
  CM   Commentary on Aristotle's Metaphysics
  CP   Commentary on Aristotle's Physics
  DM   De Malo
  DP   De Potentia
  DPN   De Principiis Naturae
  DV   De Veritate
  ST   Summa Theologiae

Introduction

AIMS AND PROCEDURE OF THE BOOK

This book is concerned with the question of naturalism in ethics. Naturalism is the view that good and bad, right and wrong, are matters of fact or knowledge that can in principle be determined by some reference to 'nature'. As I shall argue shortly, this is perhaps the most important question that any contemporary student of moral philosophy has to face. This book's search for a solution to its difficulties, however, has required going outside the limits within which that question was originally posed. In fact, it is one of the principal messages of the book that it is these limits themselves that constitute most of the problem.

The effort to think beyond the limits of modern moral philosophy has, in my case at any rate, proved to be also the effort to think back into an ancient tradition of philosophy which flourished for so many centuries beforehand, and which modern philosophers have, to their own detriment I believe, rejected or ignored. For this reason this book is an unashamedly ancient book. It might even be called an essay in discarded ideas. There are, of course, differing views about how to approach the problems raised by modern moral philosophy. It is my conviction that a return to ancient ideas is the most helpful and the most fruitful. This, I hope, will become evident from the way my argument develops from the first to the final chapters. The ancient tradition that I am following provides, I contend, just the concepts and distinctions necessary to resolve the puzzles that have gathered themselves about the question of naturalism. These puzzles are genuine and philosophically instructive; that is why they need to be faced and answered squarely. To argue round them, or to dismiss them before getting to grips with them, is to run the risk of hindering philosophical understanding. That, indeed, is the principal reason why the early chapters of this book are concerned with writings that appeared and provoked most controversy several decades ago. For this I make no apology; it is in these writings that the puzzles find their most instructive, not to say classic, expression.

Of course there is more than one ancient tradition. The tradition that I follow here is the one that leads from Plato and Aristotle to Aquinas. When I use, in the chapters that follow, such expressions as "the tradition", or "the older thinkers", or something else of the same sort, it is this tradition and the thinkers who formed it that I have in mind. One might object that Plato, Aristotle, Aquinas and the rest do not constitute a single tradition. The differences between them, especially between Plato and Aristotle on the one hand and Aquinas on the other, are profound and perhaps insurmountable (Jaffa, 1952; Strauss, 1953: ch.4). That there are differences, and that some of them are profound, is clear. But there are also similarities, and some of these too are profound. This is certainly the case in those respects in which I treat these authors as one, namely over the issue of naturalism or the knowability of good. But even were this last claim questionable, that would make little difference to my contentions. My aim has not been to give a thorough and fully nuanced account of the views of other writers, but to use their insights to understand and solve a problem. Even if not all these insights were equally shared by them, and even if the implications of the insights were not always fully realised by them, that still does not prevent or invalidate the use I have made, either of the insights, or of their implications. Ideas may be discovered by certain authors, but they do not remain those authors' exclusive property. They possess an independence of their own. Other thinkers may adopt them and follow them through in ways that the original authors may not have thought about (cf. Aristotle, *SE:* 184b3-8)

But however that may be, the insights I have culled from these authors justify themselves in practice. To each point or problem that emerges in Part One of this book as decisive in the generation and formation of the debate about naturalism, there is an answer given in Part Two that is developed from one of these insights. This is so of the idea of good itself (chapter 6), of the idea of nature (chapter 7), of the relationship between thought and will (chapter 8), and of the very idea of a human good at all (chapter 9). There thus exists, and is meant to exist, something of a symmetry between each Part of the book. The problems uncovered in Part One are each answered in turn in Part Two. The division of the final chapters (chapters 6-9), in fact, follows the number and kind of problems that emerge during the investigation undertaken in the earlier ones (chapters 1-5).

The course of research for this book has naturally led me through the writings of many thinkers past and present. I have, perhaps, not discussed all those whom I might have discussed in this context, nor examined all the works that might in some way have been relevant. But I have, I contend, discussed those writers and examined those works that were necessary for my purpose. As my aim was never to give an exhaustive account of opinions, but to understand a problem, the opinions I examined and the extent to which I examined them were, as the ensuing chapters will, I trust, show, determined by the needs of that understanding. The proper function of philosophy is to find out the truth as far as one can, not, or not just, to learn what other people think.

This should be enough to explain my aims and procedure in this book. But I said at the beginning that the topic of it is naturalism, and that this is perhaps the most important question that contemporary students of moral philosophy can face. This claim needs some justification and explanation. I can do this best, I think, if I give a brief account of the role the question has played in recent moral philosophising.

Diogenes Laertius has preserved for us the story of how Xenophon first met Socrates. "They say, he writes, that when Socrates met him in a narrow place he put his stick across it and prevented him passing by, asking him where all kinds of necessary things were sold. When Xenophon answered, he asked him again where people became good and virtuous. As Xenophon was perplexed, Socrates said, 'Follow me then, and learn.' And from that time forth Xenophon became a disciple of Socrates" (*Lives of the Philosophers:* II.48).

Socrates is regarded as the first philosopher seriously to engage in moral and political philosophy, and his influence on subsequent thought, as this has been mediated in particular by Plato, has been immense. Nevertheless, if during the earlier part of this century one had approached most of those who had, in the English-speaking world at any rate, inherited from Socrates the title of moral philosophers, it is unlikely that one would have been asked the same sort of question. For these philosophers held, or many of them held, that the question was not one to which it was proper for them, as philosophers, to give an answer. The task of moral philosophy was not to teach moral truths or to instruct one how to live, but rather to clarify the "logic of moral concepts" or "the nature of moral discourse." Moral philosophy was not about what people ought to do; it was about "what they are doing when they *talk* about what they ought to do" (Hudson, 1970: 1). But there was a price to be paid for this change in the conception of moral philosophy. Substantive moral questions ceased to be either asked or answered; they appeared only by courtesy, as illustrations, and were held away at arm's length. Moral philosophy gave the impression that "all the important issues [were] off the page somewhere" and had managed to find "an original way of being boring which [was] by not discussing moral issues at all" (Williams, 1972: 9-10; also Wilson, 1961: 1ff.).

Fortunately moral philosophy this century has not exclusively been of the sort just described. Not all practitioners of that discipline refused to discuss real moral issues, or regarded doing so as no part of moral philosophy. Moreover in the last fifteen years or so the situation has noticeably changed. Moral philosophers have tended more and more to turn towards the discussion of substantive moral questions and away from the mere analysis of moral concepts. But along with this increasing interest in substantive questions has come a decreasing interest in the one issue that, before, had seemed so dominant as to exclude every other, namely that of the naturalistic fallacy. That these two changes should be connected is not surprising given what the naturalistic fallacy was and the sort of philosophising it tended to promote.

Naturalism is (as I have already indicated) the belief that there are some things that are objectively good, or good by nature and as a matter of fact. This, it was asserted, was a fallacy, a logical mistake. There was a decisive difference, it was claimed, between the way 'good', and all value terms in general, functioned, and the way factual or naturalistic terms functioned. It was a fundamental error in conceptual analysis to suppose otherwise and to try, with naturalists, to treat value judgements as if they were a sort of factual judgement, or a judgement that could be true or false. Accordingly the most necessary thing was to expose this error. This involved in particular two things: first, showing that the difference in the way 'good' and factual terms functioned did exist, and second, showing what the function of 'good' really was (for it was not thought necessary to pay very much attention to the way factual terms functioned, since the prevailing scientific or empiricist analysis of them was generally agreed on by all). There was, of course, considerable dispute over both these points. Some confirmed naturalists persisted in questioning the first, while those who accepted it often disputed among themselves over the second.

That such disputes about conceptual questions would, on their own, be barren with respect to substantive moral questions is obvious enough. But it is also obvious that how one goes about answering the latter questions will be significantly affected by one's conceptual analysis (cf. Hare, in Daniels, 1975: 81ff.). And this is confirmed by what happened in fact, for naturalists and non-naturalists, who were divided on the conceptual issues, thought that, with respect to the substantive ones, quite different approaches required to be adopted.

The prevalence of the conceptual disputes, and the important consequences they had for one's study of moral questions, meant that one could not really start on these latter without first getting oneself clear about the former. But it was never the case that the former were determinatively settled to everyone's satisfaction for very long, and the result was that philosophers tended to become so preoccupied with the conceptual questions that they seldom got around to the moral ones; or if they did, their discussion of them was soon attacked by their opponents as flawed because founded on a faulty analysis of the terms employed. A certain ennui, one may suppose, with this interminable to-ing and fro-ing led to the following circumstance. Those, on the one hand, who had answered the conceptual questions to their own satisfaction ceased to argue, either altogether or with the same vigour, against their opponents (whom they regarded, perhaps, as invincibly ignorant) and turned instead to the moral questions directly, taking as established the results of their conceptual analysis. Those, on the other hand, who had not answered the conceptual questions turned to the moral questions anyway, hoping, perhaps, that the first would be solved as they went along, or that their study of the second would eventually put them into a better position to solve the first. They generally did this, however, with a certain unease, a certain sense that there was important business left undone (cf. Rawls, 1972: 51-53).

It is clear then that, despite these recent changes in the focus of attention, the issue of the naturalistic fallacy and the conceptual disputes it generated still remain at the centre of concerns in moral philosophy. Indeed a treatment of them, more or less substantial, seems to figure in most moral philosophy courses, and quite reasonably given their historical and philosophical importance. There is a general acknowledgement that one cannot undertake a very serious study of moral philosophy without making a determined effort to come to grips with them. Besides, there are many philosophers who have continued to speak and write about, and to consider important, the naturalistic fallacy and its disputes. One should not be surprised, then, that these disputes still remain for us those with which we must begin. For they constitute the context, if no longer the content, of our moral philosophising. It is, in fact, one of the effects of them, or one of the effects of the preoccupation with the issue of the naturalistic fallacy, that Socrates' question cannot confront us with the same urgency and the same immediacy with which it confronted Xenophon. Even if becoming virtuous, or finding out what we ought to do, is what most concerns us (and indeed, *prima facie*, this seems to be the most urgent and most important thing, as it is certainly the thing that is most effective in driving people to the study of moral philosophy), we cannot begin where Socrates began. We have, so to speak, lost our innocence with respect to that most elementary of moral questions. We must begin, not with it, but with other questions, such as: what sort of question that question is, or how it is to be understood and analysed, or whether, as so phrased, it does not hide a possible logical confusion which it is necessary first to clear up.

So the beginning for us, as students of moral philosophy here and now, is the question of the naturalistic fallacy and all that it involved. This means, in the first instance, that we must get as clear as possible about what the naturalistic fallacy is, or was supposed by the several protagonists to be. This in turn means that it is necessary to undertake a critical re-examination of the major texts. The first chapters, therefore, must be devoted to this task.

PART ONE

The naturalistic fallacy

CHAPTER 1

Moore: Goodness as indefinable

THE NATURALISTIC FALLACY

The term 'the naturalistic fallacy' first appeared in G. E. Moore's enormously influential book *Principia Ethica* (1903). It is to him, above all, that moral philosophy of the present century has been indebted for its preoccupation with this topic (Foot, 1967: 1). He himself believed that he was the first, after Sidgwick, to discover the particular fallacy for which he coined that name. In this he was, in fact, mistaken. Others had noticed the same fallacy, or one very similar to it, long before both him and Sidgwick (Hudson, 1970: 72-74). Only Moore, however, put so much emphasis on it, and insisted so forcefully on its rejection as an indispensable preliminary to any adequate moral theory. Without him the fallacy might have remained, for modern moral philosophy at any rate, a relatively minor curiosity. Moore, in other words, comes first for us. So it is he, not any of his predecessors, who has given "ethics in this century its direction," whose major book is the "*terminus a quo* of modern moral philosophy" (Hudson, 1970: 65, 80), and who advanced, in support of the contention that the fallacy really was a fallacy, the "immensely influential arguments" (Foot, 1967: 1-2). It is evidently with Moore, then, that the investigation of this issue must begin.

The first thing to try to get clear about is what Moore took the naturalistic fallacy to be. Since he describes it in a number of different ways in *Principia Ethica*, it may be well to quote some of these descriptions. The fallacy, he says, is:

> ...the failure to distinguish clearly that unique and indefinable quality we mean by good (59).
>
> ...the fallacy [which] consists in the contention that good *means* nothing but some simple or complex notion that can be defined in terms of natural qualities (73).
>
> ...the failure to perceive that any truth which asserts 'This is good in itself' is quite unique in kind – that it cannot be reduced to any assertion about reality, and therefore must remain unaffected by any conclusions we may reach about reality (114).

At another point Moore explains the naturalistic fallacy in terms of a confusion between two different questions. There are, he says, three classes under which all ethical questions fall. The first class contains the question, 'What is meant by good?'; the second class contains the question, 'To what things, and in what degree, does this predicate (good) directly attach?' or, 'What things are good in themselves?'; the third class contains the question, 'By what means shall we be able to make what exists in the world as good as possible?' or, 'What causal relations hold between what is best in itself and other things?' He then goes on to say that the naturalistic fallacy consists in confusing the first and the second of these three questions (37-38; also: 142-146, 180).

Moore also introduces in this context the term 'synthetic' (143; also: 58). This has application to the naturalistic fallacy in the following way. Good, contended Moore, was a simple, indefinable notion, and consequently no statement of the form, 'This is good,' could be a definition, or analytic, that is, true by virtue of the meaning of 'good'. It must, on the contrary, be synthetic, that is, must assert that something quite different in notion from good has the quality good as one of its properties. Naturalistic ethics supposes that at least one statement of the form, 'This is good,' is analytic, and this is a fallacy (6-7).

It is clear from these quotations that the naturalistic fallacy centres around such terms as, 'definition', 'real', 'natural', 'simple notion', 'analytic' and 'synthetic'. So in order to get clear about the fallacy, it is necessary to get clear about these terms and how they relate to it. This will require detailed discussion of certain key passages in *Principia Ethica*, mainly from chapter one where Moore devoted most attention to them, and where he gave his arguments to show that the fallacy really was a fallacy.

IDEA OF GOODNESS

In this chapter Moore's first concern is to establish what the subject matter of ethics is. He dismisses the commonly held view that it deals with the good and bad in human conduct on the ground that one cannot intelligibly talk about what good conduct is, if one does not know either what good is or what conduct is. What conduct is, he says, "we all know pretty well," so the only question that needs asking concerns good and bad. Moore declares, therefore, that he is going to use the term 'ethics' to cover "the general enquiry into what is good" (2-3). Moore begins his "general enquiry into good" by supposing that good is that property which is common and peculiar to all good things, and when he asks for the definition of this term, what, he insists, he wants is a definition that describes "the real nature of the object or notion" denoted by the word (7). However, despite making this demand, Moore immediately goes on to say that it cannot be met. There is no definition of good; good cannot be defined, and that is all there is to it. In other words (and to put the point less paradoxically), the object or notion denoted by 'good' is simple and unique, like the object denoted by 'yellow', and is identical with itself alone, being incapable of any further analysis.

The sort of definition he was asking for, Moore explains, is only possible where the object to be defined is complex, or made up of several parts. For such a definition consists in enumerating separately the parts that together go to make up the complex object. When these parts have been enumerated and reduced in turn to their simplest parts, no further definition or analysis can take place, for one has reached utterly simple notions (10). Good, like yellow, is such a simple notion, the sort "of which definitions are composed, and with which the power of further defining ceases." Good is not "composed of any parts which we can substitute for it in our minds when we are thinking of it." Moore thinks there must be many such simple notions, and he regards pleasure as another one in addition to yellow and red (8-13).

It is evident that what is governing the discussion here is Moore's views about meaning and knowledge, or, in general, his epistemology. This epistemology he has adopted virtually wholesale from Locke. Though Locke is nowhere referred to by name, it is clear that it is the doctrine of Locke's *Essay* that lies behind the treatment of good in *Principia Ethica* (a comparison between the two works will quickly confirm this fact). Now it is worth noting in this regard, first, that very few philosophers today if any would share Moore's confidence in Locke's theory (though many still believe he is right about the fallacy of naturalism), and, second, that Moore's Lockeanism is a completely unargued assumption. Nevertheless Locke's epistemology is so absolutely indispensable to Moore's thought that without it very little of what he says, in particular about naturalism, makes sense. This will be seen if one looks at his arguments in detail.

Moore agrees with Locke that words signify ideas one has in one's mind. Consequently, in order to find out what a word means one must enter into one's mind and find the idea it is the name of (7-8, 16; cf. Locke, *Essay:* bk.3, chs.1-2). To quote G. J. Warnock (1962: 38), "Early in this century G. E. Moore was conspicuous for his tendency to seek for the meanings of words by a kind of inward gazing, or groping among the contents of his mind, very much in the manner of one searching for a Lockean abstract idea." As has already been seen, Moore holds that some of these ideas are simple and some complex, and that the latter are just various combinations of the former, into which they can, ultimately, be analysed. In this he is again completely following Locke. Moreover, since his understanding of definition is determined entirely by reference to these beliefs about ideas, it is not surprising to find that his definition of definition could have been taken straight out of Locke (cf. *Essay:* bk.3, ch.4, paras. 6-7).

It is because of this Lockeanism that Moore both states the naturalistic fallacy in the way he does, and holds that it is a fallacy. Naturalism he understands to be the attempt to define good, and that can only mean, since good is a simple indefinable idea, that it attempts to equate this idea with some other idea, say pleasure. To say then, as some naturalists do, that good is pleasure, meaning by this that they signify the same thing, is to commit the naturalistic fallacy, because one will have identified good with something that it is not. For good is one simple idea and pleasure is another simple idea, and the two are quite separate and distinct. Of course it may be that pleasure is said to be good in the same way as oranges are said to be yellow (*sic;* 14), but, in that case, what is said is not that good and pleasure *mean* the same, but that pleasure, though different in notion from good, nevertheless has the property good attaching to it; just as oranges, though different in notion from yellow, have yellow as a property attaching to them. What must not be meant is that pleasure is somehow part of the meaning of good, or that the assertion, 'Pleasure is good,' is analytic and not synthetic.

What these comments bring to light is that the naturalistic fallacy, as Moore understands it, is not a fallacy confined to good. Equating any simple notion with any other notion would be the same sort of fallacy (as, for instance, equating orange with yellow). In fact, it is better to adopt the terminology of W. K. Frankena (in Foot, 1967: 57), and speak instead of the 'definist fallacy'. The naturalistic fallacy is just this fallacy as applied to good. For Moore holds that good, unlike yellow, is a non-natural property, so that defining good involves not just identifying it with something it is not, but identifying something non-natural with something natural (13-14). What Moore means by natural, and why he thinks good is non-natural, will have to be investigated later.

Another point to notice here is that the exposure of this fallacy is not a proof that good is simple and indefinable; it rather depends on that belief, for it is because good is simple that it is an error, a fallacy, to try to define it. That good is simple is something Moore holds to be self-evident. He does, however, try to argue that good is simple and indefinable by reducing to absurdity the supposition that it is not. It is these arguments that principally constitute the refutation of naturalism as Moore understands it.

There are only two of these arguments. The first is to the effect that if one defines good in some way or other, then either it will be impossible to prove any other definition to be wrong or even deny any other definition, or one will be just talking about the linguistic habits of certain speakers and not about good (11-12). To take the first alternative. Suppose someone says good is pleasure and someone else that it is that which is desired. They will be unable to argue with each other about who is right. One of them will just be trying to prove that the object of desire (which is what he means by good) is not pleasure, and this is, first of all, not a point about ethics but a psychological point about occurrences in our minds (for, says Moore, this is just what desire and pleasure are), and, secondly, not relevant. His opponent was maintaining the ethical proposition that good is pleasure, and no matter how many times it is shown that pleasure is not the object of desire, it has not thereby been shown that good is not pleasure. Moore gives a parallel case. Suppose someone says that a triangle is a circle and someone else that it is a straight line, and the latter tries to prove the former wrong by showing that a circle is not a straight line; then he has, in fact, said nothing to the purpose, for whether or not a circle is a straight line, it still might be the case that a triangle is a circle. "Which is wrong," Moore makes the opponent say, "there is no earthly way of proving, since you define triangle as a straight line and I define it as a circle." So, Moore concludes, if good is defined as something else, it will be impossible to disprove or deny any contrary definition.

The inadequacy of this argument is startling. It cannot show good is indefinable, else it would not also apply in the same way to triangle and circle, which are manifestly definable (geometers, at any rate, define them). If one can get into the position of Moore's imaginary opponents when one is defining definable things, the fact that one can get into the same position when one is defining good cannot show that it is indefinable. However, it may not have been Moore's intention to show good is indefinable by means of this argument, but only to show that one cannot define it as something that it is not. Once you define good as something else, he is saying, all your arguments about good will not be about good but about that something else. But what if one defines good as what it is? Those who define good as pleasure, for instance, surely intend this to be a definition of good as it is and not as it is not. To make the point clearer. Suppose, in the triangle case, that while one defined it as a circle, the other gave the true definition, namely that it is a plane figure contained by three straight lines. If Moore is right, then showing that a circle was not such a figure would not be at all relevant to showing that it was not a triangle, and, moreover, it would be impossible to say anything to show that it was not a triangle. But this is surely wrong.

The flaw in Moore's argument is that he conflates two different questions. If one looks carefully at what he says, it will be seen that all he really does is to present two opponents who take their definitions for granted and then rely on them to argue about which is correct. As a result they end up, not arguing, but asserting and counter-asserting; in other words, they beg the question. But to beg the question means that there is a question being begged, and, therefore, a question one can ask and not beg. This question, which is what the two opponents should be debating, is about the relation between the *definiendum* and the *definiens*, 'Is this, circle or straight line, the correct *definiens* of this *definiendum*, triangle?' Moore presents them as arguing about the relation between the rival *definientes*, 'Is this *definiens*, circle, the same as that *definiens*, straight line?' The fact that debating the second question does not help one to settle the first, tells one nothing at all about whether one can debate or settle the first. It is the difference between these two questions that allows the geometer to debate whether a triangle is a plane figure contained by three straight lines and not a circle, and which would equally allow the philosopher to debate the correct definition of good. The fact, therefore, that debating whether pleasure is or is not the object of desire is not the same as debating the definition of good, tells one nothing about whether good has a definition or not, and if so what that definition is.

In supposing, in effect, that one cannot debate about definitions, Moore seems to believe that one cannot distinguish in one's mind the *definiendum* and the *definiens* one gives of it, so that the first question, 'Is this the *definiens* of this *definiendum?*', is never a genuine one; it is always obvious straight away. If x is the *definiens* of y, then x and y must be exactly the same thought or idea, and one is not comparing two things but the same thing with itself. Hence if you equate good with pleasure, then, when you think of good, in fact the idea of pleasure presents itself to you. In that case, all disputes about good are, for you, really disputes about pleasure. 'Good' is just the name you use for this idea; it does not signify a distinct idea in itself. The same holds whether the idea in question is simple or complex, for if your idea of A is the idea of x, y, z together, then, for you, A is not a distinct idea but a name for x, y, z.

It is clear, from this, that we are back again with Locke, and it must be stressed that only in the context of Lockeanism does Moore's argument even begin to look plausible. For, in this context, simple ideas are indefinable and there can be no dispute about their definition, for all that is needed is to have the idea and it is fully known at once. Complex ideas are just combinations of simple ideas, and there can be no dispute about definitions here either, but only a verbal one about names and how one proposes to use them. If, for you, A is the idea of x, y, z, then all you are saying is that that is how you propose to use the word A. But if, for someone else, A is the idea of p, q, r, then any dispute here is not about the ideas but about the use of the word A (Locke, *Essay:* bk.4, ch.8). Moore confirms that this is what he is thinking by saying that the other alternative in his argument is that the dispute about good is verbal, merely about how people use the word 'good', whether to signify this idea or that (12).

The upshot of all this is that the disagreement between

Moore, who does not define good, and the naturalists, who do, is itself just about the use of a word. The naturalists say that the idea that 'good' stirs up in their minds is the idea of pleasure, or some such thing; Moore, however, says that the idea that 'good' stirs up in his mind is just itself and quite different from the idea that 'pleasure' or any other word stirs up. Moore's attempted refutation of the definability of good is, consequently, as irrelevant and as inadequate as the refutation of the view that a triangle is a straight line given by the person who says it is a circle. As Frankena pointed out (in Foot, 1967: 61-63), all we have is a dispute about what ideas Moore and the naturalists have in their minds. Moore claims that he always finds at least two ideas, the idea of good and the different idea of pleasure and so on. The naturalists say they only have one idea. Perhaps Moore might accuse the naturalists of moral blindness for not seeing an idea that was there, but then the naturalists might just as well accuse Moore of having moral hallucinations for seeing an idea that was not there. Indeed, if the dispute is just about what ideas one has, it presumably has to be decided by everyone for themselves. In which case it may be that some have this distinct idea of good while others do not. At any rate, Moore has hereby done nothing to show that naturalism is somehow a fallacy.

Before turning to Moore's second argument, it will be well to consider his and Locke's view of definition in more detail. Is it true that the *definiendum* is just the same idea as the *definiens* and that there can be no disputes about definitions except verbal ones? The answer must be no, as the examples of triangle and circle will illustrate. We all have clear ideas of what triangles and circles are, for we can recognise them when we see them and distinquish them from each other and from other geometrical figures; but this does not mean that we have clear ideas about their precise definition. The definition of triangle as a plane figure contained by three straight lines is perhaps well-known and so is little problem, but it is important to realise that we had, at one time, to *learn* this definition; it is not obvious as soon as we perceive examples of triangles. We have, for instance, to make explicit that it is the figure we are talking about and not the thing that has it as its shape, that it is with respect to the number of its sides that it has to be defined, and that these sides must be straight and drawn in the same plane.

Circle, however, is a more instructive example, because, while we are as able to recognise and distinguish circles as triangles, we are not as familiar with the precise definition. It is no use, for instance, saying a circle is a figure contained by a curved line, for this would include ellipses and indeed any number of peculiar shapes provided that the line that contained them was at no point straight. If, to overcome this, one replaced 'curved' with 'round', one would be using the notion of circularity to define circularity (for roundness is circularity under another name); and so the definition will not, as it should, make anything clearer. The same would happen if one put 'uniformly or regularly curved' for 'curved', since what is regular or uniform in the case of curvature is first of all ambiguous (a wave line of constant frequency is uniformly or regularly curved in one sense), and secondly dependent on the notion of circularity for its precise sense; for what 'uniformity' means in this context (what the 'one-formness' in question is) is relative to the notion of curved, and can only be explicated by saying the curvature is such as to be circular.

A correct definition, it must be noted, has to meet certain conditions. It must be informative, that is, must not use in the definition what it is that is being defined, and it must not cover more or less than it should, but just the thing in question. Yet even this need not exhaust what is required of a definition (a look at Aristotle's *Topics* book 6 would be instructive here). Contrary to what Moore and Locke think, there can be any amount of genuine, non-verbal, dispute about the correct definition of things. In the case of circle the correct definition may be stated as follows: a circle is a plane figure contained by one line, which is called the circumference, and is such that all straight lines drawn from a certain point within the figure to the circumference are equal to one another (Euclid, *Elements:* 1, def.15). It is not easy to construct such a definition; it requires study and familiarity with geometrical terms and procedures. It cannot, therefore, be the case, as Moore and Locke think, that to know precisely what something is, it is sufficient just to have the idea or fix the use of a word. It cannot, therefore, be the case that their epistemology is at all adequate to the facts of human knowing.

In order to take account of these facts, it would be more accurate to say that definition is not a matter of having ideas that are known all at once, but rather a matter of penetrating further into one and the same idea. (The word 'idea' is rather unsatisfactory here, at least in the way Locke used it. For him it meant, in effect, 'mental image', and recent writers, notably Wittgenstein, have convincingly pointed out that understanding the meanings or definitions of things is not a question of having such mental images.) Defining is a matter of drawing out and making explicit to oneself the content the idea already has, but which is present only obscurely and not evident all at once. Thus the content analysed and made explicit in the definition is somehow present in the thing to be defined (because it is its content that it defines), and also somehow not present (because this content is not grasped at the same time as, and along with, the initial grasp of the thing). This feature of human knowing is distorted, even denied, by the Lockean analysis, for as it is held that ideas are exhausted as to content as soon as the mind possesses them, wherever a predicate says more than the subject, it can only be because the predicate is a quite different idea from the subject, not a fuller grasp of the same one.

This point is worth stressing. The distortion in question would not be so serious if it were confined to Locke's theory, but in fact it has become quite pervasive in modern philosophical thought (including moral thought) through the so called analytic/synthetic distinction (cf. Hare, in Hudson, 1969: 240-241). This distinction goes back to Kant, who was deeply influenced by the empiricist tradition of Locke through Locke's successor Hume, and according to it all informative statements are synthetic, while all analytic statements are tautologous. For the former assert a connection between different ideas (so to learn this connection is to learn something one did not know in knowing the subject term on its own), while the latter assert the same thing of itself (for they repeat in the predicate what was already said in the subject), and are therefore true by virtue of the terms alone. Definitions are supposed to be analytic in this sense and therefore tautologous. All this, however, is misleading, since, as the example of circle shows, a statement can be a genuine definition, and so 'analytic', and yet informative, or 'synthetic', in that it gives in the predicate something not given in the subject. There is a definite advance in understanding involved here. In the predicate one grasps the thing at a deeper level than one grasps it in the subject, so that the quality of one's understanding of it changes. And this fact cannot be adequately explained according to the traditional analytic/synthetic distinction.

The point at issue here is evidently in need of more detailed elaboration, but this is not the best place to give it; that will be done later in chapters 6 and 7. It has, however, been necessary to introduce these anticipatory remarks at this stage (which, at any rate as to the fact, if not as to the what or the why, are attested to by the examples adduced, especially that of circle), because Moore's defective understanding of definition plays an important role in the second of his two arguments to show that good is indefinable.

This second argument contains in it the so-called 'open-question' argument, and it is this latter which has exercised the most influence over moral philosophers this century. Indeed, it is the *only* influential argument that Moore bequeathed. The 'open-question' argument is one member of another attempted *reductio ad absurdum* of the view that good is definable. Moore proceeds as follows. If 'good' does not denote something simple and indefinable, then either good is a complex whole, or it means nothing at all and there is no such thing as ethics. But good is not a complex whole, nor does it mean nothing, therefore it denotes something simple (15-17).

A number of points must be made about this argument. First of all, the conditional premise depends, for its validity, on the Lockean theory that names signify simple ideas, complex ideas or nothing; and this just goes to show once again how steeped in Locke Moore's thought is. However, the correctness of this theory is not what is of most concern here, but rather the arguments Moore uses to establish his other premise. That the second alternative it mentions is impossible, is regarded as obvious on the ground that one has only to consider attentively with oneself "what is actually before one's mind" when one talks of good, to realise that one's state of mind is quite different from what it is when one thinks, say, of pleasure, and so to see that 'good' by itself definitely does signify something (16-17). This method of proof by intuition of the contents of one's mind has already been criticised, and no more will be said about it here (though it is worth noting that it has not been popular with philosophers since Moore). It is what Moore says to establish the impossibility of the first alternative that is of special interest, for it is here that he introduces the 'open-question' argument.

That 'good' does not signify a complex whole can plainly be seen, declares Moore, from this, that whatever definition is offered of good, "it may be always asked, with significance, of the complex so defined whether it is itself good" (15). So, for instance, if one were to define good as 'what promotes the greatest happiness', one could always ask, with significance, whether what promotes the greatest happiness is, after all, good. But this would be impossible if this really were a definition, for then the question would not be significant; 'good' would just *mean* 'what promotes the greatest happiness'; and the question whether what promotes the greatest happiness is good would not be a significant or 'open' question, but a closed one, because it would be answered at once in the asking of it. Therefore, the proposed definition is not a definition. Although Moore uses this argument against any complex definition of good, it is worth noting that it would apply just as much if the definition offered were simple; say if instead of 'what promotes the greatest happiness', one said 'pleasure'.

The popularity of this famous 'open-question' argument rests, in part, on its appeal to ordinary discourse. If 'good' meant 'pleasant' or 'what promotes the greatest happiness', then, it should be possible, in all cases, to substitute either of them for 'good' without loss or change of meaning. But at least sometimes this is impossible, because in ordinary discourse one cannot, without changing the question, always replace, 'Was his action good?' with, 'Was his action pleasant?' or, 'Did it promote the greatest happiness?' The fact that the same will be found to hold of any other term one tries to substitute for good, shows that good is, in some sense, indefinable (Hudson, 1970: 79).

There are two ways in which this argument might be taken. In the first way, it is making a valid point, for it is drawing attention to a real distinction. When one says, 'Pleasure is good,' one need not be offering, and indeed is not typically offering, a definition of good; rather one is saying that pleasure is one of the things that are good, just as one says that oranges are one of the things that are yellow. In other words, one is not offering a definition of the formal notion of good, but just indicating one of the things that materially instantiate it. Now this distinction is, indeed, part of what Moore is aiming at in his exposure of the naturalistic fallacy, for he says in one of the passages mentioned at the beginning of this chapter, that this fallacy confuses the question, 'What is meant by good?' (formal notion), with the question, 'To what things does this predicate (good) attach?' (material instantiation). But if this is all Moore is saying in the open-question argument, then, while he is quite right to insist that there is a difference, this is, first, not original, and, second, not sufficient to show good is indefinable.

It is not original because it, or something very like it, is found, not just in Sidgwick or others, but even earlier in the Platonic theory of forms, where these are understood as separate from the material things modelled on them. It is also found in Aristotle's and Aquinas' distinction between the idea of the good life, or the idea of happiness, and the different things in which people suppose it is found, as pleasure, fame, wealth and so on (*EN:* 1095b17-25; *ST:* Ia IIae, q1, a7). More importantly, however, adverting to the distinction between the formal notion and the material instantiation of good, only shows that they are different; it does not tell us what they are in themselves, and, *a fortiori*, does not tell us that good, taken in the first way, is indefinable. If the open-question argument is to do this, it must be interpreted as applying directly to the formal notion of good, and not just to the difference between it and the material instantiation. This brings us, therefore, to the second way of taking the argument.

According to this second version, the argument runs something as follows. Whatever definition is given of good, to assert it will be tautologous, and to deny it self-contradictory. So if good is defined as pleasure, then to say, 'Pleasure is good,' is equivalent to saying, 'Pleasure is pleasure,' and to say, 'Pleasure is not good,' is equivalent to saying, 'Pleasure is not pleasure.' Now this would reduce ethics to triviality, for any debate about whether pleasure was good would reduce to the trivial debate about whether pleasure was pleasure (12, 21). The same reduction to triviality would ensue whatever definition was given of good. But, in fact, ethics is not trivial. Not only is the debate between hedonists and non-hedonists over whether pleasure is good a serious and significant one, but, more importantly, with respect to anything said to be good, it is always an open question, not an insignificant tautology, to ask if it really is good.

This interpretation of Moore's argument, while it can be found in recent authors (Hudson, 1970: 79, 86-87), is nevertheless shot through with Moore's Lockeanism, and gets all its force from the dubious analytic/synthetic distinction. This can be seen if it is stated in a more formal manner as follows:

(i) All definitions are tautologies – to say that triangles are plane figures contained by three straight lines is equivalent to, and as trivial as, saying plane figures contained by three straight lines are plane figures contained by three straight lines; and to say that triangles are not plane figures contained by three straight lines is equivalent to, and as self-contradictory as, saying plane figures contained by three straight lines are not plane figures contained by three straight lines.

(ii) It is impossible to find a proposed definition of good whose assertion results in a tautology, and whose denial results in a self-contradiction; for it is always an open and significant question to ask of the proposed definition if it is itself good. To say, for instance, that pleasure is good is not equivalent to, nor as trivial as, saying pleasure is pleasure, and to say that pleasure is not good is not equivalent to, nor as self-contradictory as, saying pleasure is not pleasure. The same will happen whatever definition one proposes.

(iii) Therefore it is impossible to define good.

The flaw in this argument is proposition (i). What it says about definitions is false, as has already been said above. Or, to be more precise, what it says about definitions is only true if one accepts Locke's epistemology. Moore does accept that epistemology, and that is why, for him, this argument carries weight. As Locke's theory has already been criticised, and as more detailed remarks will be made on this issue in chapters 6 and 7 below, no more will be said here.

It is worth noting one further criticism of the open-question argument, namely that there are a variety of ways in which a question might be said to be open. First, every question, no matter what it is, is open to the one who does not yet know the answer, but closed to the one who does. So, for instance, the question of the mean distance between the earth and the sun is closed to the one who has investigated and decided it, but not to someone who has not. Second, a question can be open in the sense that the answer is not to be determined from the terms, but in some other way. In this sense the question about the mean distance between the earth and the sun is still open even when one has answered it, for it is decided by observation and experiment. Third, a question can be open in the sense that, while it is decided from the terms, the answer is not obvious in the stating of the question, but requires reflection and analysis. In this sense the question whether a circle is a circle is closed, but not the question of its precise definition; though it is worth adding that this latter question is, in the first sense of open, open to the non-geometrician and closed to the geometrician. In view of these differences it is evidently inadequate, if one wants to prove something about good, to say that in ordinary discourse questions about it are open. One must go further and indicate in what way they are open, whether in one of the above ways or in some other. This, however, is not done, and it is consequently left unclear whether they are open because in ordinary discourse, which is, after all, just the reflection of ordinary perceptions, there is a great deal of ignorance about good, so that either its definition, or its instantiations, or both, are left undetermined (though they are not left undetermined by those who are not ignorant about good but have examined and investigated it); or whether they are open because there is something peculiar about good that sets them significantly apart from other questions containing other terms.

So much, then, may be said about Moore's arguments to show that good is a simple, indefinable property. But before proceeding further, it is desirable at this point, in order to avoid possible misunderstandings, to stress two things. First, nothing has so far been said in criticism of Moore to show that good is not peculiar in some way; all that has been done is to establish that Moore, at any rate, has done nothing to show that it is (though it will, in fact, be seen in succeeding chapters that good is peculiar in certain important respects). Second, despite the appeal to the examples of circle and triangle, it has not been said, nor has it been necessary to say, that the idea of good is altogether on a level with them. They were introduced in the first place because Moore himself introduced them, but they were continued with because they proved useful examples to show that he was wrong about the nature of definition. Since his arguments about good depend on his views about definition, it was sufficient, in order to refute those arguments, to bring forward examples of definitions that were contrary to his views, quite regardless of whether these examples might or might not be significantly different from good in other respects.

Moore's refutation of naturalism has so far only been examined as it concerns the claim that good is a simple and indefinable property. But Moore also maintained that good was a non-natural property. The reason why trying to define the indefinable term 'good' is a naturalistic fallacy, while trying to define the indefinable term 'yellow' is not, is that, in the case of 'good', this means identifying something non-natural with something natural (13-14). What is meant, therefore, by all this must now be examined.

The term 'natural' is nowhere made an express topic of concern by Moore in *Principia Ethica* (and what he said later in Schilp, 1968: 581-592, does not make things much clearer, as he admits), so it is necessary to pick up what he means by it from what he says by the way. A first clue is found where he says that if we start by supposing good has a definition, we will believe that it can mean nothing else than some one property that we will then try to discover; but if we recognise that, as far as the meaning of good is concerned, anything whatever can be good, we start with a much more open mind (20). It seems that, somehow or other, Moore felt that to say good has a definition is to restrict its application; but good must be able to attach to anything, so it cannot be identified with any particular thing. If good is to be universal in this sense, Moore seems to think that it must be outside, not inside, the realm of things and of being. This is the nearest one gets in Moore to a reflection of the old medieval belief that *bonum et ens convertuntur*, or that good and being are convertible. The difference is that, while the older thinkers secured this universality by identifying good and being, Moore wants, it seems, to do so by separating them. He would no doubt say that as some beings are clearly bad, good and being cannot be the same, but this reply ignores the subtleties with which the older thinkers explained their position. Besides Moore holds that good and reality are separate for other reasons.

In defining good as some property of a natural object, says

Moore, naturalism has replaced ethics "by some one of the natural sciences" (as psychology, sociology or physics). By 'nature' Moore says he means the subject matter of such sciences, and it includes "all that has existed, does exist, or will exist in time;" and by 'natural object' "something of which the existence is admittedly an object of experience" (38, 40). He reveals more of what he means here in his discussion of the Stoic injunction to live according to nature (41-45).

Moore understands this phrase as pointing to a belief that there is a natural good, and that nature fixes what is good as it fixes what exists. So, for instance, it might be thought that health is good and that what health is is fixed by nature. The result of this, says Moore, would be that ethics was based on science. But this cannot be admitted. If health is defined in "natural terms" then it can only mean the *normal* state of an organism, for disease too is something natural; but the normal is not necessarily good, because genius is abnormal and yet good. Consequently, if health is defined in such a way as already to include good in its notion, it cannot be a natural definition, and certainly not a definition of the notion as it appears in medical science. Health, when defined naturalistically, means 'normal', and does not entail its goodness; and when health does entail its goodness it is not defined naturalistically.

It is clear from this that, for Moore, the real and the natural are determined by reference to modern science, and modern science only deals with facts, not with good or value. That modern science exhausts the whole of being is taken as obvious by Moore (as it has been by many before and since), but it is not obvious. For instance, there is a quite intelligible sense in which disease is not natural, not because it does not happen by nature, but because it acts contrary to the nature of the thing that suffers it; while health, on the other hand, is natural because it works in accordance with, and preserves, the thing's nature. It is also quite intelligible to say that in this sense of nature, disease is bad and health good. If modern science, with its 'value-free' methodology, has no place for this, then that tells us something significant about the limitations of this science, and shows that its competence cannot be as total as Moore, and others, think (more will be said on this topic in chapter 7).

That modern science is one of the major factors behind Moore's rejection of naturalism is important because it plays a similar role in the case of many others who also reject naturalism. In fact, it is only against this background that Moore's belief in the indefinability of good at last takes on a certain plausibility. If defining good means equating it in some sense with being, or a part of being, and if being (or reality or nature) is identified with the objects of modern science, and if this science is understood as evaluatively neutral, then any attempted definition of good will be erroneous, since it will involve equating something in one class, the class of values, with something in another class, the class of facts. It thus emerges that, in Moore's opinion, the reason why naturalism is a logical error, a fallacy, is that it is first of all a factual error, an error about the nature of being or the nature of nature. What, therefore, lies behind his views on naturalism is not so much logic as a certain theory of physics; and since his ethics depends, for its elaboration, on his prior rejection of naturalism, it follows that if anyone's ethics is based on science it is as much Moore's as the Stoics'. It is at any rate the case that views about science lie at the root of his thinking here, for this last argument may be summarised thus: nature is not the source of good or value because nature is the province of modern science, and modern science is value-free. These beliefs, however, are left undefended and unanalysed in *Principia Ethica*.

ETHICS AND METAETHICS

Before leaving Moore, there is something else about his discussion of good that requires to be dealt with. This is the influence that his work had, not just in making the naturalistic fallacy the central theme of much modern philosophy, but also in initiating the study that came to be known as metaethics.

Moore equates ethics with the general enquiry into good

and so, in effect, equates it with the enquiry into good everywhere and in everything. This would include, presumably, the good of fishes, which Aristotle quite sensibly supposes is different from the good of humans, and which, therefore, he just as sensibly does not discuss in his ethics (*EN:* 1141a22-23). Moore behaves as sensibly for he does not examine the good of fishes either, but he does not speak as sensibly. Not only does he say ethics must investigate the truth of all universal predications of goodness (36; and also 3), he goes so far as to say that it is a mistake to regard the subject matter of ethics as confined to human conduct (40). Yet, despite this, he himself, in deed if not in word, does so confine it. (Moore did say later that there is a particular sense of good he has been concerned with in ethics, but the other senses he has in mind all seem to be ones related back to this sense, as if ethics was still somehow, in his view, the study of good as such; – in Schilpp, 1968: 554ff.)

The reason why he says ethics is concerned with good simply and not good in human life and conduct, is, one may suppose, his Lockean belief that good is simple and unique, and so the same everywhere. Hence, to see what good is in one set of things is necessarily to see what it is in all other sets. But while this helps to explain what he says, it does not help to explain what he does; for it does not explain why both he and all other ethical writers confine their study to good in human life and conduct. By contrast, for Aristotle the subject matter of ethics is not good simply, but the doable human good. That is why he excludes from consideration the non-human good, as the good of fishes, and the non-doable good, as Plato's idea of the good. In short Aristotle's procedure is perfectly intelligible in the light of what he says, but Moore's is not. One is forced, in view of this, to ask how far Moore had really thought the whole matter of moral philosophy through. One's doubts here are reinforced by a criticism of him made by later thinkers (e.g. Warnock, 1967: 15-16; Frankena, in Schilpp, 1968: 98-110, esp. 100) that shows how peculiar as ethics Moore's ethics is. It is to the effect that good has a certain 'magnetism', for there is a connection between calling something good and acting; good somehow draws to action. But what is the connection between a Moorean simple quality and action? Where is its drawing power? Why should recognising that something has this quality be at all relevant to how we should behave? Moore has left this connection between good and what it concerns us to do wholly unexplained.

It is true that Moore did endeavour to reply to Frankena on this matter (as well as others), but he seems stubbornly to keep missing the point. The most he says is that there is a connection between good and ought, but he gives no explanation of how this is so; whereas this is precisely the issue that has caused such controversy since and forced other thinkers to give radically different analyses of good to Moore's own. That Moore failed to see a problem here is an indication of the correctness of the doubts just expressed (1903: 23-27; in Schilpp, 1968: 573-581, 600-607).

These deficiencies in Moore's thought can be put down to his belief that good is altogether simple; so it is worth pointing out here that for Aristotle good is so far from being simple that it is systematically ambiguous. It is not univocal, as it is for Moore, nor is it equivocal; it is 'analogical'. 'Healthy', for instance, truly applies to urine, medicine and horse, but not in the same way, for urine is said to be healthy because it is a sign of health, medicine because it is a cause of health, and horse because it is a subject of health. They are all the same in that they are all referred to one thing, health, but different in that they are referred to it in different ways (*Metaph:* 1003a34-b1). There is also another sort of analogy where what is the same is not the one thing referred to, but a certain oneness of proportion, that is, where the first is related to the second as the third is related to the fourth. As sight is to the body so is mind to the soul (*EN:* 1096b28-29; also: *APo:* 98a20-23; *Po:* 1457b16-18). Good is, suggests Aristotle, analogical in this sort of way. Nevertheless he does not regard the investigation of good in this general sense as part of ethics (it is more proper to "another study;" *EN:* 1096b31). Moore shows no sign of being aware of this kind of meaning (he sees everything from the narrow perspective of Locke), and though his successors are not as Lockean as he was, many of them have nevertheless accepted his insistence that one of the jobs, if not the whole job, of moral philosophy is to examine the meaning of good. But if, as Aristotle had already noted, this is really a quite different study, then one should expect the inclusion of it in moral philosophy to have some serious consequences. And this has, in fact, happened.

To be accurate, the study of the meaning of good was said to belong to metaethics, rather than to ethics proper. Metaethics is a kind of higher order study dealing with the analysis of ethical concepts (as opposed to the making and justifying of moral judgements). The effect of it, however, was to narrow down the scope in which good was investigated. For metaethics is not the same as the metaphysics of older writers (where the meaning or nature of good, in its broadest sense, used to be examined). Metaethics is geared towards ethics, so that there is an inevitable tendency to study good only in the context of human action, and other senses of good are either subordinated to this context, or ignored altogether. Hence the doable human good of ethics becomes the paradigmatic sense of good and governs and influences the understanding of all other senses. This generates a twofold impoverishment of philosophical research. On the one hand (as partly explained earlier in the Introduction) attention gets focussed on what good means, and the question of what the good for humans is, or what it is that should be pursued or done, is left unexamined or dismissed to another sphere and to other professions (Hudson, 1970: 1; Stevenson, 1944: 1). On the other hand, the sense of good that is focussed on is related almost exclusively to the context of human life and conduct, and the question whether there are other senses, how many, what they are and how related to this sense, is lost to sight. It is, for instance, significant that while contemporary philosophers are quite ready to divide good into moral and non-moral senses – implying that this is an exhaustive division – they nevertheless immediately go on to assume that this is a division within things that are good in some way for human persons. They thus intimate that, for them, good only has application in human contexts (albeit some of these are non-moral), or in other words that the only good there is is the human good. This is a point that will resurface more prominently in the discussion in later chapters.

These unfortunate consequences of Moore's ethical views would not be unfortunate if good was really simple, unique and the same everywhere, for then no elaborate analysis would be needed; once good was understood in one place it would be understood in every other place. The impoverishment of philosophy with respect to the analysis of good will not take place if Moore is right about good. Very few philosophers since Moore have been prepared to accept that he was right about good. Most of them, nevertheless, came to believe that the right place to examine good was within metaethics. In the absence of a Moorean doctrine of good, however, this belief can no longer be regarded as safe. One is, therefore, forced to wonder how far moral philosophy this century was, or indeed is, capable of doing justice to the subject either of ethics or of good. But however this may be, one is certainly required to undertake a better analysis of good than Moore has managed to give us.

CHAPTER 2

Stevenson: Goodness as emotive

THE REJECTION OF MOORE'S COGNITIVISM

Moore's theory was found unacceptable by subsequent thinkers for two basic reasons. The first has already been mentioned, that it failed to account for the connection between good and action. The second was that it appealed to an unexplained kind of knowing (Warnock, 1967: 15). Good was supposed to be a non-natural and non-observable property; so how was it that we came to know it? The only solution offered was that we 'intuited' it (as Moore himself suggested, 1903: 148). But is this any more than a word to veil one's ignorance? We know how we recognize colours and other observable properties, and how we recognize real things in general, but what faculty have we got to recognize this non-observable and non-real property? If it is not part of real objects, if it is not even existent (1903: 124, 110), what is it? In protecting his property of goodness from any contamination with nature, Moore seems to have reduced it to nothing.

That there is, anyway, something dubious about Moore's appeal to intuition becomes clear when one examines what it is that he intuits as being good. Supreme goodness, the ideal, he finds to exist in the enjoyment of beautiful objects and beautiful people (181ff.), and while this might be an ideal for some (notably Moore's colleagues in the Bloomsbury Group), it is not for everyone. Mother Teresa of Calcutta, for instance, does not seem to have modelled her life on Moore's ideal, nor did St. Francis of Assisi. But, less dramatically, if intuition is the way we detect goodness, and if we all have intuition (as Moore supposes), then why do we intuit so many different things as good (Ayer, 1946: 141)? Why is the ideal of car workers, miners and any number of others different from the ideal of Cambridge professors? Does one or the other group lack intuition, or possess a defective one? And if so, which is it, and how could we know? For certainly something must be said to explain the phenomenon of rival conceptions of the ideal, if goodness is supposed to be grasped by intuition. Perhaps an answer could be given to these and the like questions, but Moore himself did not give one.

In view of these difficulties it seemed preferable to other thinkers simply to deny that good was a property at all, or something that was supposed to be an object of knowledge. This got rid of the unintelligible intuition with its associated non-natural property, and left the way open for an interpretation of good that explained its connection with action. It was the exclusively cognitive character of Moore's good that made this connection difficult, if not impossible, to account for, and if good was denied to be an object of knowledge (however non-natural an object), it ceased to be exclusively, indeed at all, cognitive. Accordingly it could be fixed instead in something more volitional, where the connection with action would be intelligible because immediate and direct. A non-cognitive analysis of good was thus attractive because it promised to solve two problems at once.

The rejection of a cognitive account of good was most emphatically presented by A. J. Ayer in *Language, Truth and Logic*. According to Ayer, all meaningful statements are either analytic (as 'bachelors are unmarried'), or empirically verifiable (as 'there are nine planets'). The former are known to be true by virtue of the meanings of the words, while the latter can only be known by observation and science. Moral and, in general, evaluative statements are neither of these; so they are literally meaningless. Or, to be more precise, ethical concepts, like good, are pseudo-concepts and are not names of properties or of anything factual. They serve only as means to express approval and disapproval, and so are analogous to exclamations like 'Boo!' and 'Hurrah!', or to the tone of voice in which one speaks. They are 'emotive' terms, whose job is simply to express feelings, or pro- and anti-attitudes. As Ayer himself put it:

> The presence of an ethical symbol in a proposition adds nothing to its factual content. Thus if I say to someone, 'You acted wrongly in stealing that money,' I am not stating anything more than if I had simply said, 'You stole that money.' In adding that this action is wrong I am not making any further statement about it. I am simply evincing my moral disapproval of it (1946:142).

The main trouble with Ayer's thesis is that it is self-refuting. The statement that all meaningful statements are either analytic or empirically verifiable must itself be meaningless since it is neither of these. Still, if the thesis destroys itself, it at least has the merit of transparency. Ayer freely admits that his ethical theory has, as its foundation, the way he analyses such terms as 'truth' and 'fact', and that these analyses are constructed in the light of modern science. In other words, he reveals that a cognitive or naturalist view of good is wrong, in his opinion, because it misunderstands what a fact, or something natural, is. It gives them a sense that is not sanctioned by modern science. He thus makes it far more evident than Moore did that what underlies the claim that naturalism is a fallacy is a prior claim about nature.

Ayer said that 'emotivism' as a theory of ethics could stand independently of his self-refuting thesis (1946: 26-27). This may be so, but it certainly has a close connection with a particular view of science and thereby of facts. How close this connection is, and what sort of contribution was made to modern moral philosophy by emotivism, especially with respect to the naturalistic fallacy, must be considered not in Ayer but in Stevenson, who was by far its major exponent. Ayer did, it is true, refine his presentation of the theory later, but it was Stevenson, in his book *Ethics and Language* (1944), who gave the most comprehensive and elaborate account of it.

Taking a lead from Moore, Stevenson conceives of his task as metaethical. His concern is conceptual analysis, in particular of the meanings of the ethical terms, such as 'good', 'right', 'just' and 'ought' (1944: 1, and Preface). He is not going to treat of matters of substance: "The most significant moral issues...begin at the point where our study must end" (336). He therefore omits Moore's second and third questions. His own study is to be "detached" and "relatively neutral," and it is not to run the risk, by engaging in real moral issues, of being "distorted" into "a plea for some special code of morals" (1).

Again following Moore, Stevenson appeals to the open-question argument to reject naturalism. To quote what he said in a different work:

> No matter what set of scientifically knowable properties a thing may have (says Moore, in effect), you will find, on careful inspection, it is an open question whether anything having these properties is good....We must be using some sense of 'good' which is not definable...in terms of anything scientifically knowable (1963: 15).

As already stated in the treatment of Moore, this argument, if it proves anything, proves only that there is a difference between the formal notion of good and what things instantiate it. The argument does not tell us anything about the formal notion of good as such, whether it is definable or not, and if so how. More than one explanation can be given of the difference in question, and more than one explanation can be given of what 'good' means. Even in the case of a strict definition the open-question argument proves nothing, because there is nothing to show that the openness it appeals to is such as to exclude definitions. The open-question argument leaves open, so to speak, the question about definitions. It is not, therefore, by relying on this argument that one can establish the truth of one's account of the formal notion of good and, as was seen, Moore relies on his Lockean intuition to establish his view that good is simple and indefinable. The same must be said of Stevenson, for he too relies on something else to establish his view about good. He appeals, like Ayer, to science (as the above quotation in part reveals), and so to the last of the factors that was discussed in the chapter on Moore.

However, it is not as obvious as it is with Ayer that this is Stevenson's court of appeal because he declares that he is, in fact, appealing to ordinary language, to the way people speak in moral contexts in daily life, and even to "the most obvious facts of daily experience" (1944: 24, and Preface). His conclusions, he says, "are based on observations of ethical discusions in daily life and can be clarified and tested only by turning to that source" (13; cf. also Hudson, 1970: 114).

This, however, is not the case. His conclusions, like Ayer's, are that moral terms are not cognitive but emotive, and do not serve to signify knowable properties but to express one's attitudes for and against things. Ethical disagreements are ultimately, and even primarily, not a question of differences in belief, or differences in opinion about what is the case, but differences in attitude, or in feelings, wants, desires, preferences and so on (1944: 3). But Stevenson is wrong to think that he appeals to ordinary language to establish this, or at any rate he is wrong to think this is all or principally what he appeals to. This is evident from the fact that ordinary language draws no such clear distinction between belief and attitude with respect to ethics. In ordinary language, the statements, 'Giving money to the poor is good,' and, 'Stealing is wrong,' are expressions of belief. As statements they are, as far as language goes, not different from, 'Stealing is more prevalent in the cities than the country,' or, 'There is only one moon orbiting the earth' (cf. Lovibond, 1983: 26-27). The linguistic facts cannot, therefore, enable Stevenson to say that ethical statements are not beliefs. The same holds if one considers the way ordinary people understand ethical statements and behave with respect to them. At least some people, and perhaps all of us at some time, treat certain ethical statements as factually true or false, that is, as expressions of belief stating what is the case (cf. Foot, 1978: 100).

Of course, none of this proves that ethical statements are matters of belief, for ordinary language, as an expression of ordinary perceptions, may be wrong, just as those perceptions themselves may be wrong (we speak, for instance, of the sun rising and setting, though it does not literally do so; yet these expressions are 'true' in ordinary discourse). Nevertheless, it does show that if one says ethical statements are not expressive of beliefs, one is not so much following ordinary language as going against it (just as if one said that the sun neither rises nor sets one would not be following ordinary discourse but astronomical theory). So Stevenson's conclusions are not, as he claims, based on "observations of ethical discussions in daily life." That they are, in fact, based on science, or his convictions about science, will be shown in what follows. But, first, it is worth pointing out the importance of his, and Ayer's, contention that ethical statements are emotive. This claim constitutes not only a radical departure from Moore, but requires a reformulation of the fallacy of naturalism. This is no longer held to be, as it was by Moore, an error within cognition, consisting in the confusion of a non-natural property with a natural one, but an error between something cognitive and something non-cognitive. This was the decisive move as far as post-Moorean ethical thought was concerned.

COGNITION AND ATTITUDES

Stevenson agrees with Moore that naturalism tries to make ethics into a natural science (1944: 108-109, 276), but he goes on to add that "wherever Moore would point to a 'naturalistic fallacy', the present writer…would point to a persuasive definition" (273). A persuasive definition, he says, is one where:

> …the term defined is a familiar one, whose meaning is both descriptive and emotive. The purport of the definition is to alter the descriptive meaning of the term…but the definition does not make any substantial change in the word's emotive meaning. And the definition is used, consciously or unconsciously, in an effort to secure, by this interplay between emotive and descriptive meaning, a redirection of people's attitudes (210).

Stevenson gives 'culture' as an example. This word carries emotive meaning, in the sense that it is something towards which we are favourably disposed, but it also has descriptive meaning, in the sense that it signifies certain definite qualities, such as being educated, well-spoken and so on. If someone were to say that A, who lacked these qualities, was nevertheless really cultured, because true culture consists in imaginative sensitivity and originality which A has, then this would be a persuasive definition. It keeps the favourable attitude attached to 'culture' but fits it to other qualities that 'culture' does not typically signify (211). 'Good', Stevenson points out, is particularly liable to being persuasively defined, since it carries a great deal of emotive meaning but is descriptively vague, so that it can be predicated of almost anything (218). Naturalism gives a persuasive definition of good, he contends, because it tries to say that the goodness of a thing is simply some property it has, say pleasure, and ignores the pro-attitude that is thereby expressed and evoked. For to say pleasure is good is never just stating something, as naturalists believe. It is above all expressing and evoking approval of pleasure, and the error of naturalism is not to recognise this element of approval as an extra, non-cognitive element in all assertions of good. To understand what Stevenson is getting at here, it is necessary to look more closely at his analysis of ethical or emotive terms, attitudes and beliefs.

In his view, ethical writers have seriously neglected disagreement in attitude, as opposed to disagreement in belief (16). In the latter case one person says that *p* and another says that *not-p*, and each tries to give proof of his belief. Examples would be disagreements about the nature of light-transmission or the voyages of Leif Ericsson. In the former case the disagreement is not in this but in purposes, aspirations, wants and so on. Examples here would be disagreements about what restaurant to go to for a meal or whom to invite to a party. Here the disagreement is in the opposed attitudes that each has to the same object (2-3). As Stevenson himself put it:

> The two kinds of disagreement differ mainly in this respect: the former is concerned with how matters are truthfully to be described and explained; the latter is concerned with how they are to be favored and disfavored, and hence with how they are to be shaped by human efforts (4).

Attitudes, moreover, are something logically distinct from, and independent of, beliefs; for after all the facts have been settled, attitudes are still open and may be favourable or unfavourable. In this respect ethics, which is principally about attitudes, goes beyond belief, and its methods beyond logic (6, 14, 113-114). Stevenson does not deny, however, that the connection and interplay between attitudes and beliefs may be subtle and complex, nor even that in some instances attitudes may be so tied to beliefs that agreement in belief assures, at once, agreement in attitude. What he does assert is that the two are always logically distinct (if they are connected it is a matter of fact, not of logic). Disagreement in attitude can never be resolved entirely by first establishing agreement in belief, for it may remain stubbornly unresponsive to any further argument (30-31).

Now it is worth noting that this distinction between belief and attitude, or between acts of thought and acts of desire or will, is by no means new, and that Stevenson is not saying anything particularly original in pointing it out. What is peculiar to him is his view of the relationship between the two things. For he holds, first, that, as far as truth or the facts are concerned, attitudes are always open and no attitude is entailed by what is the case; and second, and more significantly, that all attitude-expressing terms, or all terms of value, always include a non-factual, non-cognitive element, namely their emotive element, as an essential part of their *meaning*. So 'good', 'virtuous' and 'just', for instance, cannot be unpacked solely in terms of their cognitive content; they always have as well an irreducible volitional element. This extra element is expressed by Stevenson in two different ways according to two different analyses he gives of, 'This is good.' The first is, 'I approve of this; do so as well' (81). The second is more compendious, and runs as follows: 'This has qualities or relations X, Y, Z...,' except that 'good' has as well a laudatory emotive meaning which permits it to express the speaker's approval and tends to evoke the approval of the hearer (207). The second is said to differ from the first in that it includes, as part of the meaning, reference to the qualities of the object in virtue of which one approves of it, while the first may suggest these but does not strictly mean them. However it is less important to follow Stevenson in this difference than to notice that in each case the extra non-cognitive element is part of the meaning of good. Hence his tendency to equate ethical statements, not with statements, but with other forms of expression that are indicative already of the presence of acts other than cognitive, as imperatives, ejaculations and requests (21, 37).

Stevenson proposes this analysis of the meaning of good in order to account for its connection with attitudes or desires. He seems to think it is evident that this connection will not be accounted for if attitudes or desires are not included within good as part of its meaning. But it is necessary to point out, in reply to this, that certain of the older philosophers, who were as aware of the difference between thinking and willing, and as conscious of the connection of good with willing as Stevenson, nevertheless located assertions about good in the realm of thinking and belief (cf. Allan, in Barnes et al., 1977: 75-76, 78; for the full treatment of this idea of the older thinkers see chapters 6 and 8 below). Disagreement about what is good or desirable are, for them, disagreements, first of all, in belief, and only as a result disagreements in attitude. One's attitudes, they held, depend on what one thinks, either simply or here and now, to be good. For the good (as the proper object of the will) is something that *pro tanto* engages the will. One cannot believe that something is good and not, to that extent, be in favour of it. The connection between willing and thinking here is certainly logical or conceptual, for what one wills is a consequence of what one thinks about the good. The volitional act and the cognitive act are thus different, but the former follows the latter. When, therefore, one unpacks the *meaning* of good, that is, when one considers its aspect as conceived and thought on, or spoken in a statement, one unpacks it only in terms of the cognitive act. The volitional act (Stevenson's emotive element) is not part of its *meaning* in this sense. For the act of desiring something good is not part of the act of thinking it to be good, though it may well be that to think something as good is to think it in some relation or suitability to desire.

It is interesting to note that this distinction was not altogether lost on Moore. He adverted to it, or something like it, when he separated what one *asserts* from what one *implies*. As he put it:

> When a man asserts something that may be true or false, he implies at the same time, but does not assert, that he believes it, and likewise if he asserts an ethical judgement (e.g. that it was right for Brutus to stab Caesar), he implies at the same time, but does not assert, that he approves of the thing in question. The approving, like the believing, is not a constituent of what is asserted, it is an implication only (in Foot, 1967: 37-38).

Stevenson, it is clear, would reject this alternative account of good. He would contend that to say disagreement in attitude was reducible to disagreement in beliefs about what was good or desirable was, at best, misleading. 'Good' and 'desirable', in his view, cannot be reduced to matters of belief for they are not purely cognitive terms. But the alternative account, as much as Stevenson's, accommodates the difference between thinking and willing, and also the connection between good and choice or action. So Stevenson is wrong to think that it is because of a failure to do this that the account has to be rejected. One must, therefore, ask if there are any other reasons he might have had for dismissing it. Now there are three arguments in particular that are relevant here, and that can be constructed, without much difficulty, from the assertions he makes in various places in *Ethics and Language*.

First, no amount of agreement in belief can guarantee agreement in attitude. But this should be the case if, as is claimed, agreement as to what is good is agreement in belief, for those who agree as to what is good will evidently also agree in attitude (30-31, 113, 233, 275). Second, where matters of belief are concerned agreement can be secured by the rational methods of science and logic. Agreement in attitude, however, cannot be secured in this way, except accidentally, that is, except where certain attitudes happen to be tied to certain beliefs. But, according to the alternative account, this should be possible because agreement in attitude, essentially and not just accidentally, follows agreement as to what is good, and this latter agreement is supposed to be one of belief (30-31, 136-138). Third, the only sense of 'truth' and 'fact' that is legitimate is that neutral, or non-evaluative, sense which these terms have in logic and modern science. As the objects of belief are truth and the facts, the good and desirable, which are not neutral, cannot be objects of belief, or not simply at any rate; they must always include something more (152-156). Each of these arguments requires to be examined in turn.

As regards the first, it must be asked why Stevenson holds that agreement in belief does not guarantee agreement in attitude. The only reason that he appears to offer is the phenomenon of ordinary life where people who have convergent beliefs nevertheless have divergent attitudes. But the beliefs he has in mind are of a scientific or empirical sort (2). This is hardly to the purpose. According to the alternative account, the beliefs that yield attitudes are not these sort of beliefs, but beliefs about what is good. It is no use Stevenson saying, in reply to this, that beliefs about what is good are not like scientific or empirical ones. For what is to prevent there being several sorts of belief, of which beliefs about good are one? If pointing out that beliefs about what is good are not like scientific or empirical ones is to prove that the first are not beliefs, it must also be maintained that the latter are the only sort of beliefs there are. Stevenson does maintain this, but as it is the substance of the third argument discussion of it will be left until then.

As regards the second argument, a certain dilemma arises. If Stevenson is maintaining that rational methods are only sometimes, and not always, enough to secure agreement in belief, then this argument will prove nothing, for, even on his account of good, it will establish no difference in this respect between matters of belief and matters of good. He admits that agreement in attitude, which is what for him agreement as to what is good must be, will sometimes follow the application of rational methods, namely when the attitudes are tied to certain beliefs. If, however, he is maintaining that rational methods are always enough to secure agreement in belief, then, while this will establish a difference in the necessary respect, it is, unfortunately, false. It ignores the facts of human stubbornness. Nothing prevents people, even in science, from refusing to accept the evidence, or to follow the reasoning, and this has, in fact, sometimes happened (as seems to have been the case with Einstein's refusal to accept Heisenberg's uncertainty principle). Such refusals are particularly liable to occur where one's desires are engaged, and that is why they also occur, and more frequently, in the case of good. But if they can occur in science, which is a matter of beliefs, the fact that they also occur with good cannot show that good is not a matter of belief.

The third argument is the most significant of the three, and the one that most requires examination, for the assertions it turns on are central to the whole of Stevenson's thought. His views about the nature of truth and facts, and of belief and cognition, are determined entirely by reference to modern science, for it is this that provides him with his paradigms for them. Modern science is the ever-recurrent standard against which ethics is measured and with which it is contrasted. The methods of ethics, for instance, go beyond science, as does the content of its terms; and to the extent that they do so, to that extent it passes beyond the realm of truth, facts, beliefs, logic and validity. The emotive element of ethics is, moreover, its non-scientific element, and as ethics is, for Stevenson, a combination of the emotive and the descriptive or factual, it is evident that he regards the latter as identical with the scientific (11-13, 20ff., 36, 113-114, 152ff., 170, 245, 268). Naturalism, indeed, which holds ethics to be a matter of belief, is fallacious precisely because it fails to provide a distinction between ethics and science (20, 109). Science and scientific analysis are, as opposed to ethics, detached and neutral, concerned with knowledge and truth, and do not become moralising or emotive pleading for a cause (1, 217, 248, 271).

In view, then, of the centrality to his thought of these convictions about the difference between beliefs and attitudes, and between science and ethics, and in view of the importance they have for his rejection of naturalism, it is evidently necessary to get as clear about them as possible. As he devotes several pages to an analysis of the nature of belief or cognition, but none to the nature of science (though he is forever referring to it), clearly it is preferable to start with the former.

NATURE OF COGNITION

Stevenson begins with a somewhat surprising admission. The nature of cognition, he says, is "an involved matter that has long been a stumbling block in psychology and epistemology," but he at once goes on to add, and with considerable accuracy, that his present work cannot "pretend to throw fresh light upon it." Some "passing remarks," however, he supposes may not be "amiss" (62).

Cognition, he says, is not something that one can identify with certain mental imagery which one discovers by introspection, as Hume (and, we may add, Moore and Locke) thought. Rather it must be understood by reference to dispositions to action. Stevenson does admit that such introspective imagery is, or may be, involved as well, but it is clear that he does not regard reference to it as especially helpful or enlightening. It is the dispositions to action that occupy all his attention. Now an analysis of cognition in this way faces a certain difficulty, indeed, in Stevenson's own words, an "overwhelming complexity." How does one specify what actions a cognition is the disposition to do? His reply is again surprising. It is impossible in practice, he says, to hope here for "more than the vaguest approximation" (64). This, however, proves to be a considerable understatement.

Stevenson gives the example of a man who believes it is raining. How will this belief manifest itself in action? Perhaps he will put on his coat, but only, Stevenson is careful to note, if he also believes that the coat will keep him dry, and, more importantly, if he *wants* to keep dry. In other words, the action that results from the belief that it is raining, only results from it in conjunction with another belief *and* an attitude. Indeed Stevenson concludes generally that "no concrete action can be related exclusively to one, simple belief; it must also be related to many *other* beliefs – usually a complicated system of them – and must be related to attitudes as well" (65). Now this at once raises a number of difficulties, for it is evidently necessary, in order to distinguish one belief from another, or the beliefs from the attitudes, to find out what, in any particular action, the role of each is. The solution Stevenson suggests here is that we could do this, not by studying each in isolation (which is impossible), but by observing "what difference is made by a *change* in one of them, all else remaining roughly constant" (66). But how this could be done in practice is left unexplained. Indeed it seems altogether impossible; for how could we discover how many dispositions were instrumental in a given action, and which one had changed, when and in what way, and whether the others were still the same, if, as is admitted, they are not separately or independently identifiable? What is more, the same problem attaches to the determination of attitudes as much as to that of beliefs, for attitudes too, in Stevenson's view, are dispositions to action. But if this is the case, one must seriously wonder whether it is really possible for Stevenson ever to draw a hard and fast distinction between cognitions and attitudes, or ever to know if this or that disposition is one of belief or not.

The matter, however, is even worse than this, for talk of dispositions is vital, not just for the notions of belief and attitude, but also for that of meaning. The meaning of a term is its "disposition to produce psychological reactions" (77, and chapter 3 *passim*). The talk of psychological reactions is, however, misleading, because, as applied to descriptive and emotive meaning, these reactions prove to be themselves dispositions. The descriptive meaning of a sign is its "disposition to affect cognition" (67), that is, its disposition to affect another disposition. The emotive meaning of a sign is its disposition to affect a range of emotions, and emotions include attitudes, which are, themselves, "complicated conjunctions of dispositional properties" (59-60). In other words, when it comes to meanings, the problems about identifying dispositions are not only rendered more complex, they are doubled or trebled, for we would have all the difficulties of working out how and which disposition was affecting which other disposition. One has the feeling, after reading all this, of sinking without trace into a morass of unsolved, and insoluble, problems.

Stevenson is, to give him his due, unhappy about his account of attitude, cognition, emotive and descriptive meaning. He confesses that the difficulties attaching to the "key terms" of his book have not been surmounted, and that, though this is not "an agreeable admission," it is "difficult to see how, at the present stage of linguistic and psychological theory, any more persistent quest for a definition would be rewarding" (66-67). This admission may be disagreeable to Stevenson, but to the reader it is astonishing. How can one make sense of, let alone consider valuable, what Stevenson says, when the meanings of the vital terms, upon which the whole theory turns, are left in such confusion? One cannot help feeling that Stevenson would have been better advised to have postponed presenting his views on the nature of ethics, until he had gone much further in sorting out these other matters that are logically prior to them.

It is at any rate evident from all this that, even by his own admissions, neither he nor his readers are in a position to assess the soundness of his contentions about ethics. In particular, how could the view that disagreement in attitude is ultimately disagreement in belief about what is desirable or good be dismissed on the ground that 'desirable' and 'good' are 'emotive' and not just 'descriptive' terms? One could only do this, on Stevenson's theory, by showing that the dispositions that 'good' and 'desirable' affected were emotive and not, or not just, cognitive; and moreover if they affected these dispositions directly and not because of cognitive ones (for according to the older alternative view, thoughts about what is good or desirable, while genuinely matters of belief and cognition, have also a necessary effect on attitudes or volitions). But the difficulties that beset his dispositional analysis here are, as has already been argued, such as to render impossible the making of these discriminations at all, let alone with the precision necessary for the purpose.

Stevenson's failure adequately to define his key terms

throws him back, as he openly admits, onto a reliance on particular cases. These terms only have "such clarity as is afforded by instances of their usage," and must "for the most part be understood from current usage" (60, 67). But as has already been pointed out, it is not "current usage" that guides Stevenson's research. What guides his research is his paradigms, especially his paradigms of beliefs, but these he adopts according to the criteria of modern science. For, as has already been pointed out, ethics, as far as usage goes, may well be as much a matter of beliefs as science is. Stevenson refuses to admit that this view is correct, and since he claims this refusal is based on observations of current usage, it is clear he cannot be looking at current usage as it is. He must only be seeing in it what, for certain other reasons, he wants to see. These other reasons, it is not difficult to discover, are his beliefs about modern science; namely that it is, first, the domain and measure of the cognitive, and, second, evaluatively neutral. His dependence on science, or on his own views about science, is both crucial and, indeed, absolute.

ATTITUDE TO SCIENCE

Science looms very large in Stevenson's vision of things, and everything else must, as far as possible, be fitted in so as not to disturb that vision. He cannot avoid betraying his view that the more scientific things are, the better. "There is reason to hope," he says, that science will itself become more scientific, or that the remaining evaluative issues in it will not grow more serious (and, of course, one only 'hopes' for things or situations that one thinks are good) (290). The more science takes its "proper place" in ethics, that is, the more it is seen that the two are different, as well as how scientific elements or beliefs play a role in ethical discussion, the more will ethics receive a "needed discipline," which is, indeed, "more sorely needed" here than in any other subject; the more there will be of "co-operation" and "compatibility" and the less of "artificial opposition;" the more will moral aims become "enlightened" instead of "ignorant," and the more will "flexible" and "realistic" norms replace "static" and "other-wordly" ones (136, 319, 334, 336). Science is not only his test and foundation, it seems to function also as his basic value.

Stevenson is aware that there are evaluative issues in science, but he does his best to play them down. He thinks scientific terms are "*almost* free from emotive meaning," that their effect on attitudes is indirect, that the attitudes they do affect are of a fairly narrow range, namely "interests in knowledge," and even then that they do so in a "controlled" way. On the other hand, "all manner of attitudes directed to all manner of objects" are affected by other terms (282-284). But Stevenson is disingenuous; he conceals just how much value is involved in science. For, first, science and knowledge are values in their own right, and he cannot, in the end, avoid saying this; second, the objects of science, even its methods and procedure, are, as he also admits, determined by the views of scientists as to what it is worth doing or speaking about, or what classifications and distinctions it is worth drawing, that is to say, by the goals and wants of scientists (282-290). Science is not only a value, it is riddled with evaluation from beginning to end, and with respect to the most vital issues. For what could be more vital than aim and methods? Stevenson says that "there is reason to hope that the evaluative issues of science will not grow more serious" (290). But really there is no place for hope because we can be quite certain. The evaluative issues in science will not get more serious because they cannot get more serious – they are already as serious as they could be.

The effect of all this evaluation involved in science is that even the distinctions between belief and attitude and descriptive and emotive meaning, established by appeal to clear scientific instances, collapse. For if what facts or beliefs are is to be understood from what they are in science, and if the nature and objects of science are, as Stevenson himself concedes, determined by the wants or interests of scientists, then facts and beliefs, far from being distinguished from values and attitudes, prove to be products of them. In this light, facts appear to be themselves a sort of value, and beliefs a sort of attitude, and this, quite simply, will tear up Stevenson's theory by the roots.

One must note that these rather involuntary admissions of Stevenson's concerning the evaluative character of science just concede what must be recognised as true in some sense. For truth and knowledge are evidently values, and the primary ones as far as science is concerned. Moreover, science arose historically in large part because of the desire of its great founders and propagators, notably Bacon and Descartes, for a knowledge that would be useful as a means of conquering nature for human advantage (see chapter 5 below). It is, indeed, because of the continuing prevalence of the same desire that science is still regarded, by most peoples and most governments, as so valuable and important. But what must be stressed here is that the consequences of admitting that science is evaluative will, to a large extent, depend on what view one takes of evaluations.

There is, for instance, nothing in principle problematic about saying truth, knowledge and science are values, or even that science proceeds by making evaluations, if one also says that values are themselves truths or objects of knowledge, and that evaluations are beliefs that can be reached by the usual methods of reason and logic. For, in that case, one will be able to reason and argue about goods or values as much as about any other subject, and the judgements one comes to need be no less true, or objective, than the judgements scientists come to about atoms, planets or triangles. If, however, one says that values are not facts, and that attitudes or evaluations are not beliefs, nor subject, in themselves, to rational procedures, then as soon as it is seen or admitted that science is, in crucial respects, evaluative, it must also be admitted that it is itself non-factual and non-rational, and that judgements about it are not matters of truth or belief. Now this result is disturbing, to say the least, but it is the result towards which the logic of Stevenson's theory compels him. That is why he tries to play down the admission that science is evaluative, and why he regards the fear that science might thus be found to "totter" as a real, if hasty, one (290). For, of course, if evaluative matters are themselves matters of reason, then the possibility of such a fear does not even arise.

Stevenson, it seems, passes easily over these disturbing implications of the evaluative character of science because science, and the values of science, are "subject to a more widespread agreement...than are a great many of the broader moral issues" (287). But this can serve as no excuse. All it means is that if there is little disagreement in attitudes about science, it is because the attitudes of scientists, and most other people, are already in agreement about it; it is not because they play little or no part in it. On the contrary, they play a considerable part, and the consequences of this ought to be faced squarely.

Stevenson does not do this. He is, it is evident, very much at home in a world dominated by the progress and dissemination of science. But not everyone is as content, or as at peace with this, as he is. For one thing, science is a two-edged sword, and can cause appalling destruction when in the wrong hands; for another, its rise has been associated with, indeed has helped to create, an increasing indifference to religion. Those who care about religion and hold it to be vital to the human good (and there are many, including many scientists), cannot view this development with unconcern. Stevenson does not share their concern, nor their interest in "otherwordly" norms. Not that there is necessarily anything wrong with this, for religion may, in fact, be something undesirable as he seems to think. But whether it is or not, the important thing to note is that this must evidently be a matter of attitude. Stevenson's attitude here is clear, since, for him, science and its continued progress are central to the improvement of human life. Indeed, seeing science as the domain of facts and belief, and seeing thereby the place of ethics as the domain of attitudes and emotions (or seeing, in other words, that ethics is necessarily non-naturalist), is associated in his mind with "mental health" and "ethical development" (199, 334; and compare also the use of "distressing", 275).

Stevenson's theory of ethics, his metaethics, is based on an appeal to science as the domain and measure of the factual and cognitive. But this appeal is not argued for; it is assumed. And it is assumed because it is part and parcel of Stevenson's overall scientific attitude, or his convictions about the value and goodness of science for human and social progress. His metaethics thus emerges as dependent on a particular view of what the human good is. In other words, it is based on his (unspoken) ethics. But if this is so, what is the status of this ethics? Is this goodness of science a matter of fact or of attitude? This is, perhaps, the most damaging dilemma Stevenson has to face. If the goodness of science is a matter of fact, then Stevenson's non-naturalist theory of ethics is based on a kind of naturalism, and a most paradoxical naturalism at that, for it is to the effect that there is at least one value that is a fact, namely science, the value that requires for its pursuit the separation of facts and values. What then is the structure of this naturalism? How is it legitimate? What is the sense of 'fact' being appealed to here? And if naturalism is, after all, correct, why has he spent so long trying to reject it? To these questions Stevenson gives no answer, nor is it easy to see what answer he could give.

If, however, to take the other side of the dilemma, the goodness of science is a matter of attitude and not of fact, then what is or could be the justification of this attitude? It certainly could not, in the end, be a matter of fact or thought and reason, for, on Stevenson's view, attitudes are logically independent of the facts and of thought and reason. It must, therefore, be something non-rational; but to admit that one's theory is without rational foundation is to admit that one may, with as much or as little reason, believe any other theory – including the directly opposite one. And a theory which allows that its contrary is at least as reasonable as itself seems hardly worth taking seriously; besides, it is not at all what Stevenson had in mind.

It might appear that Stevenson could try to reply to this by saying that, regardless of which attitude one adopted, the facts were what counted; for the truth of his theory is determined by reference to the facts, and the facts are not a matter of attitude. But for him this cannot be the case. What is to count as a fact he understands by reference to what counts as a fact in modern science, for it is science that he takes as his model and measure. But he takes science as his model and measure because of his scientific attitude, or because of the overriding importance for him of the values and merits of science and its procedures. This scientific attitude, indeed, emerges as, perhaps, the most dominant fact about his book. If, however, one does not adopt his scientific attitude (and, by his own account, there is no more reason to adopt it than not to adopt it), one is not going to be under any necessity to concede that science is either the right, or the only, model and measure to use. So one will be free to deny that the facts on which Stevenson says his theory is based are the facts, or, at any rate, that they are all the facts.

This result is rather serious. If what is to count as the facts is determined for Stevenson by his scientific attitude, then it cannot be that his theory is, as he claims, a neutral, detached analysis of what is the case. It must rather be viewed as a proclamation of what is considered to be the case from within his particular scientific attitude. This is just an attitude which Stevenson has chosen to embrace. So, as far as the reader who does not embrace it is concerned, Stevenson would be left with no response save perhaps that of resorting to some of the "persuasive" methods he lists with such care, in order to evoke the necessary attitude. He would have to "propagandise" his views, and instead of standing back in a posture of "scientific detachment," plunge headlong into the task of urging and pleading for a cause. To a large extent this is, in fact, just what he does. *Ethics and Language* is a sustained propaganda exercise for an attitude towards life in which value-free science is paramount. Seizing on such words as 'fact', 'truth', 'critical', 'knowledge', 'scientific', 'analysis', 'detached', 'neutral', he exploits to the full all their "emotive" power. And what immense emotive power these words have! What intensely favourable attitudes they express and evoke! His message in the end becomes: 'I approve of my view of science, and of my view of non-naturalistic ethics; do so as well.' Consequently the naturalistic fallacy finishes up, in his hands, as the fallacy of disapproving of what he approves, of rejecting the attitude he embraces. It can thus truly be said that, for Stevenson, naturalism is a fallacy because he does not like it.

This collapse of Stevenson's theory into mere persuasion parallels the collapse of Ayer's verifiability thesis into mere nonsense. It has the value, however, of showing where work needs to be done. For as the examination of Moore's theory showed, among other things, the need for a better analysis of good, so the examination of Stevenson's theory shows, among other things, the need for a better analysis of facts and science, of beliefs and attitudes.

CHAPTER 3

Hare: Goodness as prescriptive

THE CONTRAST WITH EMOTIVISM

Moore failed to account for the moving power of good because he gave a too exclusively cognitive analysis of it, and so, to remedy this defect, Stevenson resorted to a non-cognitive volitional analysis. This was soon regarded as the right move to make by many philosophers. Among these the most influential is undoubtedly R. M. Hare. Hare, however, objected to Stevenson's emphasis on the emotions, which, in his view, had divorced things too much from reason. Stevenson's theory needed to be corrected so that the volitional element could be made more rational (1963: 4-5; Hudson, 1970: 157). Hare objected to emotivism, therefore, not on the grounds of its notion of 'fact', but of its notion of 'attitude'. While Stevenson did not simply equate attitudes with emotions, he tended in that direction (1944: 37-38), as the title of 'emotivism' suggests. Likewise he tended to regard emotive language as working by *causally* affecting one's attitudes (1944: 31). In so far as ethical arguments work, they work, in the end, because they exert, by various psychological techniques or "persuasive" methods, an influence on attitudes, and they do so, in large part, by side-stepping one's conscious thoughts (Hudson, 1970: 131, 156-158).

All this is, of course, tied to Stevenson's view that words mean the psychological states or dispositions they issue from in the speaker and tend to cause in the hearer. For words might have such an effect without one's being aware of it; one could be 'manipulated' into a change of attitude. Hence the difficulty of distinguishing morality from propaganda (Stevenson, 1944: chapter 11; Hare, 1952: 14). Hare says, on the contrary, that evaluative judgements do not express one's attitudes, emotive or otherwise, but one's decisions.

Besides following Stevenson in giving a non-cognitive theory of ethics, Hare follows him also in holding it to be concerned with language. Ethics is "the logical study of the language of morals" (1952: iii), especially of the value words 'good', 'right' and 'ought' (though it must be pointed out, in fairness, that he has never thought that this is all moral philosophy is about, or even what it is ultimately about; 1963: 6; 1979a: 242; 1981: v, viii). Hare follows Stevenson also in claiming to be appealing to ordinary language (1952: 85, 91-92, 126). But in fact he no more does so than Stevenson does. Ordinary usage permits without any difficulty a cognitive use of value-words, as well as many other uses that are not altogether consistent or even sensible, for ordinary usage is just the way people use words. Such usage does, of course, conform to some rules, but these are loose enough to allow one to express almost any opinion whatever. Ordinary usage is, therefore, not a sure guide to philosophical understanding, and even professed language philosophers admit as much. For they spend a lot of their time analysing ordinary expressions in order to find out what they really mean; and what they really mean is usually not what they appear on the surface to mean, that is, not what they actually do mean, or are usually taken to mean, at the level of ordinary usage. Hare himself, for instance, does this over the phrase "eschew evil" (1952: 173-174). What this really means is what it must mean in order to be compatible with his own ethical theory, and not what it means in ordinary usage, especially the ordinary usage of those who disagree with him. Hare does not, therefore, rely on language to establish his views about good. What in fact he relies on will be seen as this investigation proceeds.

Before turning directly to Hare's discussion of good, it is worth pointing out that he regards his analysis of it as being true for the uses of good in moral and non-moral contexts. That is to say, he regards it as being true in all contexts, if, as seems a reasonable supposition given that contradictory predicates exhaust the whole of a subject, 'non-moral' and 'moral' are meant to cover all uses of good. In other words, like Moore, he conducts a "general enquiry into good." Nevertheless he conducts it from the point of view of human action or of morals. We are forced, then, to raise again the point made earlier in the discussion of Moore. Good is to be analysed in its full extent from within the perspective of the good of human choices and actions. But what if good has senses that are not thus related to human choice, and cannot be made intelligible by means of it? And what if it is only by seeing good in its full scope that one will see it correctly in its limitation to the human and doable? Is there not a great risk of misunderstanding unavoidably attached to this question-begging methodology? These questions must cast a serious doubt over Hare's theory even before one begins to investigate it in any detail.

DESCRIPTION AND EVALUATION

According to Hare, the fallacy of naturalism is that it fails to distinguish description and evaluation, or that it fails to realise that there is a difference between saying what properties a thing has and saying it is good (in Hudson, 1969: 240). This is illustrated by an example. If we say a certain wine is a good wine, we mean that it has a certain taste, bouquet and so on, because of which we say it is good. But this is not all we mean, for we could give a name to this combination of characteristics, say 'φ', and teach someone what 'φ' meant. We could then get him to test wines to see if they were 'φ' or not, and at no point would he have to make a judgement about whether 'φ' wines were good. There is evidently more to the expression 'good wine' than is captured by the expression 'φ wine'. The sort of thing signified by 'φ', says Hare, is what he means by the descriptive meaning of good, and the something more is what he means by the evaluative meaning (in Hudson, 1969: 241-244).

There can be little doubt that there is indeed a difference here. Judging that a thing has certain properties is not the same as judging it to be good. What needs to be stressed, though, is that this fact by itself proves nothing, for *that* there is a difference does not tell us *what* the difference is. As far as we yet know it could be between two sorts of judgement that are both kinds of describing, though admittedly rather different kinds. When Hare says that the difference is between describing and non-describing, or between making a statement about what is the case and doing something else that is not a matter of making such a statement, he is going beyond the fact of the difference to elucidating its nature. It is important to note this because he sometimes gives the impression that this is not so, or that it is sufficient to recognise the difference to see that his account of it is correct. This is not because he is unaware that it is one thing to show a difference exists and another to explain it, for on the contrary he is (in Hudson, 1969: 244); it is rather because he holds that not to explain the difference in the way he himself does amounts to denying that there is a difference at all. In other words, any attempt, such as he holds is made by naturalists, to say predications of good are statements of what is the case, always ends, in his view, by equating such predications with other predications that are not predications of good (as when for instance 'φ' is said of the wine). And to do this is manifestly erroneous.

To understand why Hare believes this, it is necessary to pursue his thought further, and specifically to examine another argument he uses against naturalism (this time with the example of 'good strawberry'). Naturalists, he says, equate saying 'S is a good strawberry' with saying 'S is a strawberry and S is C' (where C is a set of properties). But, replies Hare, we sometimes want to say that S is a good strawberry *because* it is C, and this is not the same as saying 'S is a C strawberry because it is C', which it would have to mean if naturalism was right (1952: 85). Naturalism, in other words, makes it impossible for us to say things which in ordinary talk we do say; for when we call C strawberries good we intend to commend or praise them, and we cannot do this if all we do in saying C strawberries are good is to say that they are C (1952: 92-93). It is evident from this that we are back with Moore's open-question argument (as Hare anyway admits; 1952: 83-84) . But this argument is no more effective in Hare's hands than it was in Moore's. Naturalists are not, or should not suppose they are, identifying the formal notion of good with the things that possess it, or with the characteristics because of which they possess it. To say that S is good because it is C must not be construed, even for naturalists, as equivalent to saying it is C because it is C. Rather it is something like saying that to be C is what counts as the measure of goodness for S, or that this is what the goodness for S is realised in. Good, therefore, means something like coming up to standard, or being in accordance with what it is expected or desirable for S to be. That is why to say something is good is to praise or commend it. The 'extra' element in predications of goodness has thus something to do with referring to a standard of goodness.

This is precisely what Hare himself says makes predications of goodness different from other predications, namely that they involve a reference to standards. Indeed he bases his distinction between evaluation and description on this reference. It is one thing to describe S as C, and it is quite another to evaluate it as good; and the difference is that the latter involves assessment with respect to a standard of goodness, while the former does not (1952: 111ff.). But if naturalism too admits the need for such reference in its analysis of good, then this argument is of no effect against it. Hare's attack however cannot be so easily deflected, for he would just reply that in the case of naturalism this makes no difference. To evaluate with respect to a standard is not a matter of stating what is the case, or giving some kind of description. Evaluation essentially involves accepting, or assenting to, the standard of goodness by which one evaluates. But to accept such a standard is not at all like accepting a fact, or assenting to something that is the case; it is an entirely different operation. Since naturalism, therefore, makes predications of good into statements of what is the case, it fails to recognise this, and so, despite its supposed appeal to standards, necessarily fails to draw the required distinction between good and other predications. So it does in fact, whatever its supporters may say, deny that the distinction really exists.

It is clear that what this argument relies on is the claim about what assenting to a standard is. Hare's understanding of this operation brings one to the centre of his thought. In his view such an understanding is an understanding of a point of logic, or a point about the function of certain words in language; and that is why he claims that his views about it are based on an analysis of ordinary usage. It has already been argued that this claim is false, and it will be further argued in what follows. But to avoid appearing to beg the question, and indeed to facilitate the exposition, it is preferable to take Hare at his word and to begin by examining what he says about the meaning and function of descriptive and evaluative words.

According to Hare, "meaning of any kind (so far as it is words that are said to have meaning) is or involves the use of an expression in accordance with certain rules; the *kind* of meaning is determined by the *kind* of rules" (1963: 7). In the case of descriptive expressions, their meaning is determined by the rule that attaches them to a certain limited class of objects, as 'red' is determined by the rule that attaches it to the property or feature of redness. If there is no feature that one has in mind, however vague, then the term one uses has no descriptive meaning (1963: 14). It is clear that what is central to this definition is not the rule, but the feature that the word signifies, for the rule just binds this word, this vocal sound, to signifying this property. In order to understand the definition, therefore, we need to know what sort of properties these are. They are limited, says Hare, to a definite range, for a term that can be applied to anything such as 'it' has no descriptive meaning; 'it' would be so vague as to be "useless" as a description (1963: 9). They are also objects of belief, or facts, or possible and actual states of affairs, and statements are true or false to the extent that they contain them (1952: 19, 22; 1963: 28).

However none of this, as far as it goes, seems to give any conclusive evidence to show that good does not signify a feature of objects, or that evaluative judgements cannot be true or false. But Hare does not say very much else, and this makes it rather difficult to reach an understanding of descriptive meaning in terms of descriptive properties. He does, however, say one other thing that is relevant here, namely that to be "genuinely naturalistic" (that is, factual or descriptive, as the context makes clear), a definition must contain "no expression for whose applicability there is not a definite criterion which does not involve the making of a value judgement" (1952: 92). In other words, a descriptive term is a neutral or non-evaluative term, as it was also for Stevenson. But while this does provide a reason why good is not descriptive, it has the disadvantage of circularity, for Hare also explains evaluative terms as non-descriptive (they express the something more beyond the description of characteristics). Hence nothing is made clearer. To find out what he means by this distinction, it is in fact better to begin with evaluation. For he is, as it turns out, far more informative on the latter than the former.

Value-judgements such as 'so-and-so is good' are distinctive in that they do not give verbal instruction about the use of the word 'good'; they are rather 'prescriptions', or give guidance for choosing. In the case of moral evaluations, for instance, to learn that someone is a good person is to learn to "commend, or prescribe for imitation, a certain kind of man" (1963: 23). The rules, then, that govern the use of good are not mere meaning-rules, but principles of choice or action; hence evaluating differs from describing above all in that it is manifested in differences in how we *behave*, not just in how we *speak*. To evaluate is to set up a norm or standard for choosing or living by (1952: 159; 1963: 28-29; 1981: 11). Or to put it another way, evaluation differs from description in that it is essentially *action-guiding*.

It is this fact about good and value terms generally, that they are action-guiding, that is the foundation and primary principle of the whole of Hare's analysis. It is the fact that he adverts to first, the fact that gives him his orientation, and the fact that his whole theory is designed to account for (1952: 1-3). Indeed it gives him also the name for his theory, prescriptivism, for to prescribe is to guide action, and this is what value words essentially do. It also explains all his charges against naturalism, and notably the charge that naturalism misunderstands what it is to assent to a value-judgement. For the model to adopt in analysing evaluations is not that of making statements, as naturalists suppose, but (and in this Hare picks up a suggestion of Stevenson's) that of issuing imperatives – both to oneself and to others. It is, in fact, in connection with imperatives and what they entail that Hare develops the most powerful defence of his case and the most powerful attack on his naturalist opponents.

IMPERATIVES AND CHOICE

Hare presents the following argument. Value judgements, especially moral ones, entail answers to the question, 'What shall I do?' Answers to such questions take the form of imperatives, as 'Do this,' or 'Let me do this.' Hence moral judgements must have imperative force. But precisely because of this they cannot be mere statements or descriptions. For in any valid inference the conclusion must already be implicit in the premises. So if from a judgement about good the inference, 'Do this,' or 'Let me do this,' is valid (and of course it is, otherwise the judgement would not be action-guiding), then that judgment must already implicitly contain an imperative. Imperatives are not indicatives, for they are in a different mood, nor can they follow from indicatives, at least not from indicatives alone, because then there could logically be no change of mood between the premise and the conclusion, and the conclusion would have to be indicative just like the premises. But it has already been established that the conclusion is an imperative. Therefore, a value judgement cannot be an indicative, and hence cannot be purely descriptive or a statement of what is the case. As a matter of logic, then, there must be something more to it and that something more is its imperative force, its prescriptivity (1952: Part One, 163, 171-172).

Hare provides an instructive translation both of value judgements and descriptions in order to bring out the imperative character of the former. He does this by means of the words 'yes' and 'please'. A description is completed by a 'yes', and an evaluation is completed by a 'please'. So, 'This being a red juicy strawberry, yes,' is equivalent to, 'This is a red juicy strawberry;' and 'Strawberries being red and juicy, please,' is equivalent to, 'Red, juicy strawberries are good.' The parts of each sentence before the 'yes' or 'please' are the factual or descriptive content; and the 'yes' and 'please' just indicate what is being done with this content: the 'yes' asserts it and the 'please' commends or prescribes it. Hare devised technical terms for these parts, using Greek words for the purpose. The 'yes' or 'please' are the 'neustic' (the part that 'nods' assent), and the factual part is the 'phrastic' (the part that 'says' what is being assented to). This also makes it obvious how there are, for Hare, two elements in an evaluation, and what the role of each is. For the 'please' is the evaluative element, and this has the effect of transforming or altering what otherwise might be a statement of fact into an expression with essentially imperative force (1952: 17ff.).

There is a certain similarity between this pattern of analysis of good and the pattern adopted by Stevenson. But Hare's, besides being linguistically more subtle, also allows him to deny that evaluations are a matter of emotivist expressing or evoking of attitudes. Making a 'please' judgement is, says Hare, something more rational than that; it is a matter of making, or expressing, a commitment of choice, or of reaching a deliberate and conscious decision (1952: ch. 4; though this does not prevent him calling such choices desires in a broad sense; 1963: 169-170; 1981: 107-109). Nevertheless despite this there is something fundamental common to both, namely that both include, as an essential part of the *meaning* of good, something non-cognitive or volitional (1963: 198).

The reasoning in this major argument of Hare's requires to be examined in some detail, and to do that it is desirable first to reduce it to its essential elements. These can be stated as follows.

(i) Judgements about good are action-guiding, or provide answers to the question, 'What shall I do?'

(ii) Answers to this question take the form of imperatives.

(iii) Therefore judgements about good are imperatives or have imperative force.

(iv) Imperatives are not indicatives or statements of what is the case.

(v) Therefore judgements about good are not (as naturalists suppose) statements of what is the case.

This argument is formally valid, so there is nothing to object to on that score; but its three different premises are false or misleading. Premise (i) is only true in the context of human action, not of good in general, yet Hare supposes his analysis of good does hold of good in general. Premise (ii) confuses giving advice about what to do with telling what to do. Premise (iv), while correct as far as words go, nevertheless, because of the narrowness of its alternatives, obscures the fact that there might be other ways of accounting for the action-guiding force of judgements about good that do not prevent them from being statements of what is the case. These criticisms must now be pursued in detail, and for the sake of convenience in exposition, premise (iv) will be taken first.

This premise is closely connected with premise (i), because it is imperatives that Hare uses for his analysis of the action-guiding force of good. While this point about good will be taken up later, it is necessary, for the sake of clarifying the significance of Hare's contrast between imperatives and indicatives, to point out that, at any rate in the context of human behaviour, it is obviously true that good is in some sense action-guiding (Warnock, 1967: 74). What, however, is peculiar about Hare with respect to it is the same as what is peculiar about Stevenson with respect to the connection between good and attitudes or volitions; namely not his recognition of this fact, but his explanation of it. For, like Stevenson, he regards this feature of good as requiring an analysis which makes willing (or in Hare's terms prescribing) part of the meaning of good. In other words, again like Stevenson, he does not admit that there might be statements of what is the case, or cognitive acts, that nevertheless have a direct and essential connection with choosing and doing. This is precisely the point being made by the sharpness of the division he draws between judgements of what is good and judgements of what is the case, or, in his terminology, between those with imperative, and those with indicative, force. With respect to expressions of value, indeed, this division is not only sharp, it is exhaustive, for their elements are exhaustively divided into the descriptive, or factual, part and the properly evaluative part.

It has already been pointed out in the criticism of Stevenson that there is a view, maintained by older thinkers, to the effect that some judgements of what is the case, or some acts of thinking, can and do have a direct connection with choice and action. According to this older view, good is a fact, or, better, an object of knowledge, and also at the same time the object of will and desire. So judgements about what is good, which, as such, are cognitive, have *per se* an influence on the will, and consequently are necessarily fitted to move it.

Hare of course would reject this view, and that means he contends, on the contrary, that thinking does not move willing. But while he does in some sense hold this, he nowhere says it in so many words; it functions as a sort of given for him. One must ask, however, from where it is given, and it is evident that this is not from a consideration of ordinary usage. One may indeed admit that ordinary usage reflects the fact that there is a connection between good and choice or action, but there is, nevertheless, nothing in it to show that this fact must be interpreted as Hare interprets it, and not, say, as the older thinkers do. For since both views equally save this fact, they both equally save ordinary usage with respect to it. In so far as Hare reveals the real origin of his views here, that origin proves to be much more connected with his convictions about the neutrality of facts (which seem, in turn, to be connected with modern science, though this is by no means as obvious for him as it is for Stevenson), and about the freedom of the will.

As far as the reference to science is concerned, this just confirms what has already been concluded from the previous chapter, that to understand good it is necessary also to undertake some examination of modern science. Hare does not do this, and neither do Moore or Stevenson. As far as his views on freedom are concerned, these will be examined later in the discussion of the other two premises of his major argument. But before that, it is worth considering here some of the consequences of his view that expressions of good are exhaustively divisible into descriptive and evaluative elements.

This division is, as has already been indicated, the division between acts of thought and acts of will (just as is also Stevenson's similar division between beliefs and attitudes). Given the way Hare understands this, namely that the first does not move the second, and given also how it pervades the whole of his thinking, it is obvious that it will be impossible, within the limits it imposes, to express or even conceive the opposite view. It is because of this that he finds it so easy to refute naturalism. For whenever he tries to express what it is, he always expresses it as an attempt to reduce the evaluative to the descriptive, in his sense of evaluative and descriptive. But in his sense of these terms they are rigidly separated, and to say something is descriptive is necessarily to deny that it is evaluative; and to say something is evaluative is necessarily to deny that it is descriptive (at least *qua* evaluative). Hence, if one says, with naturalists, that there are judgements of what is the case which nevertheless move to action or guide choices, then one is saying something quite unintelligible. For if one says that a judgement states something that is the case, it is not an evaluation but a description; and if one says a judgement guides choices, then it is not a description but an evaluation; so to try to say that there are some judgements that are both, and specifically that they guide choices by virtue of what they state to be the case, is to say that there are some judgements that *qua* evaluative are descriptive, or that *qua* descriptive are evaluative. And this is just nonsense. In the face of this, Hare can only suppose that naturalists have failed to see the difference between evaluation and description, and so he inevitably has a strong tendency to regard naturalism as the failure to recognise that there is a difference rather than as the failure to give a proper explanation of it (in Hudson 240ff.).

This helps to explain also certain other peculiarities in his writings, and notably why it becomes axiomatic for him that if one admits that moral and value judgements are in some sense action-guiding, one must be a prescriptivist exactly like himself; and that if one rejects his prescriptivism, one must also be denying that such judgements are in any sense action-guiding (1952: 195-197; in Foot, 1967: 77-78). It also explains why it is axiomatic for him that if one says anything that at all smacks of having an influence on choosing and doing, it is no longer purely descriptive, or no longer a statement of what is the case (1963: 70; in Hudson, 1969: 247-248).

But while this helps to explain certain otherwise puzzling features of Hare's thought, it also means that his refutation of naturalism (e.g. 1952: 92) is nothing of the kind. For it means that whenever he meets naturalism he always looks at it from within the limits of his pre-conceived terminology. He never allows naturalism to be other than what he says it is, so that it is defined as fallacious from the start. Consequently his refutation of naturalism becomes just a matter of his knocking down straw-men of his own creation. These limits to Hare's thinking have their effects also in other ways; notably with respect to that aspect of good that he calls 'supervenience'. An examination of this will lead into a consideration of the first premise in his major argument against naturalism, namely that good moves to action.

Hare draws a distinction between criteria and meaning in predications of good. The criteria are those properties of a thing that make one call it good, and these differ markedly from one thing to another. For instance, what makes a strawberry good is not what makes a hockey-stick good. The meaning, however, remains constant, for to both these very different things the same term 'good' can correctly be applied (1952: 96-97). The meaning of good must thus be distinct from the criteria, and understanding the meaning must not require first understanding the criteria. But a further peculiarity of good shows that the meaning must also be somehow consequential to the criteria, for differences in goodness between things have to be accounted for by reference to differences between them in other respects. This can be seen from the fact that one cannot say that x and y are exactly alike in every respect, save that x is good and y is not, whereas one can say x and y are alike in every respect, save that x is yellow and y is not (1952: 80-81; Hudson, 1970: 164-165). This makes it evident that good itself cannot signify a property of its own, for then it would behave like 'yellow' which it does not, and also that it has to be predicated with an eye to the properties that other terms signify. Good, in other words, is 'supervenient' to other properties; or the meaning is 'supervenient' to the criteria.

That good is supervenient in some way was something well known to older thinkers, though admittedly not under this title. For this term covers, on the one hand, the difference (already often mentioned) between the formal notion of good and the material instantiations; and, on the other hand, what was formerly called the 'transcendentality' of good. By this was meant that 'good' belongs to that class of terms, including 'thing', 'true' and 'one', that are not confined to one of the ten categories, but are found in all and so transcend their differences (Aquinas *DV:* q1 a1). When predicated, therefore, they do not add or signify a determinate nature over and above the nature signified by the subject term (as 'red' adds to 'book' the additional nature of redness), but signify that nature itself considered under a certain aspect, for instance under the aspect of absence of division in the case of 'one' (Aquinas *CM:* §1980). 'One book' signifies absence of division with respect to the book's being a book, though it has many pages and may be divided with respect to them; and likewise 'one library' signifies absence of division with respect to the library's being a library, though it contains many books. 'One' is not a descriptive term like 'red' in Hare's sense, because, like 'it', it can be said of anything and would be "so vague and general as to be altogether useless" as a description (1963: 9).

'Good' is exactly like 'one' in this respect and so cannot be descriptive. It does not follow, however, that therefore 'good' does not signify something that can be grasped by the intellect in an act of knowing, just as this does not follow for 'one' either. As 'one' signifies absence of division and thus means something different in each case (for the kind of division varies with the kind of thing), so 'good' signifies the notion of end or final cause, or, to revert to the terminology used earlier, the idea of a standard (for the end is also the standard for assessing the goodness of things; cf. Aristotle, *EN*: 1152b1-3). Thus it also means something different in each case, for the end varies with the kind of thing (this topic of transcendentality is examined in detail later in chapter 6).

Hare's term 'supervenience' serves, then, to cover what was previously meant by the difference between transcendental and category terms. But it can readily be seen that within Hare's own terminology of description and evaluation this difference cannot be expressed, and, indeed, that any attempt to express it within that terminology would of necessity distort it. The difference between evaluation and description is not the same as the difference between category terms and transcendentals, for the latter is a distinction within acts of knowing, but the former is a distinction between acts of willing and acts of knowing. Nevertheless 'good' is supposed, on Hare's view, to be exhaustively divided into the evaluative and the descriptive. Some, at least, of the older thinkers would deny that 'good' was a descriptive term, if that is supposed to be the meaning that category terms have; but they would also deny that it was an evaluative term, if that means it is supposed to be expressive of an act of will and not of thought. And this just goes to confirm what has already been argued, that Hare's terminology imposes limits on the discussion that rule out, *ab initio*, attempts to state what other philosophers say, or have said, about good.

I have stated this criticism in terms borrowed from the older metaphysics, but it could in principle have been stated without them. If 'one' is supervenient in the same way as 'good' is, and if 'one' is nevertheless an object of an intellectual or cognitive act, it is obvious that there is more to cognition than Hare's term 'descriptive' allows. This is sufficient to show that the division between description and evaluation upon which his analysis of good rests is inadequate. For if there is more to the cognitive than is included in the descriptive, why may not 'good' fall into this 'something more' rather than the 'something more' of volition that Hare insists it must?

Hare's own analysis of the meaning (as opposed to the criteria) of good is found by reference to choice. When one says that something is good one is making or guiding choices, or setting up principles for choosing (1952: 101-110, 159). But choice is not a very enlightening way to explain good. One of the objections made against Hare by his critics is that good is not always linked to our choices, for our choices are linked to what we want or care about, and it is perfectly intelligible to say some things are good which we do not care about and may even hate. Examples here might be a good amoeba or a good typhoid virus. To say an amoeba is good is not to make or guide a choice of it (say for eating); rather it is to say that it is not diseased or damaged, or some such thing, but is fit to lead the life proper to it (cf. Anscombe in Hudson, 1969: 181). And to say a typhoid virus is good is certainly not to guide a choice of it, for it too is to say that it is healthy and so on, and such viruses are very effective in causing typhoid, which is something we do not want.

Now Hare does examine the claim that we do not talk about good wireworms, and says that the reason is that we do not have occasion for choosing between wireworms. But if wireworms were used as bait by fishermen for example, then the phrase would come into use to guide choices about which sort of wireworm to fish with (1952: 127-128). But this will not do. It is not the case that we have to have a need for something before we can sensibly make predications of good about it. To suppose this is to be indefensibly anthropomorphic as well as oblivious of what people can and do say. For instance, it need not be true that a wireworm good for catching fish is a good wireworm simply. It might be that a wireworm good for catching fish was bad for living the life of a wireworm, for fat ones might be best for catching fish but lean ones best for living well as wireworms.

One could perhaps save the reference to choice here by saying that this other sense of good was relative to the choices scientists make. Good typhoid viruses, amoebae, wireworms and so on would then be the kinds scientists would choose to study. But even this is inadequate, for scientists sometimes choose diseased and damaged specimens (for it is not the case that the healthy ones will reveal all one may want to know). Besides it is not the same for an amoeba, say, to be good as a scientific specimen and good as an amoeba. To say one is looking for a good amoeba because such amoebae are good as specimens, is not to say one is looking for an amoeba that is good as a specimen because such amoebae are good as specimens. One is evidently using 'good' in more than one sense, and, indeed, the first sense is needed to explain the second, since it is only because certain amoebae are good as amoebae that they are good as scientific specimens. The first sense is, moreover, *independent* of our choices.

It is possible to try to deny this by saying that a good amoeba is an amoeba that one would choose to be if choosing to be an amoeba, as a good poisoner is a poisoner one would choose to be if choosing to be a poisoner. But this seems bizarre. We cannot choose to be amoebae as we can choose to be poisoners, and if we could so choose and became amoebae, we would cease to be able to choose or to commend choices to others, for amoebae act instinctively and can be said neither to commend nor to choose. Besides, hypothetical sentences, as has been pointed out in other contexts, are inadequate to capture the meaning of categorical ones, and even more so in this case where the hypothetical contains an impossible supposition. The only way out of this is to deny that we ever use good in the sense here discussed, but this is false and is patently an *ad hoc* move to save the theory.

The consequence of the above discussion is that it is evidently necessary to distinguish between the choosable and the non-choosable good, or the good that is relative to ends we have an interest in and the good that is not. In other words not every sort of good is an action-guiding good. One may well wonder if Hare's failure to acknowledge this distinction is not due to his faulty methodology, that is, to his attempt to explain good as such from within the perspective of a particular good, the good of morality or of human action.

If Hare's analysis of good in terms of choice is wrong for some senses of good, it need not follow that it is wrong for this good of morality, for such a good is indeed a good to choose. But it is important to note that even naturalists may admit as much. What they would add, however, is that the end or standard that constitutes this good is in some sense set up by nature. This is just what Hare would deny, since he would say that the standard must itself be a matter of choice.

To recognise a standard is, for Hare, not to assent with one's mind but one's will. This is inevitable given what he says about evaluation, that it is to prescribe. For to prescribe is to give guidance for choice, or to set up a standard for choosing by. But to choose by a standard is to subordinate one's choice to that standard, or to make it authoritative for one's decisions. Otherwise the standard will not operate as a standard, that is, will not actually guide any of one's choices (it will on the contrary be "external" and "dead;" 1963: 46). But no one can subordinate our choice for us; we have to do it for ourselves. For choice is free and one can only determine it from within by oneself. Hence to assent to a standard is to "will" it for oneself (1963: 29, 219). Hare points out that it is here that the prescriptive feature of moral judgements "makes its most decisive appearance." And that is why it is here that naturalism above all falls down. In all its forms naturalism makes the standard of moral goodness an object of knowledge, a fact that can be known like any other object of knowledge, and so something that is supposed to stand above our choices and be authoritative for them just because it is what it is, regardless of what we ourselves may wish. But, says Hare, this is manifestly impossible. Human beings have the power to choose whatever they like, and can be bound by no object of knowledge whatever to choose one thing rather than another. "It is in the logical possibility of wanting *anything* (neutrally described) that the 'freedom' that is alluded to in my title essentially consists" (1963: 110). Hare believes, in other words, that to say the will or choice is free is to say that it is independent of what can be known, or of what can be an object of the mind. This is, indeed, what is meant by "neutral" description. Non-neutral description, that is, description that is not purely description but also evaluation, is not a matter of knowledge or thinking but also of willing. Objects of thought are, for Hare, neutral in the sense that they do not as such move the will for or against; they are indifferent. The will's freedom is its independence of thought and the objects of thought.

Hare is right to suppose that naturalism, even in its older form, regards standards of good and right as objects of knowledge, or truths to be recognised. For, as has been said, it regards such standards as in some sense set up by nature. But Hare is wrong to suppose that this means naturalism has to deny to humans their freedom, or to say that accepting a standard that does operate for oneself as a standard, that is, does actually guide one's choices, is not somehow itself a matter of one's willing it, or of one's making it one's own by one's own decision. Older thinkers of the naturalist school are prepared to assert as emphatically as Hare that we are free to choose whatever we like. Aquinas is one obvious example. What separates Hare and Aquinas here is that Aquinas does not admit the validity of the inference from freedom to having no good determined by nature. This does not mean that Aquinas is being inconsistent; rather it means that he does not accept that it is necessary, in order to preserve for the will its freedom, to deny that it is subordinate to thought (cf. Bambrough, 1979: 54-60, 74-77). For he is, in fact, operating here with two senses of good. There is the good that one has set one's heart on (and this is the good of one's radical freedom), and there is the good that means the goal or end that one by nature is directed to. This second sense of good is not relative to our choices but is determined for us by the sort of things we are. However, this end does not operate on us in such a way that we cannot avoid choosing it and acting on it. As rational beings, we are endowed with "lordship" over our acts (*ST:* Ia IIae, q1, a1), so that it is up to us to direct ourselves to our end. Consequently we act according to the end we conceive and set our hearts on, that is, the end we choose and make our own, as Hare quite correctly sees. But there is no necessity that this should be the same as our natural end, for we may be ignorant, or perverse, or overpowered by passion, or hindered in some other way from clear thought and action. The great task of ethics and moral education is to find out what the natural end is, and by practice so to habituate oneself to it that one always does pursue it, and without opposition or pain from within.

Hare, however, would reject this sense of good on the grounds of the obscurity and elusiveness of the sense of nature in question (1963: 70). Natural things do not have natural ends; they are not "functional" like human artefacts such as augers (1952: 99-100). A functional object is one which is *for* something, or is supposed to do something, and human beings are not objects like that, as neither are horses. Hare, moreover, analyses good as attached to functional words in terms of human choices, for such words are not purely descriptive, but already include an evaluation. Before one can call something a hygrometer, for instance, it is necessary to know "something about what would justify us in commending or condemning something as a hygrometer." The standards of goodness for artefacts are, one may say, fixed, because these artefacts only exist in the first place as a result of a human choice to make them. Natural things clearly do not exist because of human choices and so cannot be functional; they only become functional when a human end is imposed on them, as when a horse is called a charger, for then it is adapted to the human end of riding into battle on. In other words, whatever ends there are in nature are not there by nature but by human choice (1952: 145; in Foot, 1967: 78-82).

Hare seems generally to regard this point about the functionless character of nature as sufficiently obvious not to require argument. To the extent he does expressly give a reason it is that to believe nature is functional has morally objectionable consequences (in Foot, 1967: 81n.). But, as others have pointed out, this cannot show it is false (Bambrough, 1979: 8-9, 39). The only other reason that presents itself as one he might have considered, though he does not state it, is that in modern science, or at least modern physics, the account given of nature is non-functional or non-teleological. But it is not obvious that modern science must be given the last word here.

That there is something about the idea of nature that requires more consideration than Hare gives it can be seen by noting the following puzzle in his thought. He says, for instance, that his metaethical analysis of morality is evaluatively neutral, and yet he finds no difficulty in deducing from it what makes a person or a society morally "adult" (1952: 77). Morality, for Hare, is above all a matter of making one's own decisions, and if a society becomes ossified and lives "by the book" it is liable to generate a "disease." He speaks freely of "moral defectives," of "well brought-up children," of "a happy state of affairs" that "deteriorates" (1952: 71-73). It is clearly a good thing in his eyes to be moral in this way, to exercise one's powers of decision instead of relying on traditional conventions. And though he does not admit it in so many words, it would be no distortion to say that he believes this because he believes that the sort of things we are are 'freely deciding animals'. Hence a good person and a good society are ones which exercise their freedom in this way. It is evident from this that, even for Hare, there is a sense of good that precedes the (non-natural) sense of good as the freely chosen, namely the good that means the activity of freely choosing, and which is good, not because it is chosen, but because it is natural, that is, the object or end or function proper to a being whose nature is freedom. Hare regards trying to deduce morality from the "essence" of humanity as a "philosophical mystification" (1963: 222), but his own view of moral worth is deduced, in effect, from his view that the human essence is something like freedom.

FREEDOM AND REASON

The premise in Hare's major argument against naturalism not so far discussed is premise (ii). According to this premise, answers to the question, 'What shall I do?', take the form of imperatives, as, 'Do this,' or, 'Let me do this,' or even, 'This, please.' Such an answer is, however, inappropriate as an answer to the question asked. It is a mere *telling* what to do and says nothing in *explanation* of why it should be done (as Hare in effect concedes by his silent refusal to deny it, 1952: 195). There are, of course, occasions where those who ask what to do want an answer in the form of a 'do this', as when subordinate officers ask their commander for battle orders; but these are typically cases of people under authority and are not like cases of people facing moral problems or dilemmas. In this latter case what people are looking for is not a command but advice; they want help in understanding what it is good (or best or right) to do in these circumstances; and that is just what an imperative (however mildly expressed) does not provide. One can see how strange Hare's analysis is here by considering such an ordinary expression as, 'Do x because it is good.' This does typically give, and is typically meant to give, an understanding about why to do x, but it becomes nonsense on Hare's analysis. According to him, 'good' is a term with imperatival force, so to say, 'Do x because it is good,' must reduce to something like, 'Do x because do x,' or, 'Do x because x, please.' But this is not at all what 'do x because it is good' means, nor is it what anyone who says it intends it to mean. It cannot, therefore, be the case that Hare has correctly analysed this ordinary use of the word 'good'.

Hare has a reply of sorts to this, for although, contrary to ordinary usage, he does not allow 'good' itself to be a reason-giving term, he does nevertheless have a theory of moral reason-giving. But this does not really help, for the theory, while effective as far as it goes, does not go far enough and entails an incoherent view of freedom.

The method depends on the claims, already discussed above, that value terms are prescriptive and supervenient, and in addition on an appeal to preferences. Because of prescriptivity, moral judgements require one to adopt an imperative to act in a certain way, and because of supervenience, they require one to universalise those judgements, or to make them apply to all like cases. If two actions or cases are alike in their non-evaluative features they must also be alike in goodness, for if they were unlike in goodness they would have to be unlike in some non-evaluative feature as well. Consequently moral judgements must both commit one to a certain course of action and to doing or approving it universally. To these Hare adds the third element of the preferences of the people who are involved in, or affected by, the action.

One's preferences are, he says, kinds of prescriptions or ways of being committed to pursuing or avoiding something. Using these three elements Hare argues that to see if an action one is proposing is a moral one or not, one must consider if one can universally prescribe it. One must ask, that is, whether one could prescribe or prefer the action as one to be done by everyone in similar circumstances, including especially those circumstances where one is, as it were, on the receiving end of the action. Suppose one is a white and is considering whether discrimination against blacks is morally defensible. What one has to do is to put oneself imaginatively in the place of the blacks who will be the victims of the discrimination and ask oneself if one can still prescribe the action. That is, one has to ask oneself if, having the preferences of blacks, one could still choose the action. Since one could not, because then the action would be in conflict with one's preferences instead of in harmony with them, one cannot morally prescribe discrimination against blacks. Hare allows for a possible exception to this in the case of "fanatics", those who would go on prescribing the action even when it was against their preferences. Fanatics are, however, he says, either impossible or, if possible, so rare as to be easily dismissed as of little or no significance for actual life, where moral choices have after all to be made.

This theory is a form of utilitarianism, as Hare expressly says, though with a heavy debt to the universalising of Kant (see chapter 5 below). The courses of action that turn out to be universally prescribable are those that promote utility, that is, the satisfaction of the greatest number of preferences of all those involved. Hare himself gave examples of how his theory would work to produce utilitarian answers with respect to such moral issues as war, abortion, terrorism and slavery (see e.g. 1972; 1975; 1979a; 1979b).

Hare maintains about this method that over the most important part of morality it will constrain us all to adopt the same conclusions (1981: 6-7; 225-227). In other respects, though, it will not constrain us but leave us free to choose what we like. This freedom evidently covers part of morality since the method only captures the "most important part" of it, not the whole; but it also, more significantly, covers the choice to be moral at all. Amoralism, Hare says, is a consistent option and cannot be ruled out by reason or logic. There are reasons to make the choice to be moral, but they are not sufficient nor entirely laudable (1981: 182-205; 219). Finally this freedom will also cover that "irreducible and large minimum of sheer autonomous preferences which rational thinking can only accept for what they are, or will be". Or, as Hare puts it, "we remain free to prefer what we prefer" (1981: 225-226).

But how do these choices which escape the method of reasoning get made? The answer is that they get made without any reasons, or any sufficient reasons. To quote his earlier work, there is here no longer any answer to the question why choose this rather than that; everything just rests on making a decision (1952: 69). This decision must therefore emerge from the will *ex nihilo*, as it were. The will must move, not for a reason, but without one; it must move spontaneously, by itself (cf. Bambrough, 1979: 72-76). In other words, freedom is spontaneity. Nothing sets one to actually making these choices; one just chooses. But this is incoherent. When one is faced with several different possibilities that cannot all be chosen at once, one is in a state of indetermination. To choose is to determine oneself to one or other of them. But one cannot determine oneself insofar as one is undetermined, for that implies a contradiction. Insofar as one determines one is active, and insofar as one is determined one is passive, and one cannot be both at the same time and in the same respect or with the same part of oneself. But this is what Hare's thesis requires. To say the will chooses spontaneously, or chooses without any reason to choose, is to say that precisely insofar as it is not determined it acts to determine itself.

It might, of course, be that this choice is determined by some previous one because it is necessary to fulfill that previous one, as the choice of means is determined by the choice of ends. Here the determination is or can be the work of the will. But this still leaves one to ask how the previous choice was determined. If the answer is another previous choice of some further end, the question will again arise about that other previous choice. But this process cannot go on for ever, otherwise one would never will or choose anything. Hence one must get to some determination of the will for which the will is not itself responsible. What Hare calls its 'spontaneity' can only be indicative of something other than the will that has set the process of determination going. But then this would not be spontaneity any more, and consequently not freedom either, as Hare understands freedom. Hence his freedom collapses into unfreedom. In fact it collapses into something like fate. What originally determines the will is not anything we can know or reason about, for all we can know is facts which, according to Hare, do not determine the will, and in these cases of spontaneity the method of reasoning does not apply. Nor can what determines the will be something over which we have any say, for then it would have to be subject to our will and not prior to it. So it must determine our will in a way that wholly escapes our knowledge and our control. But to say this is in effect to say that our wills are originally determined by some hidden power which by-passes our conscious faculties and yet operates on us irresistibly. And this is what is meant by fate. Since, moreover, the original choice to be moral or not is a spontaneous one according to Hare, it is fate and not freedom that lies at the root of the moral life. This is quite contrary to what he wants or intends.

Whether or how the will can be said to be free is a topic that will be taken up again later in chapter 8. But it is clear from this discussion that if there is to be genuine freedom, it cannot be identified with spontaneity or with something that is independent of reason and knowledge, as non-naturalists have assumed it must be.

SUMMARY

Hare has been by far the most prominent and influential of modern non-naturalists, and his views, especially about the existence and nature of the distinction between evaluation and description, stand at the heart of the dispute about naturalism. It is desirable, therefore, to end with a summary of the criticisms made against him in this chapter.

Hare claims that naturalism equates the meaning of good with the properties because of which one calls something good and involves no reference to standards. This is a distortion of naturalism, at least of naturalism in its older form, though, as will be explained in the next chapter, there is reason to believe it is not a distortion of a naturalism which Foot has been inclined to adopt. But Hare has a further criticism. A naturalism that refers to standards misunderstands what is involved in accepting a standard, for it makes such acceptance an act of thought when it is really an act of will. This criticism is, however, based on, and leads to, ideas that are unacceptable for several reasons. Some of the ideas are false; namely that good must be analysed by reference to action and choice, and that it is not a reason-giving term. Other ideas are unproved; namely that the action-guiding influence of good requires it to be volitional or to have imperative force – for this fact, and its reflection in language, admit of other explanations. Other ideas again turn out to be logically incoherent; namely his views of freedom. Still other ideas are inadequately analysed; namely the idea of supervenience, the neutrality of facts, the non-teleology of nature and the separation of willing from knowledge. Finally other ideas limit the scope of his discussion; namely his terminology of description and evaluation which makes it impossible for him to state what naturalism really is.

Given all this, it is evident that in order to get a proper grasp of the question of naturalism we need a better discussion than Hare has managed to provide, or than Moore or Stevenson managed before him. In particular we are in need of a better understanding of willing and thinking, of good and of fact, or object of knowledge. That such understandings have so far been found lacking shows just how difficult it is to understand the issues surrounding the naturalistic fallacy within the terms set by the thinkers so far discussed.

CHAPTER 4

Critics of non-naturalism

THE NON-NATURALIST OUGHT

Non-naturalism of the English-speaking tradition may be said to have reached its most developed form in the work of Hare, but like any other philosophical theory it has had its critics. Among the first and most important of these, and perhaps the one who most set the scene for the others who followed, was G. E. M. Anscombe (Hudson, 1969: 26-27). Her original attack centred, not on the term 'good', but on the term 'ought'. For 'ought'-judgements are also value-judgements, and, as far as morality is concerned, perhaps the most common. On the non-naturalist account, such judgements are, no less than judgements about good, logically distinct from indicatives or statements of what is the case, and cannot be equated with them or derived from them. This distinction between factual and ought-judgements, or between the 'Is' and the 'Ought', is indeed the title under which non-naturalism has generally been best known.

Anscombe maintains that the sense of 'ought' used by non-naturalists in the 'is/ought' distinction is empty; it is just a hangover from a previous tradition of moral thought whose demise has rendered it meaningless. This previous tradition was the divine law tradition of Christianity that understood the 'ought' as expressive of what one was commanded to do by God. According to her, this tradition was substantially abandoned by Protestants at the time of the Reformation; but because of the way Christianity had dominated for so many centuries, the sense of 'ought' as 'bound by law' became "deeply embedded in our language and thought" (in Hudson,

1969: 180-181). However, without the notion of a law-giving God, this 'ought' was no longer intelligible; but instead of giving it up, moral philosophers (first in the person of Hume) tried to retain it by saying 'ought' had a special sense in moral contexts. It is this special sense that cannot be inferred from any 'is'-sentences because it has, she says, only "mesmeric" force and no content, and so cannot be inferred from anything at all (in Hudson, 1969: 182; cf. Foot, 1978: 162-163). Anscombe, therefore, suggests we give up the term altogether.

This criticism is completely wrong. First, the concept of 'ought' and indeed of other value terms is not at all empty in the work, for instance, of Hare and Stevenson. On the contrary, it has a very definite and intelligible role in expressing prescriptions and attitudes, or commitments of will. Second, the concept of 'ought' they use is not particularly a moral one, even if they concentrate on this aspect, for they both make it clear that their accounts of it, as of other value terms, cover the non-moral as well as the moral uses. Third, a study of their writings shows that in neither case do these views have any connection with divine law theories of ethics or their vestigial elements. Fourth, the sense of 'ought' she is attacking, where it is held to be 'autonomous' and independent of the facts, does not derive from Hume, who, despite distinguishing 'ought' from 'is', or rather from a certain sort of 'is', has no such conception of 'ought'. It derives, in fact, from Kant (as will be explained in the next chapter). Fifth, it is implausible to suppose that a concept could still endure embedded in our thought four hundred years after the demise of its only intelligible support. If it survives with so much vigour, as indeed it does, and not just in the thought of recent English-speaking philosophers (cf. Bambrough, 1979: 77-78; Strauss, 1953: chapter 2), it must be because it has a support that is still operative. It will in fact be argued in the next chapter, when Kant is examined, that it derives from the sense of freedom and nobility (combined, however, with a scientific and sceptical account of knowledge); and the sense of these things is indeed perennial, and can and does endure quite independently of vagaries in the history of religion.

Sixth, Anscombe's hypothesis does not explain what it is supposed to explain, which is the separation of the 'ought' from the 'is'. For even if one needs a law to give sense to this 'ought', why should not nature, instead of God, be the lawgiver? We may have lost the notion of divine law but we have also lost the notion of natural law; and the latter is the crucial one, for if it were the support of the 'ought' and the relevant sense of nature was lost, it would be very easy to explain why the 'ought' should be divorced from the 'is'. The same would not be so if a law-giving God was lost but a law-giving nature retained, for then, while the 'ought' would be separated from religion, it would not be separated from the 'is'.

Seventh, this brings to light an error in Anscombe's history. The Reformation did not cause an abandonment of divine law ethics; if anything it introduced one of a more thorough-going kind, for it introduced a divine law divorced from the natural (as MacIntyre pointed out; in Hudson, 1969: 49). In Catholic doctrine, at least as this was developed over the centuries (D'Entrèves, 1970: chapter 3), human nature was understood as fundamentally good, possessing still the mark of divine wisdom and containing the decrees of God in itself in the form of natural law; but Reformation doctrines of total human corruption effectively prohibited attempts to provide a foundation for morality in human nature. God's law came to be understood rather in terms of something imposed, if not necessarily in opposition to nature, at any rate regardless of it; and so the 'ought' of morality could simply have no ground in the 'is' of nature. Whether the 'ought' used by modern non-naturalists has anything to do with a lost sense of law is questionable, but that it has a connection with a demotion of nature from the realm of value there can be no doubt. It is this down-grading of nature that is responsible, if anything is, for the 'is/ought' distinction, not the loss of a law-giving God.

Anscombe has, despite, or perhaps because of, her strong dislike of non-naturalism, just not got to grips with it. Her failure here is well illustrated by the analysis she herself offers of a legitimate sense of 'ought'. It is the 'ought' used in 'the machinery ought to be oiled or it will not work,' and is equivalent to 'needs' in 'this plant needs this sort of soil to flourish' (in Hudson, 1969: 179, 181); and this 'needs' and 'ought' are inferred from the characteristics of the thing in question. Anscombe appeals, therefore, to a functional sense of 'ought', a sense which Hare, as has been seen, rejected for natural things. If she wants to establish her analysis against Hare, therefore, she needs to pay more attention to this dispute about nature and rather less to the history of divine-law ethics.

THE NON-NATURALIST GOOD

Anscombe has another criticism of non-naturalism. She argues that it is senseless to say, as non-naturalists must and do say, that one can logically desire anything or call anything good (it is one of the consequences of the separation of facts from values that one can take up a pro-attitude towards, or commend, any fact whatever). It only makes sense to say, for instance, 'I want a saucer of mud,' if there are desirability characteristics about mud that make one want it, and there is a limit to what can coherently count as such a characteristic (1963: 70-73).

Phillipa Foot has deployed a similar argument. She says there is a necessary internal relation between good and the things called good, and not, as is the case with non-naturalists, a merely contingent or external one dependent on what one's attitudes or choices happen to be. She points out that pride, for instance, cannot be felt except about something one sees as one's own and as constituting an achievement or advantage (in Hudson, 1969: 198-199). The same holds, she believes, for good and other value words, for these too have a necessary relation to certain things, and specifically matters of human benefit and harm. However, she does concede that such internal relations will only establish a limit as to what one can sensibly call good, if the relation is between good and certain things and not just between good and certain words; for if these words were themselves unlimited in application, as they could be, then one could assert them, and consequently also good, of anything one liked just as before. Her reply is that the relation is indeed to certain things, as she tries to show with the term 'injury' (in Hudson, 1969: 201-205). Not just anything can be thought of as injurious. One could not say one had been harmed if the hairs of one's head had been reduced to an even number, or if a bucket of water had been taken out of the sea. The same applies to good. One cannot, for instance, count clasping or unclasping one's hands three times an hour as a good action. No special background, she insists, must be brought in to show that such an action is desirable, say, because it is part of a religious ritual. For if it is to be genuinely possible to say good of anything, as non-naturalists affirm, then it must be possible to do this directly, and not just indirectly, or not just because what one is talking about (clasping and unclasping one's hands) falls under something else (religious ritual) to which good directly, and quite intelligibly, applies.

Hare's reply to both Anscombe and Foot is the same – they are talking about words, not things. Their point, he says, might be taken in one of two ways. If, on the one hand, they are claiming that nothing can be called good except in virtue of some desirability characteristics it has, and that these characteristics must not be viewed just as characteristics but also as desirable, then he entirely agrees with them, for the first is just another way of referring to what he calls the criteria, or descriptive element, of good, and the second is just another way of referring to what he calls the meaning, or evaluative element, of good. But, he is careful to insist, as far as this goes anything could be called good because one might have eccentric desires. If, on the other hand, they are claiming that there are logical ties between calling something good and also calling it pleasant, interesting, beneficial and so on, then again he agrees with them. For he is quite prepared to admit that if one claims to desire something, then logically one must not use certain words of it (say 'injury'), and may even have to be ready to apply certain other words to it (say 'pleasant'). But this does not get us beyond words and cannot show that there are certain things that must or must not be called good. Hare insists, against Anscombe and Foot, that there just is no limit to what one might, however oddly, come to want.

Bonum est multiplex, or good is multiple, he says, quoting Anscombe, and there is no way of putting a logical limit to its multiplicity (in Hudson, 1969: 247-252).

There is an important sense in which Hare is right here. It may be conceded that to be desired a thing has to be viewed as desirable, and even that to be viewed as desirable a thing has to be viewed under certain sorts of respects, as that of being pleasant, or agreeable, or interesting and so on, but this does not seem to set limits to the things that can be desired. For anything whatever, however odd, can be viewed as desirable and so be called good; and there are certainly enough people around with sufficiently odd desires to do this. If they use 'good' for what they desire, they cannot be accused of abusing words or of offending logic. But, on the other hand, Anscombe and Foot are also right. If the sorts of desires or value-judgements they object to are not logically impossible, they are certainly bizarre. What this debate shows, in fact, is that there is an ambiguity in the 'cannot' and 'makes sense' that they use (cf. Hudson, 1970: 308). There is a 'cannot simply' and a 'cannot sensibly', and the 'cannot' of 'one cannot desire a saucer of mud' and 'one cannot say one is harmed if one's hairs are reduced to an even number' is the latter, not the former. It is necessary, therefore, to draw a distinction within good between the sensible good and the non-sensible good (cf. Crombie, 1962: 274; Aristotle, *EN*: 1112a18-21). But it is also necessary to find some way of explaining this distinction. The distinction of older thinkers between the real and the apparent good is similar to it, but this distinction relies on there being ends or goods by nature, or on nature being teleological. Neither Anscombe nor Foot seem prepared unambiguously to assert a teleological view of nature, and it is fair to say that it is because of this that neither is able to establish their point against Hare. For one could only limit good to certain things, and even then only in the form of the sensible good, if the things were somehow, as a matter of their being, ends or goals, and hence if they were ends by nature.

Foot has also been criticised on other grounds by Phillips and Mounce, who say that her talk of internal relations already involves evaluation and not just description. For the fact or thing that is the object of the internal relation is not just a fact, but a fact assessed with respect to a norm. Pushing, for instance, is only 'rude' or 'offensive' if it is so assessed, not if "pure facts" alone are mentioned (as, say, in a physiological account of pushing). This is proved by the consideration that if it were just a matter of facts agreement would eventually be reached, for the facts are "incontrovertible," but in matters of morality one soon reaches "deadlock" (in Hudson, 1969: 232-239).

This argument will not work. Facts are not incontrovertible in the sense that no one will controvert them; for not only are there commitments that some people will deny anything to maintain, there is also sheer perversity. In morality perversity is more of a problem because it touches human desires and interests so closely, while science does not. Terrorists, for instance, who want to go on committing murder, will not be concerned to deny the impossibility of squaring the circle, but they will be concerned to deny that there is anything really bad about murder, or that what they are doing is really murder, no matter what one says to show the opposite. One must distinguish between 'incontrovertible' where it refers to what one can do, and where it refers to what the facts will allow. The facts of plane triangles do not allow them to have angles equal to more or less than 180°, but that does not mean one cannot deny this if one so wishes. There is nothing, even in science, that is incontrovertible in this sense, but of course that does not mean there is nothing incontrovertible in it in the other sense. With respect to the phenomenon of disagreement, therefore, one has no reason to suppose that morality is any different from science. It does, indeed, suffer more from perverse controversion than science does, but that is not surprising given how it may, and often does, cross our desires. The fact, however, that it is often controverted in this sense cannot show that it is controvertible in the other sense. One cannot, therefore, determine whether morality has to do with facts or not by adverting to "deadlocks" in moral disagreements.

Nevertheless if Phillips' and Mounce's argument fails, their objection does not. If by "pure facts" is meant something non-evaluative then no moral term is purely factual and it would be false to say it was. Moral terms involve assessment with respect to a standard and if there is no standard referred to the term is not being used morally. The question, as already stated in the previous chapter, concerns not the reference to standards but the status of them, whether they are set up by nature or not. It is not at all clear whether Foot realises this, and, therefore, not at all clear whether she wants to equate 'values' with 'facts' in the value-free sense of 'fact' used by Hare, Stevenson, Phillips and Mounce. It is thus not clear either whether she realises that one must challenge as much the sense of 'fact' used by non-naturalists as their sense of 'value', though she is aware that the way these words are defined by them, namely in terms of each other, begs the question (1978: 100). It is this lack of clarity in her position which serves to provide some excuse for the way Hare distorts naturalism when he tries to refute it; for the distorted naturalism that results is the sort of naturalism towards which some of his opponents are inclined.

Foot, however, like Anscombe, has another line of attack against non-naturalism. She maintains that saying something is good need not have any connection with choice. The criteria of goodness for some things are established just by what they are independently of choices, as is the case with 'good knife'. The same is true of 'good father', for a man who offered up his children for sacrifice could not be called by us a good father (in Hudson, 1969: 219). As the example of knife shows, this is just another recourse to a functional sense of good, and leaves her open to her critics' retort that moral good is not functional. Foot consistently fails to develop a reply to this objection.

Nevertheless, she pursues her point in another way by saying that choosing something is not a mark that one thinks it good, and that one's thinking something good, even in moral contexts, need not involve any disposition to choose it. Hare rightly regards this view as "not very plausible" (in Hudson, 1969: 209, 254). There may, indeed, be a sense of good in which it is not connected with choice, as she insists, but there is also a sense in which it is. But she seems to believe that if she asserts the former she must deny the latter, and this is not at all necessary (unless one is committed to some Moorean sort of view according to which good is always the same everywhere).

FOOT'S COGNITIVE GOOD

Despite these criticisms Foot has persisted in her opposition to non-naturalism, and to see where this leads her it is necessary to examine her own ethical theory. This, like Hare's, is centred round the connection between good and action. At first she accepted that good has action-guiding force, but instead of identifying it with some extra 'volitional element', she tried to explain it in terms of the facts with which the goodness of a good act is connected. Some things, the virtues for instance, are such that they give anyone a reason for choosing them because everyone has need of them (1967: 8-9). Courage, temperance and prudence proved easy to explain in this way but justice did not. Thrasymachus had argued in Plato's *Republic* that justice harms the just because it prevents them getting what they want, and could seize, if they were strong and unjust. As Foot was concerned to show that everyone has a reason to be just, and as she believed that the only reason for action that could be appealed to universally was self-interest (1978: xiii), she found herself, unlike Plato's Socrates, unable to justify justice against Thrasymachus' attack. The most she could manage was to show that the profitability of injustice was "very dubious" (in Hudson, 1969: 213).

Foot was, therefore, faced with a dilemma; either she abandoned the belief that justice was a virtue, a good worth having, or she abandoned the belief that everyone has a reason to be moral. She was initially inclined to abandon the first belief because, as she says, she was at one with her opponents in maintaining the second. Eventually, however, she abandoned the second instead, having been convinced by examples of good in non-moral contexts (as 'good knife') that good has no necessary connection with choice. This led her to the view that just as only those have a reason to choose good knives who have an interest in possessing one, so only those have a reason to be just who have an interest in being just, and not everyone has such an interest (1967: 8-9; 1978: xiii). Judgements of good, she declares, are in themselves not connected with choices, nor do they furnish reasons for choosing, nor do they have action-guiding force, but only when in conjunction with an interest or desire to be good (1978: 177). It is evident from these remarks that we are back, not only with Moore, who ignored the action-guiding force of good even if he did not deny it, but also with Hare. Like him she believes that thinking does not move the will, only willing itself does, so that if a judgment guides choices it can only be if one's will is already engaged in favour of what the judgement is about.

Foot thinks she is moving away from the position of Hare and Stevenson (1978: xii), but, at least in the crucial respect, she is not. 'Good', she is in effect saying, is only to be used with 'descriptive' content, and the action-guiding element, the 'evaluative' content, is to be located, not in the meaning of 'good', but in the interests or wants of individuals. In other words for her, just as for Hare, thinking and willing remain quite accidental to each other, and the 'gap' that divides them remains unbridged; also facts, or objects of knowledge, remain without action-guiding force. The only difference in Foot's case is that acts of willing are to be regarded as external to judgments that something is good and not as constituent parts of them. As Hare said, though not in the sense he intended, the dispute between them is about words (but see his later remarks; 1981: 189).

Foot has, in fact, misunderstood in what sense she and Hare are opposed. She is principally attacking the view that everyone has a reason to be moral, but while some may hold this view, Hare does not. He holds that it is quite possible to drop out of morality and refuse to make any moral judgements at all, though he does regard this as rather hard to do given the facts of human life (1963: 51, 200-201; 1981: 186-

187). Where the disagreement between her and Hare really lies is in her rejection of autonomous evaluations, or autonomous 'oughts', that lack a sufficient justification in anything factual (1978: 96). In other words she rejects the idea of ultimate decisions and spontaneous acts of will. What she wants to do instead is to reconnect choices with reasons for choosing, that is, with interests and desires. To this extent she initiates a return from Hare to Stevenson. The interests she has in mind are those one just happens to have; they are, in her words, "contingent ends" (1978: 169; cf. also 167). This means they are more like Stevenson's attitudes or feelings than Hare's decisions of principle. This shift back to Stevenson deserves to be pursued further, because it has serious consequences for her theory in two important respects, namely as to how one becomes moral and what status moral judgements have.

Hare insisted on the fact that what is involved in morality are decisions that one makes in one's capacity as a free and responsible agent. For Foot these are replaced by contingent interests. She does, indeed, admit that these interests must be interests in morality for its own sake and not for some 'pay-off' one might get out of it (a mistake she had made when trying to justify justice, and for which she had been taken to task by Phillips and Mounce; Foot, 1978: 165-166; in Hudson, 1969: 233). But she stresses that not everyone has them, and that they are contingent to those who do have them, so that there is reason to fear that one might find at some point that one had ceased to care about morality (1978: 167, 170). Yet, having said this, she then goes on, paradoxically, to say that we must regard ourselves as if we were "volunteers in the army of duty." Does this mean then that we choose to be moral? This is what she appears to assert, but she fails to spell out what it means in the context of her theory. How, for instance, is this choice made? It could not be based on any reasons unless they referred to interests one already had, for she is operating on the view that only thus would they actually be reasons. If these interests were non-moral they could hardly ground a moral choice, since then one's moral behaviour would be for the sake of non-moral ends, and this is precisely not to behave morally (as she admits). If the interests were moral then there could be no question of volunteering to be a member of the moral army, since one would already be a member of it, for it is surely a principal mark of moral persons that they have moral interests, or take an interest in morality for its own sake. One might choose without reasons, but that would make the choice arbitrary and Foot wants to get away from such unfounded choosings. Besides, how could an arbitrary choice be a subject of praise and blame, and yet surely those who are moral are rightly praised?

The result of this is that it proves impossible to volunteer to be moral. If anyone is moral it cannot, therefore, be a result of choice but rather of various involuntary factors like birth, heredity, upbringing or the chances and changes of life, which, for some reason, had given one these interests instead of those. This would make it unreasonable to blame those who were not moral, if they were not responsible for this and could not change save by some unforeseen accident; nor could one praise those who were moral, since the same would be true of them. And there is yet this further consequence, that for all those who have no interest in morality, morality is, at best, useless and more probably harmful, since it would require the suppression of their non-moral interests, the only 'good' they have. To say it is not good to be moral, at least for some people, comes pretty close to being an immoral thesis. To quote Archbishop Whateley:

> If anyone really holds that it can ever be expedient to violate the injunctions of duty, – that he who does so is not sacrificing a greater good to a less (which all would admit to be inexpedient), – that it can be really advantageous to do what is morally wrong, – and will come forward and acknowledge that to be his belief, I have only to protest, for my part, with the deepest abhorrence, against what I conceive to be so profligate a principle (1877: 316).

Foot does indeed assert that the person who does not care about morality cannot be shown to be wrong. Now whether one considers this Thrasymachean view serious depends on whether one thinks morality to be important. Foot clearly does, so she ought to find her own theory morally disturbing; but she does not (1978: xiv).

This brings us to the second point about Foot's ethical theory, namely what status she gives to moral judgements. They have no necessary connection with choices and decisions, nor are they themselves decisions, so what are they? It transpires, in the end, that they express merely conventional beliefs. When it comes to moral rules what we actually have are "rules of conduct adopted by certain societies and individuals within these societies" (1978: 171); and moral judgements on their own, without connection with interests, are on a par with rules of etiquette, which are confessedly conventional (1978: 162, 164).

Foot does not say anything about any objective basis on which morality might rest. Consequently she leaves certain important questions unasked. Is this morality good? If it is conventional, is it any more than the expression of other people's prejudices, and so, quite possibly, bad? Ought one to care about it even if in fact one does not? In short, ought one to be moral? All Foot will say is that the sense of 'ought' involved here is just the way society is apt to voice its demands, or is tautologous, or makes no sense (1978: 166, 169-170). But this is to miss what is really important, for this sense is perhaps the most urgent and pressing sense that the term 'ought' can have. Foot endeavours, it is true, to mitigate the effect of her words by saying that the person who does not care about morality cannot escape moral censure (1978: 172). But if this morality is conventional what can moral censure be other than a mere calling of names? It just reflects the personal standards of some individual or group of individuals, and to use it to measure everyone else by is to force everyone into one's own subjective mould. To call people uncharitable because they do not care to be charitable in our sense, is like calling everyone who does not follow the teachings of Trotsky capitalist lackeys. But morality, whatever it is, is surely not like this.

Some have thought, and with good reason, that Foot's theory subverts morality because it shows morality to be bad.

She makes moral judgements into conventions, renders being or not being moral a matter of chance, and only allows 'ought' to give a reason for action when it is relative to one's actual desires, that is, when it means something like, 'You ought to do whatever you desire to do' (as she virtually admits; 1978: 170). One is reminded of the belief of Plato's Thrasymachus that morality, or justice, is just what the stronger impose on the weaker. Foot is by no means as colourful or as rhetorical as he is but she cannot help ending up on his side, however much she tries not to. Both are opposed to the idea that the moral 'ought', an 'ought' that is supposed to bind irrespective of one's wants or the facts about one's wants, is anything other than an unjust and senseless imposition (Foot, 1978: 162, 167, 177). Foot's opponents, disturbed by this iconoclasm, resort to reinforcing the same 'ought' all over again. To preserve morality from contamination with contingent wants, they invent, in the manner of Kant, an 'ought' that is categorical, or not relative to ends at all.

One must note, in respect of this, that there is a crucial ambiguity in Foot's central thesis that reasons are relative to interests. She speaks as if the only way one can have an interest in being moral is if one actually takes an interest in it; she fails to consider the distinction between taking an interest, which is a matter of actual desires, and having an interest, which is not. True, she does say that people who do not care about morality may find their lives "sadly spoiled" (1978: 167), which certainly suggests that they did have an interest in being moral though they did not realise it; but she does not spell out how this could be possible, especially if, as she is prepared to admit, they get what they want. This could only be, in fact, if there were objective interests independent of our thoughts and conscious desires. And this itself requires explanation in terms of natural ends or natural goods. Foot, however, like Hare, does not seem prepared to resurrect this belief of older thinkers.

This, in fact, is another important belief she has in common with Hare. In speaking of interests or preferences both confine themselves to those that people may actually have or feel, and which, therefore are contingent and can change over time (Hare, 1981: 180, 226). Neither adopts the view, which was central to the older naturalism, that there are natural desires, or inclinations, that belong to the structure or being of things, and which are accordingly not contingent but necessarily always present, whether consciously felt or not. To say there are such ontological desires, as opposed to purely experiential ones, is, of course, just another way of saying nature is teleological. Such a view does need explaining, and all the more so nowadays given the prevalence and success of modern non-teleological science; but it must not be dismissed automatically and without argument.

Foot's failure to separate 'having an interest' from 'taking an interest' exposes her to another criticism, for it is because of this failure that she adopts the belief that one will only have a reason to be moral if one wants to be moral. She wishes to get away from unfounded 'oughts', or the autonomous evaluations of Hare, and the only way she finds it possible to do this is by connecting 'oughts' with actual or conscious desires, which are the only interests she considers. But it has been urged against her that it is not true that operative moral beliefs, those one actually follows, must be grounded in wants, for rather the reverse is the case. Someone who says that she does not want to have an abortion, or to marry an unbeliever, is not necessarily expressing her "psychological state;" she may be expressing a judgement based on convictions of what it is good or bad to do (Hudson, 1970: 269-270).

Some hold these convictions to be part of a basic moral stance which is beyond argument (Phillips and Mounce in Hudson, 1969: 238-239). Others that they are the result of seeing things in a particular way (McDowell, 1978: 13-29; Murdoch, 1970; Platts, 1979; cf. also Wiggins, 1976); but little is said as to what this 'seeing' precisely is (cf. Lovibond, 1983: 11-17). Murdoch, for instance, says it is a seeing reality as it is and is especially the effect of art and literature, but she does not give any detailed account of what such a reality must be like if seeing it as it is somehow reveals good (1970: 91-93). Nevertheless, the claims that there is value to things themselves, and that it is possible to see this if one views them in the right way, along with the associated claim, certainly present, if only implicitly, in Murdoch's sort of position, that thinking can and does move willing, deserve to be carefully considered. They cannot be assumed to be wrong.

THE NATURALISM OF LOVIBOND AND LEE

Anscombe and Foot have been the most discussed and most followed of the critics of non-naturalism. Indeed some of their positions have been taken up again recently, though for rather different reasons, by Lovibond (1983) and Lee (1985). An examination of the writings of these later authors will give an idea of how little the contemporary debate about non-naturalism has changed.

Like Anscombe and Foot, Lovibond rejects the non-naturalist claim that there is a distinction between descriptive and evaluative modes of language. The reason, she says, is that language is "homogeneous" and "seamless", and not differentiated in the way non-naturalists say it is. This is because the functions of describing and evaluating pervade the whole of language. All assertoric discourse is both at once, and facts and values "coalesce" into one (1983: 25, 27). The theory of language which she relies on to say this is given the name "expressivism". A language embodies or gives expression to the shared way of life of a community. Consciousness and thought do not exist independently but only when embodied in a language, and a language is a social product, a social practice. In other words there is a certain way of life in which the use of terms such as 'chair', 'table', 'horse', as well as 'courage', 'theft', 'deceit', are more or less definitely prescribed, and if one uses these words one can do so only because one is part of the common way of life embodied in that usage. If it is the practice of the community to use the word 'chair' in this way and the word 'courage' in that way, then it is 'wrong' or 'false', not to say incoherent, to use them in a different way. The norms of what is to count as true, rational, correct and so on are established by consensus or agreement in ways of acting; there is no distinction between the "actually true" and the "held true by us" (1983: 37, 58-65, 148).

Given this view of the nature of language it is easy to see how value-judgements can be regarded as statements that are true or false, and how factual judgements can be regarded as evaluations. Value-judgements can be true or false because the words in them are governed in their use by the rules of the linguistic and social practice of the community that the language expresses and embodies. A certain use will be true if it follows the agreed rules for evaluating things and false if it breaks them. Descriptions are evaluations because to describe something as a chair, say, is not to assert the presence of some objective fact that exists out there in its own right and to which the speaker's judgement has to conform if it is to be true (as non-naturalists have supposed is the case with scientific facts), but to give expression to the prevailing or agreed upon evaluation as to what is to count as a chair in this social practice.

This position about limitations on what can correctly or intelligibly be called good or bad, while like that of Anscombe and Foot, differs in that what is said to determine the limitations is not some 'facts' about human benefit and harm that are presumed to be ascertainable independently of social practices, but just such social practices or ways of life themselves. It is for this reason that it is a position that labours not just under some of Anscombe's and Foot's problems but also under certain difficulties of its own.

To take first the non-naturalist point about the connection between good and willing or action. Lovibond's answer is that all language involves desire and has a connection with practice, for language as a whole, as an expression of a way of life, is an expression of human interests and concerns and doings. The difference between moral words and non-moral words, the reason why the former especially give reasons for action, is that they express "unconditional" concerns, concerns that are integral to one's whole vision of an intrinsically admirable and praiseworthy life, while the latter express only concerns that are contingent and passing. To ignore the former is necessarily to give up, if only temporally, one's interest in living an admirable life. This is not so in the case of the latter (1983: 52-54). But while this answer does establish a difference, it raises the same question as was raised earlier about Foot. Since these "unconditional" concerns can come and go, how, if one has lost them, does one recover them, and how, if one has them, did one come to have them? Either there are reasons here or there are not. If there are not, then whether one is moral or not is a matter of accident or fate or something else not in our control, and this makes nonsense of moral praise and blame as well as of any attempt to say that those who do not bother with moral concerns nevertheless should. If, on the other hand, there are reasons, then we need to be told what they are and how they operate. They could hardly be internal to the vision that establishes what is to count as admirable and what is not, for then they would not be reasons for those who had abandonned, or did not yet share, that vision. Nor could they be external, because Lovibond is operating on the theory that giving reasons is only possible within an agreed way of life and social practice, and not from some point outside (1983: 38-40). In short there are, and could be, no reasons for adopting this vision rather than that. If one has adopted a certain vision, this will be because of the accidents of history, or of coercion by some authority, or something else of the sort. All the criticisms, therefore, directed above against Foot's position can be directed with equal justice against this one as well.

This highlights, in fact, a flaw in the whole theory of language Lovibond adopts, namely its fundamental irrationalism. Lovibond is not so much a naturalist or realist as a cognitive relativist (Lee, 1985: 37-46; cf. also Rosen, 1969: chapter 1; Strauss, 1953: chapter 1). Whereas, with non-naturalists, only part of our discourse is unfounded in any independent reality, namely values, and facts do possess such foundation, with Lovibond everything becomes unfounded. The claims of non-naturalists are not overcome; they are just rendered global. We are what we are and we do and say the things we do, not because there is any objective truth or reality for us to know (there is not), but because our social practice is the way it is. There are, of course, other such practices or ways of life different from ours, but there is no way of judging between them, or of making an informed and unbiassed assessment about which is right or better. All judging takes place from within a form of life, for there is no speech or thought outside a form of life; consequently judging will always beg the question in favour of the form of life from within which the judging is done. The very notion of an 'outside' is incoherent.

We might express this in another way by saying that for Lovibond everything has become a value, including 'reality' and the 'facts', because nothing can be for us except as mediated through the prism of that most fundamental of values, our way of life, our way of looking at and doing things. In other words the irrationalism that Stevenson, despite himself, finally collapsed into, Lovibond embraces willingly and with open eyes. What she does not realise, however (though she appears to at times; 1983: 147, 151-158, and compare 5 with 141), is that her position cannot be a refutation of non-naturalism nor a moral realism when it is, in fact, nothing but a non-naturalism of a more thorough-going kind.

Lee, unlike Lovibond, has the merit of seeing and rejecting the irrationalism in Lovibond's thesis (1985: 37-46). She attempts to overcome non-naturalism in a more rational and direct way. She does not, unlike most other critics, deny the validity of Hare's distinction between description and evaluation; what she says is that there is a relationship of implication between the two, or that there is such a thing as descriptive evidence for an evaluative claim. This implication is not strict implication, such as one finds in logic and mathematics; it is rather what she calls "epistemic implication" (1985: chapter 3). Epistemic implication is not something peculiar to ethics. It is in fact pervasive throughout the domain of science and ordinary knowledge. The point, she says, is this. No evidence of any sort is ever sufficient to prove conclusively the assertion that is said to be based on it; all that the evidence can do is more or less confirm the assertion. For example, no amount of empirical or perceptual evidence could guarantee the claim, 'This is a cow' (1985: 102), but such evidence could more or less confirm it, and one would be justified in believing it unless, or until, one was faced with contrary evidence. Non-naturalists, she says, have grasped this truth as regards ethics, for they have seen that no 'ought'-proposition is strictly implied by any 'is'-propositions. But they have not seen that the same is true of most other domains of knowledge as well. If they did, they would realise that the lack of strict implication cannot mean that 'ought'-propositions are unfounded and arbitrary, for then most other propositions would likewise be unfounded, and non-naturalists have not wanted to say that. They have said, on the contrary, that scientific propositions and ordinary empirical claims are, or can be, well-founded.

According to Lee, therefore, what one has to say instead is that while 'is' does not strictly imply 'ought', 'ought' does nevertheless "epistemically" imply 'is'. In other words, while no set of 'is'-propositions compels one to assent to some 'ought'-proposition, nevertheless one cannot adopt any 'ought'-judgement one likes in total disregard of all the facts, just as one cannot assert any other judgement in total disregard of all the facts. One has to cite some relevant evidence in support. For instance, one cannot say that this cow is ill because it has two eyes, for a cow's having two eyes is not relevant to its being ill. One has to say something like this cow is ill because it is refusing to eat. Likewise one cannot say that a certain person should be imprisoned because it is Wednesday today, for the fact that it is Wednesday is of no relevance to the necessity or duty of punishment. But if one said that the person was guilty of some serious crime, then that would be all right (1985: 93-96). One is, moreover, obliged to say something like this because 'ought', like other assertions, does epistemically imply 'is', that is, it does require some relevant evidence in its support; it cannot just be asserted arbitrarily, without regard to any such evidence at all.

It can readily be seen that this position is very similar to that of Anscombe and Foot. Like them, Lee says that one cannot adopt any moral commitment whatever, however arbitrary; one must give reasons and these reasons must be serious and not trivial ones. But, as was argued earlier, this is not sufficient to refute non-naturalism. Certain commitments might be arbitrary, but provided they are not impossible, then the logic of 'ought' is such that it requires no necessary connection with any 'is', and this is all that nonnaturalism needs to establish itself. Epistemic implication, therefore, fares no better in this respect than Foot's internal relations or Anscombe's desirability characteristics.

Lee's position, in fact, misses the point. The reason why the 'is/ought' distinction is asserted by non-naturalists such as Hare, is not because of a lack of strict entailment between evidence and conclusion (something that might well, as Lee points out, obtain in the descriptive sphere), but because of a difference in mood between 'is' and 'ought'. An 'ought' commits one to action in a way that an 'is' does not; that is why 'oughts' are in the imperative, as opposed to the indicative, mood. No amount of talk about epistemic implication is going to answer this point; it has to be faced directly by itself. Lee, however, has not done this; indeed, like many critics of non-naturalism, she has failed to appreciate the force of the non-naturalist case in this respect. For instance, she gives as evidence that torture is to be avoided the fact that people typically avoid pain (1985: 94-95). But Hare would readily retort that saying what people typically do is not the same as saying what they ought to do, precisely because of the change from 'is' to 'ought'. Lee cannot claim to have answered this by her talk about relevant evidence, for this change needs to be explained and one cannot explain it just by repeating that change oneself and then carrying on as if nothing had happened.

Besides these failures to refute non-naturalism, Lee's theory is also suspect in itself. This is because of its scepticism about the possibility of attaining final truth in any matter. Lee is, in her own terms, a "fallibilist", someone who does not believe that any position or assertion can be shown to be infallibly correct; all conclusions are no more than tentative, open to further criticism and possible overthrow by new and contradictory arguments (1985: 194-195, 196-201). Epistemic implication is clearly fallibilist in this sense. However one can ask the same question about this theory as was asked earlier about Ayer's theory, namely what happens when it is applied to itself? Is the theory of fallibilism infallibly correct or not? If it is then fallibilism is not true of the theory of fallibilism and at least here we can reach final truth. But once a breach has been made in the theory at one point, why not at other points also? If we can in this case reach final truth, we have reason to believe that we might be able to do the same again elsewhere, so we ought not to blind ourselves to that possibility by adopting a theory that rules it out in advance. If, however, the theory of fallibilism is not infallibly correct, but, like everything else, open to future revision, then do we any longer have a fallibilist theory? Clearly not because the possibility is now expressly left open that fallibilism might be found out, and infallibly found out, to be false. So, whatever we say, fallibilism overthrows itself.

WARNOCK'S COGNITIVE HOBBESIAN GOOD

It is clear that the later critics of non-naturalism have not managed to advance beyond the earlier ones, and that both groups have failed either to give any convincing criticisms or to present rival theories of their own that are acceptable. This should be sufficient to dismiss further consideration of them. However there is a reason to examine one more critic, G.J. Warnock. This is not because he has any new arguments against non-naturalism, for the ones he puts forward are not significantly different from Foot's and fall foul of the same difficulties as hers did. It is rather because of the doctrine of naturalism that he himself puts forward. An examination of this will serve the valuable purpose of highlighting what, in the context of the modern debate about the naturalistic fallacy, certainly needs to be highlighted, namely the extent to which that debate is indebted, for its form and presuppositions, to the writings of some of the great thinkers of the past three or four hundred years. By seeing this historical connection, and tracing the common elements to their origin (which will be done in the next chapter), one is enabled to see with greater clarity that, as has in part already been argued, what is really most important in the modern debate about naturalism has not been regarded as most important by the protagonists in it, but has been passed over, usually without argument, and sometimes without notice.

In his attempt to establish a real or natural basis for morality, Warnock has recourse to a pessimism he consciously adopts from Hobbes. The human predicament, he says, is such that things tend to get worse. There is a lack of resources and a lack of knowledge (especially technological); human needs are complex and contradictory; and life is short. This results in a competition for the satisfaction of wants – a satisfaction however that is in principle unattainable. People also have limited sympathies; they are naturally selfish and tend not to do what would benefit others, and even themselves, in the long run. It is this selfishness that is the crucial factor in whether the human predicament will get better or worse in those respects in which it can be bettered by human action. The object of morality is to make people less selfish and in this way to ameliorate the human condition. In other words, morality is necessary because nature is cruel; while we want by nature to behave selfishly, our lot by nature is such that we cannot get away with it, and the job of the moral virtues is to put a constraint on our natural tendencies (1971: 17-26). Nature, then, is not on the side of humanity nor of morality; it is opposed to both.

This conception of nature and virtue is distinctively Hobbesian; indeed it virtually originated in Hobbes. It is, moreover, not the only respect in which Warnock follows him, for he also declares, like Hobbes, that humanity has no ultimate end. There is no 'good life'; that is a "senseless question" (1971: 89-90). The job of morality and moral virtue is to make a depressing human condition less so (cf. Mackie, 1977: 107-114).

Hobbes' view, to put it briefly (a fuller discussion will be given in the next chapter), is that the only goods that people pursue are their own selfish pleasures. We find pleasure in diverse things, so there can be no one end for us but an infinity of different and conflicting ones. Since, however, the unhindered pursuit of pleasure leads to misery and war, it is necessary to put some stop to it, and this is the function of morality and the state. This view is obviously very close to that of Warnock, but Warnock, it must be pointed out, notes something about Hobbesian morality that Hobbes ignored. If morality's job is to hinder one in one's natural but selfish inclinations, this must furnish a reason for regarding morality as bad, because it is thus shown to be unnatural and liable to produce "neuroses" and "a general psychic malaise" (1971: 161-162). This objection cannot, Warnock says, be ruled out as unreasonable, though he himself thinks that while morality may have bad consequences, things would be worse without it.

Such a 'paranoiac' morality differs from that of the older naturalists in precisely these two respects of nature and ultimate ends. The moral virtues were understood as promoting one's natural inclinations, and as indicative of nature's generosity and good will, not its meanness and hostility. It was also held that humanity does have an ultimate end, namely the perfection and fulfilment of nature, and that morality is to be understood by reference to this.

That humanity has no such end is not only rejected by Hobbes and Warnock, it is also rejected by Stevenson (1944: 202-204, 329) Rawls (1972: 325-332), and Hare (1963: 147-156; cf. also MacIntyre, 1984: 119). The sorts of reasons given for this are, first, that it is irrational as well as fanatical and destructive to subordinate or sacrifice the many ends people have to some one particular end among them (e.g. Rawls, 1972: 553-554), and, second, that the attempt of the older thinkers to base this end on some distinguishing mark of human nature is impossible because there is no such mark. The things people can do are many and various, and some of them are good and some bad. There is, in fact, a crucial ambiguity about human qualities that indicates a radical freedom in human nature, that is, a radical lack of orderedness to one thing rather than another. Human nature is too complex to justify one moral ideal (Williams, 1972: 73-76; Hare in Foot, 1967: 81n.).

These points will be taken up expressly in chapter 9, but it is worth adding here, by way of anticipation, that the sort of end the older thinkers had in mind was not an excluding but an including end, and that the phenomena of human diversity are not necessarily incompatible with the idea that human nature is ordered to such an end. It is, nevertheless, important to note how common a theme the rejection of supreme ends has been in most moral philosophy since Hobbes, even when, like modern naturalists and non-naturalists, they have sharply disagreed about other things.

The debts, however, of modern moral philosophers to great thinkers of the past do not just concern this matter of supreme ends. Hare's indebtedness to Hume has often been remarked on, both by himself and others, but he is far more indebted to Kant, particularly as regards the claim, which is the very essence of his theory, that evaluation is a matter of will, not of thought (e.g. 1963: 34, 219). In fact he makes his dependence on Kant particularly explicit in his latest book (1981). He bases his ethical theory on what he claims to be the 'logic' of moral words like 'good' and 'ought', meaning by 'logic' their function in language, or their usage. This logic is itself, he says, the expression of the "linguistic intuitions" of language-users, or their discernment of what is permissible and impermissible usage. But, he adds, it is above all Kant whom we must thank for giving us our understanding of this logic (1981: 4, 8-11). In other words Hare's logic is Kantian philosophy.

What this shows is that, in order to understand the issue of the naturalistic fallacy, it is not enough to consider what modern moral philosophers have said about it; one must also consider what those other thinkers said who are their principal sources. This more historical question must be treated before the philosophical issues themselves are directly faced, for the light that the former can throw on the latter is considerable.

CHAPTER 5

Historical origins

REVIEW

This investigation began as an attempt to understand the issue of the naturalistic fallacy as it has been discussed in modern moral philosophy. The results may be summarised as follows. First, no convincing argument has been found to show that naturalism, the view that there are goods by nature, is wrong let alone a fallacy. Second, very little has in fact been found to show that naturalism, as it exists at any rate in its classical or traditional form, has been understood. Third, while it is, as a consequence, impossible within the limits of most modern moral philosophy to treat properly the question of naturalism, those matters nevertheless have been uncovered, namely good, being, willing and thinking, that must be dealt with if such a treatment is to be given.

That modern authors have generally failed to get to grips with naturalism is as true of its professed supporters as of their non-naturalist opponents. The views of the latter, however, are of greater significance for this study, partly because these views are, in important respects, also shared by most of the former, but mainly because they constitute the basis of the attack on naturalism and serve to make clear what that attack amounts to. These views may be summarised briefly as follows. The factual or natural, the realm of the 'is' and of knowledge, is the preserve of modern science and is evaluatively neutral; good is not part of the natural or the 'is' and is not an object of knowledge but an expression of volitions; thinking does not move willing; there are no desires save actual or contingent ones; there is no highest good for human beings. These beliefs taken together express a vision of how things are, or of what humanity and the world are like.

The importance of this point must not be overlooked, for it means that, in some sense, the basic fact for non-naturalists is the nature of things, or their view of the nature of things. In other words, for them, as for naturalists, nature is the fundamental thing. This is evident, indeed, even from the statement itself of the non-naturalist position, for when Hare and Stevenson, for instance, say that facts and values are radically distinct, they are in effect saying that this is the fact of the matter, or that it is a fact that values are not facts. And 'fact' here, where it is used to express how things generally are, is just an alternative for 'nature'. In other words, views about ethics even here are dependent on views about nature. This point has indeed been adverted to in passing in the previous chapters, but it must now be looked at directly, for in the light of it one must say that what separates the older or traditional view of ethics from the modern non-naturalist one (and even the modern naturalist one), and what therefore lies at the heart of the debate about the naturalistic fallacy, is a difference in views about nature.

The discussion in the preceding chapters confirms this conclusion, for what the naturalistic fallacy amounts to is the charge that naturalists are confusing two different things: goodness or value on the one hand, and nature or facts on the other. But this charge rests on the belief that the two are distinct in the way non-naturalists say they are. This belief is assumed rather than proved, and it leads, in addition, to a mistaking of the point at issue. For the point is not whether it is possible or legitimate to reduce the good or the evaluative to the natural or non-evaluative (that is, not whether this sort of 'naturalism' is a fallacy), but whether 'good' and 'nature' must be understood in such a way that of necessity they exclude each other. The issue, in other words, does not begin with the naturalistic fallacy, but at one stage further back, at the presuppositions or foundations on which the non-naturalistic case rests.

If the real issue is this question about nature and one's

views about nature, it is this that most needs examining. Unfortunately, however, modern non-naturalists have not said very much in explanation or defence of their views in this respect. They have, as has already been pointed out, taken them pretty much for granted. It is evident, nevertheless, that these views are derived, first, from their belief in the more or less universal competence of modern science, and, second, from their acceptance of the teaching of certain of the great thinkers of the past, notably Hobbes, Locke, Hume and Kant. In order, therefore, to understand better the vision of nature that modern non-naturalists (and even modern naturalists) are operating with, it is necessary to understand something about these thinkers, and about the way modern science emerged and developed. It will be found that these two issues can be considered together, for they are both part of the same tradition of thought, which, for the sake of convenience, and indeed with considerable fidelity to the facts, may be called the modern tradition. This tradition is not only the one that is still most dominant today in several of its various forms, it also had its beginnings in that same period of European history when, by the common consent and terminology of historians, the modern world was itself emerging.

THE MODERN VISION OF 'REALISM'

It is saying nothing new to point out that during this particular period there was a general feeling, expressed by many of the important figures of the day, that the bonds of the past were at last being broken. In matters both religious and secular a self-conscious departure was made from the ideas that had prevailed up to then. It was a claim of people like Luther, on the one hand, and Bacon, on the other, that their age was witness to a new birth of the human spirit. Whereas previous ages, whether ancient or medieval, laboured under various degrees of darkness, the present was at last emerging into the light. It is not the place in a properly philosophical work to dwell on religious developments (though as Kant, and even more Hegel, well knew, there is a close connection between their philosophies and certain fundamental ideas of the Reformers); what is of concern here is to note the change in moral and political thought that took place.

This change centres round the question of the *summum bonum:* the supreme or highest good. This notion was, one may say, the very substance of the previous tradition of moral and political thought. According to that tradition, there is by nature a highest good which can be discovered by reason, and the best life is the life governed by and directed towards that good. Modern thought may be said to begin with the denial of such a good.

This denial is found most emphatically in Hobbes (*Leviathan:* ch.11), though it is worth noting that Hobbes was just following here a path previously marked out by Machiavelli (cf. *Discourses:* Bk.1, ch.37, Bk.2, Preface; Strauss, 1953: 177-180). According to Hobbes there is no supreme good such as is mentioned by the "old moral philosophers", because human passions are not fixed on any one thing, but are continually passing from one object of desire to another. The human quest for satisfactions is interminable and insatiable. Everyone is dominated by a "perpetual and restless desire of power after power that ceaseth only in death;" for what everyone wants is not just satisfaction now but an ability to secure satisfaction for the future (*Leviathan:* ch.11). This inevitably brings people into conflict, since they are competing for limited goods and so striving to get the better of each other. From this results the "war of everyman against everyman" where, far from being satisfied or secure, each is in continual fear of violent death. In such a condition the most urgent and most necessary thing is peace (*ibid:* chs.13-15).

Peace, one may say, is the universal and essential condition for the attainment of any satisfaction whatever, and for the procurement and safe enjoyment of any of one's private goods. It becomes, in effect, Hobbes' substitute for the highest good. It is indeed not the complete object of desire or the final perfection of human life, but it is the criterion by which to judge of political and moral realities.

It is, more to the point, a good that is 'realistic' as opposed to 'idealistic' or 'utopian'. By 'realism' here I mean the view that in political and moral matters one must begin with goods that people can and will appreciate just as they are, without needing first any reformation or elevation of their selfish desires. This is not true, for instance, of Plato's ideal city in the *Republic*, where the goodness of the ideal can only really be appreciated and loved by those whose desires have been transformed, or purified, by philosophical training. But it is very clearly true of Hobbes' peace. There is nothing ideal in Plato's sense about this. It is a good that is so constructed as to appeal immediately to everyone's unreformed, selfish desires. Only through peace will there be any safe chance of satisfying any of them. It was by appealing to these selfish desires that Hobbes hoped to develop a realistic theory of politics and a realistic system of government, one that would almost inevitably come into being and never collapse, at least from within (*ibid:* ch.29), for the desires of everyone, just because they are ineradicably selfish, would always work to preserve it. One could not say this of Plato's ideal city, nor indeed of Aristotle's.

It is an essential part of this realist position that no one desire can be fundamentally superior to any other. By nature all the passions are equal; there is no natural order in the human soul, as the ancient thinkers taught; there is no hierarchy of wants. It is true, indeed, that for Hobbes one can distinguish the warlike and the peaceful passions, and that politics is the device for using the latter to overcome the former. But this division is based on the priority of peace, which is itself based on the ceaseless search for satisfactions, or on the fact that by nature the good is just whatever one has a passion for. Provided peace is secured nothing else very much matters.

This levelling of the human soul, this reduction of wants and interests to the same worth and status, is one significant part of what I here term 'realism'. But there is also closely connected with it a certain view of knowledge, a view which regards knowledge as power or technique, or as a means to the conquest of nature for human advantage. For 'advantage' in this context comes to mean little other than a Hobbesian satisfaction of passions. It is not in Hobbes, however, that one finds this idea of knowledge as power and technique especially developed and emphasised, but in Hobbes' older contemporary, Francis Bacon. Bacon is, of course, acknowledged as one of the great founders of modern science, for it was he who did so much to establish the scientific method. But that method is expressly designed by Bacon to extend and establish human empire over nature. For in his view a knowledge that conquers nature for human use is more important for the attainment of the political good than political action proper. As he himself said (in implicit criticism of Machiavelli), it is not the successful prince or founder of cities who deserves true praise, but the inventors of "new arts, endowments and commodities towards man's life" (*Advancement:* Bk.1; in *Works:* III.301-302).

One of the more significant elements of Bacon's method is the divorce it creates between the world and human beings, both with respect to value and with respect to knowledge. As has often been remarked, Bacon's new science describes a world of bodies and efficient causes that operate according to mechanical laws without reference to ends (e.g. *Novum Organum:* Bk.II, §2; *Advancement:* Bk.II; in *Works:* III.357-359). Nature is denied its own inherent values. It also ceases to be an object of reverence. This, indeed, is a necessary consequence if nature is something to be conquered, and conquered by violence or the torturings and vexations of art (*Works:* I.141; *Novum Organum:* Bk.II, §98). Taken together with the levelling of the human soul already mentioned, this creates a vision of the world where things are neutral, and where there is no natural pattern to follow. Non-human nature is just goalless facts, and human nature just a collection of unordered interests or passions.

This implicit separation of facts and values, already present at the beginnings of modern thought in people like Bacon and Hobbes, is created because of the desire of conquest, or because of the adoption of a certain value. This was something noted earlier in the case of Stevenson, and it is neatly expressed by Max Scheler: "to think of the world as value-free is a task that man posits to himself for the sake of value: the vital values of *mastery* and power over things" (1980: 211, note 86). It was Locke who took up this value in *Two Treatises* and used it, in combination with a Hobbesian understanding of human passions, to construct a theory of politics that is, in all essential respects, the foundation of modern capitalism.

But Bacon's method also separates nature and knowledge. Previous science, in his view, had not only corrupted the study of nature by the introduction into it of final causes (*Novum Organum:* Bk.I, §48); it had also followed a faulty method. It set too much store by the "immediate and natural perceptions of the senses," and tried to use these to get to the realities of things. But this is a hopeless procedure because the senses are too gross to judge nature directly; they can only judge it by means of artificial aids; that is, they can report the truth about experiments but it is the experiments that must report the truth about nature. By this reliance on experiments Bacon hoped to restore familiarity between the mind and things (*Works:* I.121, 138; *Novum Organum:* Preface). It is, however, clear that this restoration by means of an artificial method is only required because by nature the mind and things are divorced. The human mind has, as such, no direct access to the nature of things, and though mechanical aids enable it in part to overcome this, it only ever gets indirect access; the original divorce is never abolished. It remains the case that the mind and the senses are not by nature fitted to know nature.

This divorce is even more evident in the case of Descartes, another of the great founders of modern science, who also, like Bacon, saw in it a means of the conquest of nature for human advantage (*Discourse:* Part VI). His famous 'doubt', his use of scepticism to reject the natural and ordinary operations of the mind and the senses, has, as its result and indeed its intended result, the setting of the world of things beyond human access behind a screen of 'ideas', or inner mental entities. The picture of the real world Descartes ends up with is one of pure mathematical extensions, devoid of all sensible properties; something, in other words, quite foreign to what we are familiar with through the unaided senses. Both Descartes and Bacon consider this divorce necessary in order to establish modern science (for this, they held, requires for its success a picture of the world quite unlike our ordinary one); and they consider the purpose of modern science to be the conquest of nature. In other words, this conquest of nature, which was their principal object, proved to require first a conquest of the natural mind.

In this is displayed a noteworthy feature of modern thought generally – the combination of confidence with despair. There is confidence in the practical power of humanity to conquer nature for its own use, but despair of the theoretical power of the mind to get to the essence of things. This despair of speculation was not just bound up with the project of conquest; it was also believed that its truth was confirmed by the miserable state of the sciences in the schools of the day, where speculative reasoning, unchecked by the ascetic discipline of modern science, continued to flourish, and where ceaseless disputing appeared, to Bacon and Descartes among others, to be a sign of nothing so much as ignorance.

The explanation that was devised to account for the prevalence of such disputes, and also for the failure of people, up to then, to discover the methods of modern science, was similar to the one used to justify those methods themselves, namely that the natural and ordinary operations of the mind are unreliable. For, it was said, the natural tendency of the human mind is to fly off beyond the sphere of its competence into useless speculations which generate disputes that cannot be solved, because they are about matters of which it has, and can have, no genuine knowledge. And, for the same reason, the mind is diverted from studying those matters where it is competent and can have knowledge, and from discovering the methods appropriate to those matters, that is the methods of modern science.

It thus came to be held that what was required to conquer or overcome this natural but fatal tendency was to set about establishing the limits of the human mind so that one could fix, before the commencement of any other investigation, what it was and was not fitted to know. For then one would be able to impose on it the necessary discipline and restraint, and be able to direct it to matters where it could be successfully employed. This is the position particularly characteristic of Locke, Hume and Kant (and latterly of A. J. Ayer as well), and it leads, in the case of all of them, to a serious reduction in the kind and number of things that the mind can hope to know. As Locke put it, the mind is of too narrow a scope for us to "let loose" our thoughts into the "vast ocean of being." If we do so (as the ancient thinkers and the schoolmen of the day certainly did) we just increase doubts and insoluble questions (*Essay:* Bk.1, ch.1, para.7).

This, one may say, is the original inspiration of Locke's empiricism, whose significance for the attack on naturalism in Moore has already been remarked on. Though it is true that Moore's successors did not follow Locke as he did, they have all, nevertheless, been significantly influenced by empiricism. The open-question argument, for instance, which was not confined to Moore, relies on the analytic/synthetic distinction and this has empiricism as its basis. Moreover the term 'fact', as used by Ayer, Stevenson and Hare, means more or less an empiricist property. This has the same effects in their thought with respect to narrowing down the scope of knowledge as it had previously in the thought of Locke, Hume and Kant. These effects were many, but what is of most interest here is what they were for the idea of good.

THE 'REALIST' TRANSFORMATION OF GOOD

It is a thesis of the realism of Hobbes that the only natural good is the good of the self-regarding passions, or in other words, the selfishly pleasant. The same thesis is adopted by Locke for reasons of his epistemological as well as political thought; for pleasure is about the only empiricist property that can plausibly be identified with good (and Locke was still sufficiently naturalist to believe that good was an object of knowledge). It is a consequence of Locke's empiricism, and one which he points out, that to know such a good it is necessary first to experience it, that is, to feel some pleasure (*Essay:* Bk.2, ch.20, paras.1-2). What this claim amounts to is that there is no good without first a movement of desire or appetite; nothing can be called good if one does not first actually desire it or feel pleasure with regard to it. Good, in other words, is determined by acts of appetite and these acts must precede any knowing of good.

It was Hume who really brought this point to the fore. His statement that there is a distinction between 'is' and 'ought' is not intended to mean that no 'ought' follows from an 'is', because he makes it plain that duty or obligation is tied to, and follows, some interest we have and cannot just be willed into being nor can it arise on its own; he has no sense of disinterested duty or unfounded, autonomous 'oughts' (*Treatise:* 484, 498, 517-519, 523). What Hume means is that 'ought' follows from a certain sort of 'is', namely an 'is' that must be given by 'feeling' or 'sentiment' and cannot be detected independently by reason. The 'is' or fact that is meant by value terms such as 'good', 'bad', 'virtuous', 'vicious' and so on is a "fact of sentiment" (*ibid:* 469; also *Enquiries:* §132.), for there has to be an act of appetite before there is anything reason can know. Hume does, indeed, present an argued treatise on the virtues that he thinks can be shown to be objectively true, but only because the sentiment that 'creates' value (*Enquiries:* §246) is a natural one and is found to operate pretty much equally in everyone.

That the good is not an object of knowledge before it is an actual desire follows from Hume's sceptical and empiricist epistemology. He limits the scope of reason to facts, or sense data and collections of sense data, and relations between them (*Treatise:* 463ff.). It is because he confines reason in such a way as to cut off from it its openness to being (which was the central element of ancient epistemological thought) that he denies to it the capacity to know good independently of actual desires. It is this limitation of knowledge, this epistemological scepticism or despair of speculative reasoning, that is the historical origin of the claim that thinking does not move willing. Nevertheless it is not in Hume that this claim reaches its most forceful and systematic expression, but in Kant. The examination of Kant, however, must be prefaced by a discussion of Rousseau, as well as by some further remarks about Hobbes, Locke and Hume.

The realist political philosophy of Hobbes, modified and brought more into line with the increasing dominance of trade and commerce at the time by the capitalist politics of Locke, was founded on the view that everyone is moved by the selfishly pleasant. It accordingly lacked a sense of the noble and generous – those goods that one acknowledges as goods for themselves independently of any advantage that may accrue from them to oneself; goods, in other words, that are importantly selfless and involve a certain self-forgetting. These had been acknowledged in the thought of older thinkers, but had been forgotten or ignored by Hobbes and Locke. It was Hume and Rousseau who tried to recover them. In Hume this is particularly marked. He takes exception to the "selfish systems" of morality (citing Hobbes and Locke by name; *Enquiries:* §248), and is fertile and compelling in the way he calls upon the evidence of our ordinary experience to establish the fact of the selfless and the noble in human motivation. "The voice of nature and experience seems plainly to oppose the selfish theory," he declares (*ibid:* §174). Hobbes' realism is evidently unreal. It concentrates on some facts to the exclusion of all the rest, and Hume is valuable for the way he points this out. But Hume, because of his empiricist epistemology, still understands the noble as the pleasant. He locates the noble and the virtuous in a special non-selfish pleasure that arises from contemplation. Like Hobbes and Locke, the good he recognises is the object of some actual desire, that is, some actual sensible feeling or passion. None of them speak of a good that is connected with a distinct, rational will. It was left to Rousseau to do that.

Hume directed his attack against the realism in the writings of philosophers, but Rousseau directed his against the realism that was actually present in the people and manners of the day. Capitalism he found particularly abhorrent. From it he appealed back to the ancient world and to virtue, and also to the classical ideal of the city (for this he regarded as the home of virtue; *First Discourse*). However, in his attempt to understand this he relied heavily on the teaching of Hobbes.

Virtue does not, for Rousseau, belong to nature as such, for by nature there are only certain primitive and non-social instincts. In saying this he was following Hobbes' conviction that human beings are not by nature social, or not directed by nature to communal living. The non-sociality of human beings is inevitable given the claim that they are only moved by private goods. As Hobbes himself put it, nature "dissociates men" (*Leviathan:* ch. 13). Rousseau, however, was more consistent than Hobbes in holding this belief in non-sociality. For if human beings are by nature genuinely non-social, then by nature they cannot be such as to live or need to live in society. Yet they do now live and need to live in society. This can only mean, in Rousseau's view, that the properly natural element has been submerged beneath a multitude of non-natural and social additions. It was Hobbes' failure to realise this, and his consequent failure to separate the natural from the social, that made him believe that people naturally lust after power. But for Rousseau this is a picture of socialised, not natural, humanity, for such a lust would make no sense where people were living a genuinely non-social, that is, solitary life. By nature humans must rather be primitive animals, solitary and non-violent by instinct, keeping to themselves and caught up only in the immediate needs of existence without concern for the future. They must lack any distinctively social and, indeed, human characteristics. These must be the result of a process of history whereby, departing from their original simplicity, people declined to a state where they could not live without society (*Second Discourse*).

While Rousseau thinks that the social is not the natural, nevertheless he still holds that the natural is the determinant, even for society, of what is naturally right. That right reduces, in his view, to two basic and primitive instincts – the desire for self-preservation and natural pity. Measured by that right most existing states, particularly modern capitalist ones, are fraudulent because they have not been founded according to its requirements. The political task, however, cannot be to restore natural right simply (for once socialised human beings cannot return to their original state), but to restore it at the social level. This means recovering natural pity and natural freedom, or each one's natural right to decide for themself what is necessary for self-preservation. These can only be recovered by the work of reason and so cannot be recovered in their source (for they are by nature instincts), but just in their effects (for in society reason achieves the equivalent). (*Second Discourse:* Preface *af finem.*)

This recovery requires the creation of a society founded on a social contract to which all members are party. Everyone gives up their natural individuality and "alienates" themself totally to the whole. A new collective unit, a new individual, is created which has its own life and its own will. This secures, first of all, the effects of natural pity, because it becomes impossible to attack or offend one of the members without attacking the body as a whole, so that there is an obligation on all to aid each other mutually and to hinder cruelty and oppression. Secondly and more importantly it secures the effects of natural freedom, because the will that governs society and decides its laws is the general will, and this is the expression of the will of everyone in the whole, or the embodiment of their freedom. Obedience to the general will thus becomes obedience to one's own will, and obedience to the legislation of the general will becomes obedience to the legislation of one's own will. And "obedience to the law that one has prescribed for oneself is liberty" (*Du Contrat Social:* Bk.1, ch.8).

Liberty is thus autonomy, and it is in this autonomy of the general will, where reason takes the place of instinct, that people become moral agents and that virtue is first realised (*ibid:* Bk.1, chs.6-8). It is this sort of society, with this sort of autonomous virtue, that is Rousseau's version, or rather transformation, of the classical idea of the city and of virtue; and it serves, in some measure, to justify or redeem the historical decline of humanity from the natural state, for it is only here that one possesses genuine moral worth.

This identification of virtue with freedom and freedom with autonomy is taken over and developed more systematically by Kant. Kant's systematisation, however, includes an epistemology that develops the tradition of despair of speculative reasoning begun by Bacon and Descartes and pressed to an extreme in the empiricism of Hume. It is a combination of the empiricism of Hume and the autonomy of Rousseau that lies behind Kant's moral philosophy.

KANTIAN AUTONOMOUS MORALITY

Following the empiricists Kant makes the object of knowledge empirical data. But this data on its own does not constitute knowledge; there is need also for categories or principles of unity for combining this data. The content of knowledge is always some sensible experience, but the form or unity it has, which gives it meaning and coherence, is imposed on it by the mind in the act of thinking. The mind possesses these patterns of unity (categories) *a priori*, or possesses them already from itself and does not derive them from experience. Knowledge is a matter of subsuming experiential data under laws or patterns given prior to that data.

Kant expressly models himself here on the procedures of modern science as practised by people like Copernicus, Galileo and Newton. Bacon had already pointed out the importance to science of experiments, and Descartes that of mathematics, but it was Kant who stressed the importance of hypotheses. Science is, in Kant's view, a matter of the refutation or confirmation by experiment of hypotheses (*B:* xviii, note; xxii, note). The experiment and its (usually) mathematical results tell us something, or are significant, because the experiment is designed according to the principles of a theory, already thought up by the scientist, which it is designed to test, that is, to confirm or refute. Science is a matter of constructing in the mind a model of the world which is to be set against the world, in the form of its experimental data, as a possible framework for arranging or synthesising that data (*B:* x-xiii; and compare also the useful analogy in Wittgenstein, 1961: 6.341ff.).

What is important about Kant is not that he notices this fact of modern science, but that he applies it indiscriminately to cover all knowledge. He did this, in part, because, like many in his own day and since, he was deeply impressed by the success of modern science and became convinced that it had the key to knowledge in general (*B:* xvi; and also the conclusion to the *Second Critique*). But in part it was also due to his acceptance of the empiricism of Hume. Hume confined knowledge to ideas and impressions (immediate sense experiences and their copies in imagination) grasped at the level of sensation; and he showed, with fair success, that in such a gutted experience there is nothing universal or necessary. Kant accepted that Hume was right about what experience in itself is like, but because he recognised that there was no science without the universal and the necessary, and because he accepted the reality of science, he was driven to look for another source of these properties and found it in the mind.

This reduction of knowledge to empirical, scientific data on the one hand, and theories or frameworks for unifying and organising this data on the other, governs the rest of Kant's philosophy. The view of older thinkers that knowledge is above all a matter of coming to grips with self-subsistent beings that have their own natures, their own inner intelligible order, is rejected. This rejection, which Kant shares with Hume and many others, including those already mentioned in the same tradition, is responsible for the claim that the good is not an object of knowledge.

One of the immediate consequences of Kant's epistemology is the claim that we can never have knowledge of anything but what can be given in sensible form, either purely quantitative, in mathematics, or sensuous as well, in the natural sciences. There is no such thing as genuine metaphysical knowledge, that is, knowledge of supra-sensible being, or being abstracted from its sensible conditions. In Kant's view we can only know appearances; what things may be in themselves is hidden from us. This leads him to distinguish two worlds: the phenomenal world, the world of appearances that we know, and the noumenal world, the world of realities, that we do not. The phenomenal world is the world of natural science, and as such it is governed by rigorous mechanical necessity; it is also the world of particular selfish interests and desires. For as Kant accepted mechanistic science, so he accepted the other element of realism, namely the contentions that human beings, insofar as they are objects of knowledge or belong to the phenomenal realm, are governed by selfish passions, and that all these passions are on a par with each other, having no natural order among them (*Second Critique:* AA, V, 21-25, 35; Abbott: 107-112, 125). It is not surprising, therefore, that when he comes to examine morality, what most strikes him about it is that it cannot be accounted for within the knowable world as he had defined that world. There are three aspects, in particular, which he points to.

First, moral judgements have a special claim or authority that applies independently of one's actual and contingent desires, or the goods of one's selfish passions. If morality is made to depend on such goods, one ought only to behave as the moral judgement requires if one will satisfy some desire in the process; and if one has no such desire, or one's desires change, then one no longer ought to do it. But the sense of 'ought' used in morality is not hypothetical like this. It does not vary with the state of one's inclinations, but rather stands independently of them, even in opposition to them; it is, as he says, in some sense "categorical". Second, morality is something "sublime", but if one subordinates it to particular inclinations, which are all selfish, one will make of it something mean, and destroy all its peculiar worth (*Groundwork:* AA, IV, 428, 442-444). These two features of morality or virtue, that it is independent of one's actual desires and good in itself, not for the sake of some 'pay-off' one gets out of it, are not first noticed by Kant; they are just the particular way he recognises the sense of the noble. For the noble has nothing to do with the selfish, nor does it depend for its nobility on anyone's desiring it; it carries its desirability in itself. Third, morality is bound up with freedom. In judging and acting morally, one does so without external constraint or compulsion from natural causes; one is exercising free choice or one's rational will. All these three features were lost in the thought of Hobbes and others, and in restoring them Kant is so far returning to the tradition of older moralists. The way he treats these features, however, is quite different.

The noble, as traditionally conceived, is something one can grasp by reason; it is the selfless good. But since for Kant there are no goods one can conceive that are selfless, he either has to abandon the idea that there is something selfless in human action, or he has to abandon the idea that the noble is something knowable. To abandon the selfless is to abandon morality, which Kant was not prepared to do, so he abandoned the idea that the noble is a good to be known instead.

This simple but necessary move had an immediate and profound effect on Kant's understanding both of the 'ought' of morality and the 'is' of knowledge. Neither of them could any longer be understood in terms of the good. The 'is' of knowledge is no longer morally good because all it contains is the good of the selfish passions, and the 'ought' of morality is no longer dependent on a prior grasp of good because there is no good one could grasp that is worthy of it. As a result the 'is' and the 'ought' have to be radically separated. The 'is', as already seen, is the 'is' of modern science and empiricist epistemology; the 'ought', by contrast, is the autonomous will of Rousseau.

If one takes an 'ought'-judgement and removes from it any reference to an object (some knowable good) to which the 'ought' is relative or which is to be attained by following what the 'ought'-judgement prescribes, one is left merely with the formal character of the 'ought' as a prescription or a command. This command, since it can have no origin in knowledge or the 'is', must be purely volitional; it must spring directly and immediately from the will by itself. The will is here acting spontaneously out of its own ground, and the moral command or 'ought' it prescribes can have no foundation outside the will's own operation. If the will is nevertheless also subject to this 'ought', as it is in moral choice and action, this can only be because it has legislated it to itself. For since the pure formal 'ought' has no source besides the will, nothing else except the will could be in a position to legislate it or command it to the will. So the will, for Kant, turns out to be free because it is self-moving or spontaneous, and autonomous because it is self-legislating or self-imperating (*Second Critique:* AA, V, 44-46, 62-63, 71-72; Abbott, 134-135, 153-154; *Groundwork:* AA, IV, 452). It is in terms of this freedom and autonomy of the will that Kant is able to give nobility to his moral 'ought'. Such an 'ought', because it is autonomous and independent of all connection with selfish passions and inclinations, is at the same time categorical, selfless and free.

It is this Kantian doctrine of the 'is' and the 'ought' and the autonomous will that is really decisive, historically, for the emergence of the 'Is/Ought' distinction. Up to this point it had been possible to relate the 'is' and 'ought' to each other, because the good had been conceived as part of the 'is' and the 'ought' had been conceived as subordinate to the good. But Kant had removed this possibility when he denied moral worth to any good associated with the 'is', and then also, as a result, let loose the 'ought' to float free as a product of a spontaneous, self-legislating will which does not operate because of any prior awareness of good. Only at this stage did non-naturalism come, as it were, fully of age. That is why it is Kant, rather than Hume or any other philosopher, important though they were, who is principally responsible for its emergence.

While this is, in the context of the naturalistic fallacy, the most significant aspect of Kant's moral thought, there is another that deserves discussion and that follows from the first. The purely formal character of the moral 'ought' was understood by Kant as not just prescription, but universal prescription (the reason given is that what is formal is also necessarily universal). The 'ought' in which the will expresses itself, the so-called categorical imperative, requires that any proposed course of action must be examined to see if it can be made a universal law for everyone and still stand, and only if it can is it compatible with right and duty. This has an interesting consequence. It enables Kant to give a moral dignity to the purely selfish character of human desires. For while it remains true that the only desires or interests that one can know to exist in human beings are their particular felt and self-interested passions, it is nevertheless possible to put these desires on a higher moral plane, provided they can be subsumed under the categorical imperative, the principle of morality, and be made into universalised prescriptions or laws. Morality, in other words, becomes a kind of universalised self-interest (cf. Hare, 1963: 104-105).

It would be false, however, to suppose Kant was content to get human preferences universalised and paid no attention to their motives. On the contrary he expressly distinguishes the legal from the ethical, the former signifying the external conformity of actions to duty or the moral law, the latter the conformity of intention to it, namely that one does the action for duty's sake and not for one's private pleasure. It is also true that he has a system of virtues which are, in general, the qualities that promote this rightness of intention in oneself and others (as is explained in the *Metaphysic of Morals*). But none of this alters the fact that all the interests that are relevant for morality are actual or felt ones, or that, taken by themselves, these interests or desires lack any order or pattern; nor does it alter the fact that what is primary for Kantian morality is the moral law, or the purely formal criterion of universality. The rightness of both actions and intentions, or of both the legal and the ethical, is determined by reference to this principle. For those actions are right whose rule can be universalised, and those are wrong whose rule cannot. Similarly, those intentions are right which are directed to this universalising for its own sake, and those are wrong, or at any rate not morally worthy, which are not.

Kant, indeed, expresses the categorical imperative, or the moral law of duty, in more than one way, and specifically he does so in the form of an injunction always to act in such a fashion that one treats oneself and others as ends and never simply as means. This, however, makes no difference to the present point. Not only does Kant himself regard it as just another way of formulating one and the same imperative (*Groundwork:* AA, IV, 436-437); he is quite clearly right to do so, for it does nothing to affect the purely formal character of this imperative. To treat people as ends is, for Kant, to treat them as autonomous authors of universal law, and this can only be done if, in one's acts, one does not subject them (or indeed oneself) to any rule which cannot be willed as universal. Hence, in order to treat them as ends, all that is necessary is to ensure that one's acts conform to the criterion of universality, or are universalisable. In other words, this purely formal principle is here also the sufficient determinant of what is right (*Groundwork:* AA, IV, 427-434, 437-440).

That Kant manages to develop a system of virtues, or material duties, which are right because of their matter or content, and not just because of their form, is only because, as he admits, he is able to take the formal principle of duty and make it itself the matter or content of these virtues. Duty itself becomes their object. As Kant explains it, one first takes the idea of right established by the formal principle of universality, and then makes this into an end. Hence what was originally something purely formal becomes something material and a goal and object of pursuit (*Metaphysic of Morals:* AA, VI, 379-382; Abbott, 292-293). The virtues Kant then gives are all ultimately reducible to this goal. This means, paradoxically, that since the formal principle itself becomes an end, the 'ought' of this principle, the categorical 'ought', itself becomes a good, and moreover the standard or ideal by which to determine other goods. It is not, however, a cognitive good, for it is just the original 'ought' looked at in another way, and that 'ought' is something purely volitional. But by being thus assimilated to 'ought', good too becomes something essentially prescriptive and lacking in any cognitive content.

It goes without saying, of course, that all this is quite foreign to the older conception of ethics. There good does have cognitive content because human beings have an end determined for them by nature, namely the natural perfection of their being, independently of what their particular, felt desires happen to be. Moreover, of the various things that belong to this perfection, some are higher or more central to it than others. What is, therefore, of importance here is to discriminate this pattern and try to realise it in oneself. Whether or not a particular goal can be safely pursued by all, or be 'universalised', is hardly to the point, for this is not going to set up an ordered pattern among such universalised aims, and even if it did the fact of universality could not, on this older view, be the reason for it, since rather one's natural end would be. Moreover to the extent Kant does have a pattern of values or virtues, it is a pattern whose principle is respect for universalising as such and for its own sake, and therefore, by implication, of disrespect for any vision of human perfection based on some natural teleology.

This is in fact just what we find in Kant. His hostility to the ancient understanding of morality is particularly marked. When he speaks of their vision of human perfection, he calls it "fanaticism," by which he means "the delusion of seeing beyond the boundaries of sensibility (sense perception)" (*Third Critique:* §29, AA, V, 275); or, specifically in the case of "moral fanaticism," the attempt to base morality on something other than the stern rule of duty, and in particular the attempt to base it on some presumed knowledge and love of the noble (*Second Critique:* AA, V, 85-86; Abbott, 179).

The ancient claim to know human perfection, or the noble, is rejected by Kant because, if the perfection is non-sensible and non-empirical, it will be empty, determine nothing and so be useless; and, if it does determine something, it must really be empirical and so must reduce to some kind of selfish interest (*Groundwork:* AA, IV, 441-444; *Second Critique:* AA, V, 35-41; Abbott, 124-130). This just brings back to prominence the extent to which Kant's moral views depend on his empiricist, or empiricist-motivated, epistemology, or on his despair of speculative metaphysics. It is the combination of this with the sense of the noble and of freedom that is the source of his moral thought, as is well illustrated by the following:

> Duty! thou sublime, mighty name...what is your origin, and where is found the root of your noble descent, which proudly strikes out all kinship with inclinations?...It can be nothing less than what exalts man (as part of the sensible world) above himself....It can be nothing other than personality, that is freedom and independence of the mechanism of the whole of nature, yet viewed at the same time as a power of a being which is subject to special laws, pure practical laws given by its own reason (*Second Critique:* AA, V, 86-87; Abbott, 180).

It has been necessary to dwell on Kant because he has been the most decisive influence on modern moral thought. To see something of his views and what their causes are is of considerable value. The mood of much modern thought is a result of his vision of how things are, his vision of what human nature on the one hand, and non-human nature on the other, is like (cf. von Wright, 1963: 1). This vision is an expression of the attempt to recover the idea of the noble in the context of a 'realist' understanding of knowledge and nature. With empiricism in knowledge, mechanism in nature, and selfishness in human inclinations, the noble is only able to return as an unfounded 'ought'. The rational will also, for the same reason, can only return as a pure spontaneity, freely making its choices without a basis in anything that can be known. The moral good, as a consequence, becomes an expression of the will's free self-determination, or something volitional and not cognitive.

SUMMARY

Ancient naturalism is the doctrine that there is by nature a supreme human good that can be known by reasoning. Non-naturalism, in its complete form, is the doctrine that there are no goods at all by nature, and that good is not a matter of knowledge but is constituted by, or expressive of, one's own volitional acts. The shift from the one to the other is what is manifested in the historical development traced above. That this is so can be seen if one reviews that development as a whole.

The first step is taken when it is denied that there is a supreme end by nature or a supreme good. Instead the good by nature is just whatever one may happen to have a passion for, and so is contingent and varies from each to each, and indeed from moment to moment. But it is already a necessary part of this position that the good is in some sense constituted by volitional acts, for it is determined by what one's particular passions happen to be. It is Hume especially who brings this out. He does, it is true, restore the idea of a desire, or sentiment, that is not contingent but is present and operates in the same way in more or less everyone, but it is only from the exercise of this sentiment, not independently by reflection, that the mind can see what the objects of it are. So here too the volitional act is prior.

However, in all this there remains something of nature because the passions are understood as operating by nature, so that even if good is constituted by the volitional acts of one's passions, these acts, whether held to be contingent to each or common to all, arise from nature. It is only in Rousseau that one gets a rejection of this natural element as well. For in Rousseau's view, the volitional acts that set up the moral good are the free self-legislating acts of the rational will, not the more or less automatic operations of the passions. Yet still in Rousseau there remains an appeal to nature. The autonomy of the will is understood as a rational substitute for a natural passion or instinct, and so, in some sense, takes its measure from that instinct. It is left to Kant to deny even this residue of nature in the determination of the human good, and to establish the free acts of the will as having no ground or measure in the natural and knowable at all.

These moves in the understanding of good were made because of a narrowing down in the scope of knowledge and because of an abolition of ends from nature. This was the result, in both cases, of the dominance of the methods and values of modern science. It is these new 'realist' conceptions of knowledge and nature, combined with the old sense of the noble and of freedom, that lie behind the final emergence in Kant of the doctrine of non-naturalism.

It is made particularly evident by all this that Kant, and modern thinkers generally, differ in moral thought from those who preceded them only because they first differ in more general epistemological and metaphysical thought. To focus on the former and ignore the latter is to mistake the point at issue. If one is to make headway on the serious ethical questions, one must consider the prior non-ethical ones. To rely on 'intuitions', or so-called logic, is really to beg the question.

Given this review and examination of the historical origins, it may now be possible to bring together the results of the preceding chapters, and summarise the problems that are seen to emerge as central to the question of naturalism. These are, first, the questions of good, being and nature, together with the question of knowledge, including the question of the knowledge of modern science. Second, there is the question of willing and thinking and how these two operations relate to each other. And finally there is the question of the noble and of the highest good, and whether there is such a good, and, if so, how we could know it. The thought of older philosophers contains definite positions on all these questions that are importantly different from those of their modern counterparts. Given the deficiencies of the latter, there is evidently a strong case for taking the former more seriously than is usually done. One may find there useful insights for the resolution of the difficulties encountered in the first chapters, or at any rate for a more helpful way of looking at them.

PART TWO

The defence of naturalism

CHAPTER 6

Good and being

PRELIMINARIES

It has already been argued that among the things required for a proper understanding of ethics is a proper understanding of good. The present chapter is an attempt to give such an understanding. It is an understanding, however, that has as its foundation two basic contentions: first that good must be analysed cognitively, not volitionally, and second that it must be analysed in terms of being, not in terms of facts. Or at least it must not be analysed in terms of facts when 'fact' means what it has generally been taken to mean by contemporary authors, namely the empirical or observable properties of things. For 'fact' can sometimes be used simply to mean whatever is the case or whatever is an object of cognition, and in this sense my contention is that good can and must be analysed factually. Usually, however, these two senses are not distinguished because they are supposed (especially by non-naturalists) to reduce to the same: empirical and observable properties are held to be all that can be known in things. It is this supposition that, in contending for a cognitive analysis of good, I reject, even though in what follows I will mainly use 'fact' and its cognates in the first and more restricted sense.

Both contentions – namely that good must be analysed cognitively, not volitionally, and in terms of being, not in terms of facts – are, if not necessary consequences of the preceding investigation, at any rate strongly supported by it. This can be seen if each is considered in turn.

A volitional analysis of good, such as Stevenson and Hare

give, has two serious shortcomings. First, it has to limit good to human contexts, and second, it cannot, even there, account for all senses of good. Both Stevenson and Hare say good is expressive of desires or choices, and if this is the case it cannot be used except where human beings are concerned. Animals do not choose, and even if they may be said to emit emotive expressions, as cries, pantings, cooings and so on, they do not use the word 'good'. Plants, however, do not even emit emotive cries.

It has already been argued in the chapter on Hare that such a limitation of good is not adequate. There are legitimate uses of good that cannot intelligibly be explained with reference to our choices and desires, and the verbal expression of them. One talks, for instance, of what is good for fish and spiders, as that it is good for fish to swim in unpolluted rivers, or that it is good for spiders to catch flies. Yet it is not the case that these things are good for fish and spiders because they have anything to do with our choices and desires in the matter. One can also use good of plants, for one can say what is good or bad for daffodils, as a certain soil, a certain temperature and a certain degree of sunlight. Now all these predications of good are said with an eye to what benefits or harms the things in question; indeed, one can say generally that anything that contributes to a thing's generation, and, after its generation, to its continued growth and existence and the exercise of its powers, is its good. Conversely, one can say that whatever does the opposite is bad. If the natural sense of these expressions, which is certainly the sense that prevails in ordinary speech, is to be preserved, then some account of good must be given that allows these predications to stand as they are, without any reduction, plausible or otherwise, to human desires and choices.

When one turns from non-human to human contexts one again finds senses of good that a volitional analysis has to exclude. There is sometimes a difference between what we choose or desire and what is really good for us. For instance, we may take a medicine to cure a disease and in fact only make the disease worse. One would say here that a wrong choice had been made, and that what was chosen was bad, even though it was chosen as good. And the implication of this is that its badness was independent of our choice. The medicine was not good because we expressed ourselves in favour of it, nor has it become bad now because we have changed our minds and expressed ourselves against it; rather it was always bad for us quite independently of what we said or thought. The same goes for the medicine that should have been chosen instead, for this too was good all the time regardless of the choices made. In other words, the badness of the one and the goodness of the other were something independent, or inherent in the things themselves, and not relative to any human acts or speech. But this is just what a volitional analysis has to deny, for it does, of necessity, make good and bad relative to what people wish and say. So here also there is a sense of good, quite commonly found in the ordinary course of things, that such an analysis has to reject.

Another non-volitional sense of good is found in the thought of Stevenson and Hare themselves. Both admitted a good that is, in some way, good as a matter of fact. For Stevenson this factual good is science, while for Hare it is something like the exercise of freedom. These goods, about which they said nothing expressly but which lay beneath the surface of their thought, are not only, even for them, factual or cognitive, but, what is more, serve as the justification or ground of the non-factual, volitional good about which they did expressly speak.

There is also this further point. To say something is good gives, in human contexts, a reason for doing it. But giving a reason is not like issuing an imperative or expressing a favourable attitude. All these may, it is true, have in common that they direct to action, but they do not do so in the same way. An imperative does so directly, and no reason is needed for it, especially when it comes from someone in authority, as from a general to a private soldier. To express a favourable attitude may well be to indicate one's desire or wish that such and such be done, but it does not by itself constitute a reason for doing it; indeed, no volitional act however expressed does this. To give a reason, however, is to direct to action by giving information about what it is really worth choosing and doing.

Hence saying something is good is far more like a statement (even in its logical, to say nothing of its grammatical, form) than like an imperative or an exclamation or a wish.

If a volitional analysis of good is inadequate, a cognitive analysis in terms of facts is no less so. Good cannot be taken to signify any one fact or set of facts. The goodness of a good strawberry, for instance, is not the fact that it is red or juicy, nor is the goodness of a good action the fact that it causes pleasure. Mere redness is not by itself good, or at least not always (the redness of sunburn is not), and, of course, it is a commonplace that not all pleasant actions are good. Moreover, different things are said to be good for different reasons, and a property that is good here is bad there (as softness is good in a sponge but not in a hammer).

Nor can one say that good is some peculiar fact of its own, for, as Hare has rightly pointed out, one cannot say of two things that they are exactly alike save that one is good and the other not, whereas one can say of two things that they are exactly alike save that one is yellow and the other not. Nevertheless if good is not a fact or a collection of facts, the facts are not irrelevant to it. A strawberry that is not red and juicy will not usually be called a good strawberry, even though its being good is not the same as its being red and juicy; and, further, to call a thing good is generally to call it good in virtue of something about it, some property or properties it has – for one calls a red, juicy strawberry good because it is red and juicy, and one calls a smooth, soft sponge good because it is smooth and soft. Good is, to revert to Hare's term, supervenient: it both says more than the facts or properties of a thing, and yet it is somehow attached to, and dependent on, those facts as well. It is, indeed, just this supervenience of good that, above all, rules out a factual analysis of good.

The conclusion one must draw from this is that, while one cannot give a volitional account of good, one cannot give a cognitive account either unless one increases the scope of the cognitive beyond that of the factual. Indeed the necessity so to increase it, if one is to give a cognitive account, may be said to be the principal message of the last chapter. For it was the severe reduction of knowledge, the prevalence of empiricist epistemological despair, that led originally to the separation of good from cognition. The overcoming of this reduction is precisely what the appeal to being is meant to achieve.

THE IDEA OF BEING

Being is something of a contentious issue for philosophers today. Some dismiss it out of hand as nonsense; others embrace it as the all-absorbing object of their attention. But whatever others may have said of being, it is meant here to be something simple, straightforward and obvious. Understanding it does, indeed, become rather complex the more one goes into the details, but there is nothing complex about the beginning. Recovering the simplicity of this beginning is, however, itself something of a problem. For, strictly speaking, there is nothing one needs to do to recover it. Being is already there facing us and all that is required is to look at it. Indeed, in one sense, we are looking at it all the time, only we do not pause to step back and reflect on it. Going about to search for it, in fact, as if it were something mysterious and hidden, is the one sure way of not finding it. It would be like going about searching for one's glasses not realising that one was wearing them all the time. For when one talks of being, one is not appealing to some object separate from the objects of experience, nor is one appealing to some knowledge separate from the knowledge of these objects; one is appealing directly to these objects themselves. Being is just what is given in experience and just what is known from experience.

It must be admitted, however, that if one is to sustain this contention one must certainly deny that experience is what empiricists say it is. For empiricists, at any rate of the sort Locke and Hume were, and also Kant, insofar as he followed Hume, experience as such is little more than a series or collection of sense data, or, in other words, the sensible world taken at the level of sensation. But being, if it is manifest at all, is only manifest to thought. The world of experience is, indeed, an object for thought; in fact it is as much an object for thought as it is for sensation. Moreover there is for thought more in sensible objects than there is for sensation, or than is grasped at the level of sensation. One recognises by intellectual reflection what one cannot recognise by perception on its own. However this needs more explanation.

The sensible world is the world that we know, and we know it because of the senses; there is no need for recourse to any special sort of innate ideas to explain this knowledge. But there is more to the sensible world than the senses explicitly grasp, and there is more to knowing and thinking than the knowing and thinking of sense data or sensible images. By the senses we perceive sensible things, but, strictly speaking, we only judge by the senses the particular sensible properties; we do not judge by them the being as such of sensible things. Nevertheless it is sensible things that we perceive, and these are beings, or things that in some sense are; their being-ness, in other words, is something we are aware of. It is the function of the mind to make that being an express object of attention, or to raise it from something implicit to something explicit. Thinking, in other words, involves an ascent from a lower to a higher cognitive level, namely from perception to mind. What is thought, however, is not something other than sensible experience, but rather sensible experience itself. In other words, what is thought is the same as what is perceived, but it is *thought*, and to think is not to perceive a second time (as Hume in particular seems to have supposed). This difference is marked precisely by the fact that when it is thought it is thought under the aspect of its being (cf. Simpson, 1985).

The senses and the mind, in other words, grasp the same realities, sensible beings, but the one grasps them as to their sensible properties and the other as to their being. The latter, moreover, embraces the former as the whole embraces the part, for sensible properties are just a mode of a sensible thing's being (being red and juicy, for instance, are ways in which a strawberry is); being is thus a more comprehensive object.

It is one of the more important implications of this view of the mind and the senses that the mind must be supposed to have in experience its own proper objects, and objects that cannot be reduced to, or equated with, the proper objects of the senses, such as colours, sounds and the like. To deny this, and to say that the objects of the mind are not being and the kinds of being but rather the same as the objects of the senses taken precisely as the objects of the senses, and to divide the mind's objects according to the divisions of sensible properties, as Locke in particular did, is not only to evacuate experience of all that is unique to mind, but also to evacuate it of the greater part of its own reality.

But what is meant by saying that the mind, when it knows sensible objects, knows them in their being, or that what it knows, first and foremost, is being and not, say, immediate sense impressions? This point may seem obscure, but, as has already been suggested, this is less because it is difficult than because it is easy; so easy, in fact, that it is all too often overlooked. This overlooking is something that can be found in all periods of human knowing, but it is particularly prevalent now because of the dominance and success of modern physical science. Modern science is not particularly concerned to make the ascent spoken of. It does, indeed, do more to sense data than entertain them; for it measures and quantifies them and also traces their relations, particularly their mathematical relations, and expresses them in formulae and general hypotheses. Nevertheless, it generally sticks to these observable and measurable data, and its grasp of the world of experience is confined to them (as will be argued in more detail in the next chapter).

This way of looking at the world has become so familiar, and has proved so successful, especially in its useful applications, that it is not easy to adopt any other. We have lost, one may say, the habit of reflecting on the being of sensible things. This, however, is not the same as losing the awareness of their being altogether; and, in fact, this awareness remains just as much alive as it ever was, and continues to manifest itself, if not in philosophy, at least in ordinary thinking and ordinary speech. Science may speak of a world of observable data, and empiricist philosophy may do the same, but ordinary speech and ordinary thought speak of things and realities, of objects that are out there, that exist as independent entities with their own nature and their own properties, and that act and are acted upon in their own distinctive ways. Our experience is, quite generally, one of continual contact with beings; and we are made unavoidably aware, however much we may fail to make it explicit, that, whatever else is true of them, it is certainly true that they *are*. It is this immediate experience of the reality of things, of the fact that things are, that is the original and all-pervasive experience of being. Being just means the 'is'-ness of things. Ordinary experience is suffused with being in this sense, and ordinary language, which reflects it, is suffused with talk of being and beings. One cannot do justice to either if one does not talk, first and foremost, about being.

It is this ordinary and pre-philosophic grasp of being that forms the starting-point for the more elaborate philosophic grasp of being. The difference between the two is principally that, at the pre-philosophic level, being is not made an express object of reflection, for that involves an effort of thought and a certain detachment and is the result of practice and learning. In this respect, indeed, modern physical science is more accessible, because, while it requires effort like any other study, it does not make the same ascent from sensation; and its objects have, accordingly (except when they become elaborately mathematical), a certain immediate accessibility to sense and imagination that is lacking in the case of being. And that, I think, is part of the reason why reflection on being is less common, despite the pervasive experience of it.

There is one obvious objection to all this, or at any rate one that is often made, namely that this claim about the reality of things is just assumed and not proved, and therefore, before one accepts it, one must be given some inference to justify it. The short answer to this is that it does not need proof. The grasp of being is not inferential; it is immediate. The being of things is the direct object of the mind, as colours, sounds and so on are the direct object of the senses; and so the intellectual grasp of being is as immediate as the sensible grasp of colours and sounds. It is as futile to try and prove the one as to try and prove the other. One can only, and indeed must, appeal directly to experience itself, and leave each one to decide on that. If some still refuse to accept the reality and being of sensible things there is nothing more to be said. The final decision lies with the immediate evidence, not with argument. And philosophers have all admitted as much, for, whatever their views, they have eventually had to rest their case on an appeal to such evidence. In the end, experience is the only, and sufficient, arbiter.

But to make being the topic of concern, the being that we are confronted with in the form of the sensible things of daily experience, may seem nevertheless to do something trivial or ridiculous, since, if 'being' is a term that has any sense at all, it can only be at such an abstracted and universalised level as to reduce statements about it into insignificant platitudes or grandiloquent-sounding truisms. Whether or not this charge is fair can best be judged from the analysis that follows. What informs and instructs the mind, what gives it knowledge where before it was ignorant or confused, what deepens its conscious and reflective grasp of things, even ordinary things, is not insignificant. It is true that one must not expect scientific or empirical information from such an analysis, but then the contention here is that this is not the only information that there is. The knowledge that comes by philosophic contemplation is knowledge of things with which we are already quite familiar. There will be no exciting new discoveries of hitherto unknown objects or natural processes as there is in science, but only a deeper appreciation of just what the being of ordinary common beings is.

It may still be objected, however, that all this must collapse, in the end, to mere word-play. For being is not one thing, if indeed it can be said to be anything at all; it is, in fact, just a general name that is used in any number of disparate ways, and has no sense outside specific contexts; it has to be taken case by case. The force of this objection is that being is only one as an equivocal name is one. But this cannot be so. Those things are equivocal which have the name only in common as 'perch' when said of the fish and of something a bird sits on, and hence where there is no likeness or connection. But this is not how being is taken when it is said of anything that is in any way. Clearly, what it is for a horse to be is not what it is for a colour or a thought to be, but yet all these things can be said to be in the way proper to them: a horse as a horse, a colour as a colour and so on. To say this is to say something common to them, for as the being of a horse is to a horse, so is the being of a colour to a colour or of a thought to a thought; in each case it makes the thing the thing it is. This is not to say something entirely the same nor is it to say something entirely different; it is rather to say something that is analogically the same: the proportion or analogy between the different terms is the same even if the terms are different. So Aristotle speaks of diverse things as sharing a common proportion; as bone is to an animal so is fish-spine to a fish, and as the Iliad and Odyssey are to tragedy so is the Margites to comedy (*APo:* 98a20-23; *Po:* 1448b38-49a2). This is sufficient to establish a unity such that one can speak of what is applicable in all cases.

What then about the being of things? What is it that becomes evident when things are reflected on in the way suggested, that is, with respect to the fact that they are? First and fundamentally that they are not in a single way, but in many ways. The being of each thing is complex. A thing's being white is not its being here or its being round or its being simply; these are all distinct kinds of being. If they were not then a thing could not be white without being here or round, and could not cease to be here or round without ceasing to be white, nor could it be at all if it were not white or round or here. But all this is absurd. Things exist after a variety of manners and can change in one without changing in another; and one can think of their being in one way without thinking of their being in another way. Nevertheless, each individual thing exists in all these ways at once, as a single totality. Ontologically each thing is a whole, but a complex whole.

To grasp what is complex the mind needs to divide it up and see it in its parts. Consequently to get a grasp of the complexity of the being of things it is necessary to try and reduce to order the manifold ways in which things can be and be said to be, and, if possible, give a complete list of them. For instance, a being can be considered, first of all, just as something self-subsistent, or as something that exists in its own right and not as the modification of something else. This independence of being is what is meant by the term substance. One can also consider a being precisely as to its modifications. Here not its being simply is considered, but its being in a certain respect, as so many feet long, or as so coloured or so shaped. These are what are called accidents, and in this case the accidents of quantity and quality. Compiling and explaining such a list was the aim of Aristotle's famous doctrine of the ten categories. These were taken as the principal divisions of being, but there were also divisions within the divisions, as that there were four kinds of quality and so on (Aquinas, *CP*: §322; *CM*: §§890-892; Avicenna, *M*: §§3, 9-10). A full understanding of the categories would require going into such details, but it is not the intention to do that now, nor is it necessary for present purposes, for one does not need to accept Aristotle's categories to agree with the basic point being made here.

Reflecting like this on the diversities of being, not only between things but within individual things themselves, means reflecting not just on the idea that they are diversities, but also on the idea that they are diversities of being. 'Is' applies to all of them and with respect to all of them a thing can be said to be. As has been indicated already this commonness of being to all of them is analogical. To be a substance, as a fish, and to be a quality, as white, are not alternative ways of being as, say, being a dog and being a cat are alternative ways of being an animal. The one nature of animality is present equally in dogs and cats, so that with respect to animality they do not differ; but there is no one nature of being that is common to being a substance and being a quality, for it is precisely with respect to being that they differ. The 'to be' of one category is not the 'to be' of another, even though both are kinds of 'to be'. Nevertheless, since in every category its 'to be' makes existent something in that category, each 'to be' has a likeness of proportion to every other: the 'to be' of this category does for things in this category what the 'to be' of that category does for things in that category, just as, to use Aristotle's example, bone in an animal does for animals what fish-spine does for fish.

Further reflection after this fashion on the being of things reveals not only that being is analogical, but that there are also other terms we use, besides the term 'being', that are applicable to everything in a way rather like 'being' itself. Such terms appear to be, as it were, the inseparable companions of being, that follow it everywhere and in everything throughout all its kinds and divisions. The term 'one' is such a term, for just as it is possible to think of the being of a thing as a substance and the being of its modifications, so it is possible to think of the oneness of this substance and the oneness of each of its modifications. A horse, for instance, is one as a horse, its colour is one as a colour, and its five foot height one as a five foot height. 'One' is thus found to apply across the board just like being and to be, as it is said, coextensive with it.

But if 'one' is coextensive with being and is applicable to all being simply, then this has a quite serious implication for understanding its sense. For when 'one' is said of some being, whether a substance or a quality or anything else, it cannot be understood as adding to it a further property of its own. To say, for instance, that this horse is one or that this white thing is one is not like saying that this horse is white or that this white thing is round, for no further property is hereby added by the term 'one'. A property is itself a particular determination of being, and this particular determination is what is signified when a property is predicated of something. When a horse is said to be white, the 'white' expresses and adds to 'horse' a further specification of the horse's being, namely its being as coloured in a certain way. But the term 'one' cannot be functioning like this when it is predicated. For if it were limited, like this, to expressing some particular sort of being, or some particular property, then it could not apply to all being equally (both substantial and accidental), or follow all being everywhere.

Consequently it must be said that when the term 'one' is predicated of something, as when a horse or a cat, or even something white, is said to be one, it cannot be signifying any other sort of being than just the being expressed by the subject term itself. Nevertheless this does not mean that it signifies this being in the same way, or that it is the same in 'notion' (or *logos* to use Aristotle's term; *Metaph:* 1003b22-25). To say of a horse it is a horse is not the same as to say it is one horse, and, generally, to say of any being what it is is not to say it is one. For 'one' says something more than 'horse', not because it says an additional property, but because it expresses something that 'horse' by itself does not express. 'One' expresses the fact that a horse, just because, and just insofar as, it is a horse, that is, just because, and just insofar as, it is this particular sort of being, is undivided in itself. The idea of 'absence of division' is what 'one' says over and above what 'horse' says. In other words, while 'one' signifies the same sort of being as that of which it is said, it signifies it as taken under a certain aspect, the aspect of undividedness.

This aspect of a thing's being is found in every sort of being whatsoever just because, and just insofar as, it is that sort of being. Everything is one just as the being it is, even if it is many in its parts. A library is one as a library, and a horse as a horse, even though a library has many books and a horse has several legs (yet each of these parts is, in its turn, one as a part; a book as a book, and a leg as a leg). This is why it is that 'one' converts with being and universally follows every being. This is also why it is quite different from other terms that do not do this but are limited to expressing some determinate sort of being, as in the case of 'white'. For a horse is not white just because, and just insofar as, it is a horse, but only because it has the additional determination of being white.

There are other terms that can be seen, by reflection, to convert with being like this, and to signify the same nature as what they are said of but to add a difference of respect or consideration. The term 'thing' is itself such a term (when used broadly, and not when confined, as it sometimes is, to referring to substances), though it is not as obvious as with 'one'. 'Thing' appears to be so close to 'being' that it seems to be a complete alternative, but it too, like 'one', may be understood as expressing a difference. To say of a horse it is a being expresses the idea that it is an existence or reality, while to say of it that it is a thing is to express rather the idea that it is a certain kind of reality, or a determinate somewhat. Just as a horse is one because, and insofar as, it is a horse, so it is a thing because, and insofar as, it is a horse; it is both by virtue of the being that it is, and not because of the addition of something else. 'Thing' like 'one' expresses the same nature but, again like 'one', it expresses it with a difference of consideration, the consideration that a horse is, as a horse, a determinate sort of existence, having a determinate nature.

It can fairly be said of such terms that they are in some sense 'supervenient'. By contrast with other terms (those that are confined to some particular category), they do not signify a property of their own, but are tied to, and take their determination from, that to which they are applied. 'One' said of a library signifies the oneness of a library, not the oneness of a book or a colour, and 'thing' said of heat signifies the thingness of heat, not the thingness of a horse or a circle; for each being is one in its own way and a thing in its own way. Nevertheless these terms do not just follow and repeat the subject they are said of, they take it under a certain respect; in other words, they add a 'something more'. This something more depends on the respect that is taken; in the case of 'one' this is the respect of absence of division, and in the case of 'thing' this is the respect of being a determinate somewhat.

THE IDEA OF GOOD

It at once appears evident that if 'good' can be analysed similarly to 'one' and 'thing', it will have been analysed in just the way required to account for the peculiar character of its supervenience. For it too, like 'one' and 'thing', will signify being, any and every being, just as that being it is, but with the addition of a something more, the something more of a certain respect or consideration. It will not signify some special being or property of its own, some fact peculiar to itself. This possibility must now be examined.

Since the term 'good', as almost all writers have freely admitted, has something to do with desire, some connection with what is broadly called 'volition', it may help to examine a suggestion that likens the term 'good' to the term 'true', and understands both as implying or involving a reference to something else that may be related in a certain way towards them (Aquinas, *DV:* q1, a1; q21, a1). This something else that may be related in a certain way to being is, on the one hand, mind, and on the other hand, desire and will, for as mind is related to being in the way of knowing it, and thus gives rise to the idea of truth, so desire may be related to being in the way of loving it, and thus gives rise to the idea of good. One must be careful in this last case, however, because one must not so interpret desire as to confine it only to human, or perhaps other sentient beings. 'Good' has, or can have, application out of these contexts, as already argued, and one must not explain it in such a way that it does not. Nevertheless the notion of desire, especially and first our own desire, is a useful one from which to start.

But to get hold of the basic idea here, it is preferable to begin with the term 'true'. Truth, one may say, belongs to knowledge, at least in that knowledge is knowledge of some truth. To know something is of course to know that thing just as it is, either wholly or at least to some extent (if something is taken as it is not, there is rather error than truth). So to know is to know things as they are. But if this is also the same as to know truth, as it is, then truth can only be this: 'things as they are'. In which case truth and being or things must in some sense be one and the same, and it must just be the being of things, the fact that they are as they are, and are not as they are not, that is what truth signifies. Things or being in general do not thus receive the predication 'true' because of any addition to their being, for it is just by being as they are, no more and no less, that this predication will attach to them.

Nevertheless truth is not altogether the same as being; it adds a 'something more', and the something more it adds is the respect or consideration that this is how things are. Such a respect or consideration cannot arise, however, without some reference back to thought or mind or some operation of judging and forming propositions, for it is only in this way that one can get, in addition to the idea of being, the idea of 'this is how being is'. This latter is a proposition and so belongs to the realm of mind and thought (which forms propositions). Indeed, it has often been pointed out that truth belongs essentially to propositions. One cannot, clearly, predicate truth of isolated terms; one cannot, for instance, say, 'that a cat, is true', but one must add something further and say, 'that a cat is an animal, is true,' and so on. Of course one can say such things as, 'this is true,' but here the 'this' will stand for a proposition; it is not a purely isolated term. One might also say, 'he is a true man,' but here again the 'true' points to a proposition, perhaps of the form, 'he is all that a man should be,' or, 'he is what it is to be a man;' or perhaps the term 'true' here has a different sense and signifies that the man has the qualities of honesty and decency (and of course honesty means telling the truth, and here 'truth' has the first sense, so 'true' as 'honest' refers to 'true' as in propositions). But these are side-issues that need not detain us, for they do not alter anything that has been said about the basic idea of truth, that it signifies being in the sense of 'this is how being is', and hence in the sense in which it becomes an object for the judging mind. This is why truth is said to express the conformity of being and mind, or to express the idea that mind, in judging truly, is conformed to how things are, because it judges things to be as they are.

The term 'truth', then, like the other terms 'one' and 'thing', does not signify any peculiar property or determination or fact of its own; for something is not true because some other property of being is added to it (as a thing is only white because something else, the being white, is added to it), but rather just because and just as it is. There is nevertheless a something more that true says that being by itself does not say, namely the idea of 'this is how being is', which, as was said, indicates some reference back to thought and mind.

The term 'good' is like the term 'true' in that it too, while it attaches to all being just as such, says a something more that the term 'being' by itself does not say, and which is understood, at least implicitly, by a reference back to something else. The something else in question is desire.

As was said (and while this may be initially misleading), it will help to begin by considering our own desiring first, and then to lead on to a broader grasp of the idea. The object or objects of desire, the things we want and pursue, are all evidently in some sense beings or degrees or aspects of being, for after all we call them things and objects of pursuit. This is so whether we understand by object of desire the thing wanted or the action or operation by which we possess it, as for instance food is the thing we desire and eating it the action we desire, because it is by eating that we appropriate the food. We want these things or these actions, moreover, just because they are what they are. Food is not wanted because of some addition of being to it over and above what it is as food, nor are eating and drinking wanted because of some addition of being over and above what they are as eating and drinking. It is just because, and just insofar as, each of the things we desire is what it is that we desire them.

Of course if something more were added we might desire the object more; if, say, to the strawberries we desired was added also cream, we might desire the strawberries more. But this would not necessarily mean we desired the strawberries only because of the addition of the cream, as if it was the cream alone that, by being added, made the strawberries desirable and the strawberries were not desirable on their own. Someone might, indeed, just like cream and therefore only want strawberries because there was plenty of cream with them, and someone might just like strawberries with cream on them, and neither on their own. But whatever combination one adopts, if one considers these objects that are desired, insofar as they are desired, whether strawberries or cream or both, it is just these objects themselves, being as they are in themselves, that we desire in desiring them, not the addition of something else to them – just as it is by being what they are, without addition, that things, when known, are known to be as they are. In neither case is that which makes something to be known or desired anything other than that thing itself taken in its simple being by itself, quite regardless of, and prior to, any knowing or desiring there might be of them.

As it was contended that true signifies the being of things but with the further consideration of a reference to judging, so it is also contended that good signifies the being of things but with the further consideration of a reference to desire and desiring. For if it be said, as is quite reasonable, that we desire things that are good and because they are good (either really so or because we supposes them to be so), so that the term 'good' signifies that about things which we desire in them, or that about them which makes us call them good, then 'good' would appear to signify nothing other than those very things themselves which we desire. What is it, for instance, about strawberries that makes us desire them and call them good? Nothing other than that they are strawberries, and strawberries of the sort that they are – having the properties of being red, juicy, large and so on. In other words it is just the being of things we desire that we have in mind when we call them good and desire them – it is just this that makes them desirable or attractive, and draws us towards them. 'Good' does not signify any additional being peculiar to itself which when added to a thing makes it good (as the being white, when added to a thing, makes it white whereas before, without this additional determination of being, it was not white or not understood as white). What it signifies is just that thing itself as the being it is. Things are good in the same way as they are 'one' or 'true', namely just because, and just insofar as, they are what they are – neither more nor less.

But again, of course, like all the other terms, 'good' adds a something more, for it does not signify being just as being – it says more than the term 'being' says. The something more it says is just the something more of a certain respect or consideration, the consideration that arises from viewing a thing in the light of a reference to desire, in that, just by being what it is, each thing also is or has all that desire desires in it.

One must not mistake the bearing or thrust of these remarks, and suppose that the goodness of a thing is somehow not real in that thing, but is subjective and belongs only to the desiring, as if a thing could only be called good insofar as someone or something desired it. 'Good' does not refer to the desiring, rather it refers to the *object* of the desiring, the thing that is desired because and insofar as it is what it is. So, for instance, it is the strawberry that is good because it is the strawberry it is, and that is why it is desired; for one who desires strawberries desires the strawberries for what they are, because in being what they are they are or have what is desired. The goodness one wants in wanting strawberries is precisely the being of the strawberries, so the goodness must be really in these strawberries and not a mere external and subjective relation that may attach to them.

The reference to desire that is involved in the idea of good is thus not a reference to the fact that the thing called good is or has been desired; rather it is a reference to the notion or concept of desire, and to the fact that what desire desires in things is just what they are. By being what it is, a thing, any thing, is already a good, a something that is already all that it has to be in order to be an object of desire, or a something that desire would desire in it. So it is not necessary for a thing to be or to have been desired to be called good; it is good in and by itself (for it is a being in and by itself).

For this reason one may say that the good is the desirable, where the term 'desirable' is something analogous to such terms as 'visible' and 'audible'. 'Desirable', one may say, signifies the being of a thing with a view to the idea of its being, as such, an object of desire, or such as to be desired. Likewise 'visible' signifies a thing with respect to its being an object of sight, or that it is such as to be seen; and the same with 'audible' as signifying the object of hearing.

Moore, it is true, objects to this likening of the desirable to the visible. He argues that whereas 'visible' means 'able to be seen', 'desirable' does not mean 'able to be desired' but rather something like 'ought to be desired' or 'deserving to be desired' (1903: 67). But one must say to this that 'visible' and 'desirable' are only akin when they are used to signify the objects of sight and desire as such, and that, taken in this way, 'visible' is not best interpreted as 'able to be seen', nor is 'desirable' best interpreted as 'ought or deserving to be desired'.

The visible, in the sense of the proper object of sight, is strictly speaking colour, or coloured things (taking white and black also to be colours in this sense). But it is not the case that these are always able to be seen, for it may be dark, or they may be hidden, or something else may intervene to prevent one's seeing them. The visible is, in fact, more accurately understood as that which is fitted or adapted to sight, rather than as that which is able to be seen. The phrase 'able to be seen' would only be accurate if it was interpreted just in this way to mean, not what can actually be seen, but what is such as to be seen, though it need not be seen if there is no light or something is in the way or one is blind.

Likewise not everything desirable ought or deserves to be desired. To say of some object, as a car, that it is desirable is not to say one ought to desire it (one may already desire some other car instead). Indeed, it may be that one ought not to desire it, say if it belongs to someone else. One must rather say that here 'desirable', like 'visible', means something like fitted or adapted to desire, for a desirable car is one that has what fits it to be desired (as speed, comfort, efficiency and so on), quite regardless of whether one ought also to desire it. So, contrary to Moore's contention, 'desirable' and 'visible' are, when properly interpreted, comparable in the way asserted.

It must be admitted, however, that there is a sense in which 'desirable' differs from 'visible', for the desirable is divided into the real and apparent while the visible is not. If anything is seen it must be really visible, but if anything is desired it need only be apparently desirable. As will be argued in the ensuing chapters, the really good or desirable for each thing is determined for it by its nature. In the case of human beings, however, desire follows the good as they conceive it, and since one may conceive falsely, so one may desire falsely and choose that as good which is not really or by nature so, but only apparently or in one's conception of it. 'Desirable' may, therefore, sometimes be used to signify the real as opposed to the apparent good, and in this sense it does mean something more like 'ought or deserving to be desired'. This is the sense Moore seems to have had in mind. However, in this sense 'desirable' is no longer being used in its full scope to cover all possible objects of desire, and so is no longer being used in the way it must be if it is to be truly like 'visible'.

Given that all this is so, it is evident how, despite its supervenience and its connection with desire, good is nevertheless something cognitive and signifies being or things in a way in which they may be known and judged. For the whole of being is an object of cognition, and 'good' is just a name for being in one of its several considerations or aspects, just as 'one', 'thing' and 'true' are also. The respect or consideration that 'good' signifies is, as much as any of these other aspects, an object of cognition, to be grasped and thought by the mind. For, after all, what is in question here is precisely the consideration of this reference of being to desire, and to consider being along with this reference is an act of thinking, and so something cognitive, not an act of desiring; just as to consider something in its reference to sight or in its reference to hearing, as with the visible or the audible, is an act of thinking and not an act of seeing or an act of hearing.

NATURAL DESIRE AND EVIL

It is not enough, however, to leave the notion of good at this level of signifying being in its relation to desire. This, by itself, might imply that, even if things are good independently of whether they are desired, there was a necessary reference in the idea of good just to that realm of being where desire is or could be found, and this might be thought to imply a reference to the human world.

But besides this question there are also others that arise and need to be clarified. There is, for instance, the question of the drawing power of good, or how it moves to action. While this is, in an important sense, sufficiently answered by saying good is the object of desire (for it is desire that moves to action, and so what moves desire must move to action also), there is still a need for a more particular explanation of it in human contexts. But as this is more properly dealt with in the discussion of thinking and willing it will be left to chapter 8. There is also the question of bad and evil, and of how there can be bad and evil in things if good goes along with being and if thus every being is good; and there is also the question of how there can be a good by nature, or how it is that, if everything is good, there can be a particular natural good for each thing. This second question will be taken up expressly in the next chapter, but certain remarks in what follows will also be relevant to it. The question of bad and evil will be taken up expressly in this chapter.

To come then to the question of the scope or extension of desire. The object of desire is the end or goal which desire seeks in seeking its object, and which it naturally pursues. Desire is in general a directedness towards an object, a tending or even moving towards it. One does, after all, speak of the goals of movement, meaning that what the movement is a movement towards is its goal. When one talks of desire, however, one generally has some consciousness or at least sensation in mind. One describes the tending towards objects of sensing and thinking things as their desires. But the same structure, I mean the structure of tending or moving towards objects, exists also in things that lack sensation and thought. Flowers, for instance, tend toward the sunlight (one even says they *seek* the sunlight), and the ordinary processes of growth that one finds in things are just the movements of these beings towards their full maturity. It is by noting these facts, namely the structure of desire and the structure of tending towards in the being of even non-conscious things, that one may admit the legitimacy of the concept of natural desire, that is of desire that exists in things as a matter of their nature, and not of anything conscious. And of course, the objects of these natural desires, these natural tendings towards, will be properly described as goods – the goods of the things in question.

One may also look at the matter from the point of view of the ideas of the potential and the actual, and of the realisation of the potential by the actual. A thing is said to be potential with respect to what it can be but not yet is, and it is said to be actual with respect to what it now is or has become. But to take a thing in terms of its potentialities is to take it in its relation and directedness to the respective actualities. 'Potential' simply indicates a thing under the aspect of what it can be, or of how it is disposed to being; and this just means that, *qua* potential, it tends towards or is directed to that particular actuality. Since this is the same structure as desire, one may say that the relation of the potential to its respective actuality is the same as the relation of desire. And given that the natural world in general is a world of things that are in a state of change and becoming (things come to be and cease to be, are born, grow, decay and die), which is the state of becoming actual, or ceasing to be actual, with respect to the potentialities to be that each thing has, one may say that the idea of desire, in its broadest sense where it does not include also the idea of consciousness, is found throughout the natural world. Thus the idea of good, as the idea of being in the sense in which it is an object of desire, is an idea that has reference outside human contexts altogether.

This way of understanding things has become opaque because of the dominance of empiricist thinking. In Hume, for instance, it is impossible to speak intelligibly of motion or change, and hence of the actualisation of potentialities; for change requires the permanence of the subject that undergoes change, as water endures throughout when it changes from cold to hot. For Hume, however, there is no such subject, but only a succession of ideas, each of which is complete in itself and distinct from all others. Change is, therefore, reduced to something else, namely a succession of sense data or a series of instantaneous creations and annihilations. There is no dynamism in any of these data; they do not develop or grow or move; they are static; they are entirely complete and fixed as what they are. The most that happens is that at one moment they are, and at the next they are not (that this follows from Hume's position is evident from his discussion of space and time). To the extent that all empiricists speak of data in the same way and make them first and basic, all of them lack the sense of motion and change. To the extent, moreover, that the methodology of modern physical science is empiricist, or to the extent that, as Kant indicated, it just subsumes such empiricist data under models and theories and traces the proportions and relations of their mathematical properties, it too lacks a sense of motion, and hence has no place for the doctrine of the actual and potential. Therefore, it is difficult, if not impossible, within the perspective of modern science to speak of the natural appetites of things. (More will be said on this issue of change and of how things have potentials to be, the realisation of which is their good, in the next chapter.)

The idea of good, the idea of object of desire and of the actuality that completes and satisfies desire (desire in the broad sense of any tending towards, any relation of potentiality to actuality, not necessarily implying consciousness), is the idea of finality. It is being as final being, the being towards which things tend as to their ends and goals, and which perfects or completes them. So in understanding how goodness is found in things, and hence ultimately also evil, for evil is understood by contrast, one needs to understand how things have this aspect of finality to them, or how they may be complete and perfect in their being. There are, in fact, two basic ways here, for a thing may be considered either as perfect or as perfective, or as that which is realised and that which realises (Aquinas, *DV:* q21, a2; *DM:* q1, a2).

To take the first way. When a thing has fully realised its potentialities and been made actual with respect to them, or when a thing is completely all that it can naturally be and has the fullness of being that belongs to it, then it is said to be good just because it is so actual, for that actuality makes it, as such, to be perfect. But things may be wholly or only partially realised, and so may be said to be wholly or partially good. Thus of a selection of strawberries one may say that some are good and some not, because some have realised their potential, that is, have grown, developed and matured as strawberries, while the others have not, or to a lesser extent. But even these last, while they are not said to be good simply, can nevertheless be said to be good in some respect, namely in that respect in which they actually are strawberries, however poor they may otherwise be. For to the extent that they actually are strawberries, they are realised and perfected in some way, and so are, thus far, as strawberries, good. The same applies to anything whatever. Everything is, insofar as it is, good. Any degree of being a thing has attained, however minimal, is an actualisation of it, or a respect in which it has realised its capacity for being, and so is perfect. As regards those respects in which it is not yet actual, it is not yet good, and its goodness is related to it as something aspired after but not yet attained. In this respect it is not said to be good in fact, but good in aspiration; and this is the way that that which is in potential to good is said to be good.

To take good in the sense in which it signifies that which is perfective, this may be either because it is the end and actuality of a potential, or because it assists or leads to it. So if the being of full formation, with all limbs and parts in place and in due proportion, is the term of the generation of an animal, then this is the good as end; and what assists this generation, as food, the health of the mother and so on, is the good as means, or as the useful. Likewise, not only what contributes to the attainment of a good is good, but also what contributes to the retention of that good when once attained is good, for the good still remains a good after it is possessed, since it is then a good, not as pursued, but as enjoyed. Hence, whatever conserves beings in their being is good.

In this sense of good, in which something is said to be good as perfective of another, or as assisting and conserving the perfection of that other, the thing is taken with reference to the desire or potentialities of that other, not with reference to its own potentialities. So a thing may be bad for another, in the sense of destroying it or hindering it in its tending towards good, while good in itself, as a perfect typhoid virus is good in itself but bad for humans, because it tends to destroy them. Conversely, a thing may be bad in itself but good for another, as inert or dead viruses are bad in themselves because so far imperfect, but good for humans because, when used in innoculations, they stimulate the body to build up its defences against the active viruses, and so assist the body to preserve itself.

But good is not just divided into these senses of the perfect and the perfective; because it follows being as such, it is divided also through all the categories. A thing may be said to be good with respect to its substance, or its size, or its shape, or its colour. So a large, red, juicy strawberry may be viewed as good with respect to its being a strawberry, and with respect to its being large, as well as with respect to its being red and juicy; for all these are ways, though different ways, in which its being is perfect. However, just as being is not the same in each of the categories, so neither is good. Good taken in one of the categories is taken partially and not wholly. Moreover, not every good can be found in every being, for some beings are simply incapable of having the necessary actuality. Trees are incapable of speech and so speech is not a good for them, but it is a good for humans. So here also, to take a good that belongs only to one sort of thing is to take it partially. This is what happens, in both respects, with the moral good. For the moral good belongs only to voluntary agents as humans (and not spiders or cats), and only with respect to acts and qualities (and not with respect to substance, for even morally bad people are human beings, and so, as actually such substances, good, though not morally good). The study of the moral good, that is to say the study of good insofar as it is an object of pursuit by voluntary human action, is thus a distinct study, and separate from the study of good simply. It is not, therefore, strictly part of metaphysics (though, as will be seen in chapter 9, there is a close connection with metaphysics), for it takes good in a limited respect, not in its entirety (cf. Aquinas, *DV:* q21, a2, ad 6; *DP:* q9, a7, ad 5). Hence it is, or can be, misleading to try and understand good as such from the perspective of the moral good.

Given these further specifications about the idea of good, it is possible to explain the idea of bad or evil. Evil, as the opposite of good, must be capable of being said in as many ways as good; but, more importantly, if good is being then evil must be non-being or nothing. It is not, however, simply nothing, but rather nothing in a certain way; just as good is not simply being but being in a certain way. If to say something is good is to say it is actual in some way, or the actuality that perfects another, then to say something is bad is to say it is not actual in some way, or that it is destructive of another.

In the first sense, when it is said that something's not being actual is bad, this absence must be the absence of an actuality for which the thing has a potentiality; for the absence of sight in a stone is not bad for the stone, since a stone has no capacity for sight. An absence that is bad is, thus, properly a privation. A privation presupposes not only a subject that lacks something, but a subject that is ordered to have what it lacks (else, as has been said, it would not be deprived, as a stone is not deprived because it lacks sight). Bad, therefore, says not just nothing, but nothing in a something, a something for which that nothing is a privation.

Because good is only found where there is something to be deprived, it follows that bad is only found where there is good, and only found in good. For if it is only found as an absence in something, that something is, to the extent it is, a being; hence, for the same reason, it is good. This is not as strange as it may appear at first sight, for to say a thing that is bad is good insofar as it is, is not to say it is good in the sense in which it is bad. In the sense in which it is bad it is deprived of being; but in the sense in which it is good it has being. Rather what one says is that that which is bad is bad to the extent to which it lacks something due to it; and this does not compel one to deny it has being in other respects which it does not lack, and as regards which it is good. Thus there is no contradiction and no incongruity.

As bad in this sense is opposed to good as perfect, so bad in the sense of destructive is opposed to good as perfective. And just as the subject of bad in the first sense is good, so the cause of bad in this second sense is good. What destroys a thing or deprives it of something and so causes bad to it, is itself some kind of thing or actuality, but an opposed actuality. Deer, for instance, destroy grass by eating it, and wolves destroy deer by eating them. But in each case the destructive agent is destructive because it is realising its own good, or exercising the powers of its own being in some way; the only thing is that, by doing this, it destroys, at the same time, the good of another. What the agent is tending towards primarily and principally is its own good, or its own realisation of its own being; and thus far it is good and tending towards good. The bad is caused because this good is opposed to, and destructive of, the good of another. The bad, however, that it causes is a privation, the privation of being in the thing destroyed; and this cause of bad is bad only because its good is opposed to the good of another, not because the bad is something in its own right. So that, in either case, bad is, strictly speaking, nothing.

There are two other points that it is worth making about good here. One of them refers backwards to something already discussed, and the other refers forwards to what will be discussed later, especially in chapter 9. The first point concerns the fact that good signifies the idea of a standard (as mentioned in the chapter on Hare). This is indeed the case if good is being in its finality or completeness, for this means that things are more or less good the more or less they realise or attain the standard of their completeness as the things they are. So a strawberry is more or less good the more or less it realises the fullness of being red, juicy and so on. One must, however, remember here that there might be a certain relativity of the standards. A thing may be good either because it is complete with respect to its own potential to be or with respect to another's potential to be, and these need not coincide. A strawberry that is successful or complete as a strawberry need not be the same as one that is desirable to eat, for a certain level of redness and juiciness may be just right for eating but too much if the strawberry is to function well as a strawberry, that is to assist propagation and so on. Or if this is not true of strawberries, it certainly seems to be so with the fattening processes that certain animals are made to undergo, as turkeys at Christmas or Thanksgiving. The standard here of course is what people want out of turkeys when roasted, and not what turkeys need to be to flourish and live as turkeys. But this does not alter the point that good signifies a certain actuality of being, and that this being is the measure by which to judge how far a particular example really is good (fatness for turkeys as far as we are concerned, leanness, perhaps, as far as the turkey itself is concerned).

The other point concerns the capacity we humans have to conceive and know the idea of goodness as such. Because of this we are able to discern goodness in all things and in all contexts, just because we are able to discern being in all things and in all contexts, and to see how far each thing is or is not perfect and complete in its being. We are not limited only to discerning and pursuing goodness in the sense of that being which we ourselves might be moved towards. So one can discern (as just mentioned) not just how a turkey is good with respect to our eating of it, but also with respect to how it is good in and by itself, and with respect to its own flourishing, not ours. This capacity to discern good independently and, so to speak, objectively, and hence also to love and admire each good for what it is in and by itself, will be found to have important implications when it comes to understanding the operation of the human will and the determination of the human good (as will be explained in chapters 8 and 9). For it means that we, unlike all or most other things around us, are not just moved towards good in the sense of the immediate objects of our own preservation, survival and perfection (in the way that, say, a plant is moved just towards such flourishing as best it can as the plant it is), but can also be moved towards, in the sense of loving them and wishing well to them disinterestedly, the goods of all other things generally. Though, as again will be seen, this phenomenon also reflects back on our being itself, and has an important consequence for how our true perfection must eventually be understood.

CONTRAST WITH NON-NATURALISM

This, then, is the doctrine of good as given from the perspective of being, and it is possible, in the light of it, to provide a solution to some of the questions discussed in the first chapters. For the difficulties that have beset philosophers and driven some of them to deny that good is an object of knowledge all arise from the peculiarity of the sort of object that good is, namely that it is supervenient. These difficulties are most revealingly brought to light in the context of the open-question argument and the various moves that Moore, Stevenson and Hare, in particular, felt compelled to make because of it.

The essence of this argument is that no matter how many properties or facts one says of a thing one will never get something that adds up to its good. Good always says a 'something more'. Consequently there must be some sort of gap between facts and good, a gap that can never be filled by the addition of any other fact or facts. To this extent, indeed, the open-question argument captures a genuine truth about good, even if, as an argument, it is unsound. The trouble with

Moore, Stevenson and Hare is that they give inaccurate accounts of this truth.

Moore thought that it was necessary to say that good was a peculiar fact of its own, or that the gap is filled by a fact that is not like any other fact, but is, as he put it, non-natural. As was seen, Moore was compelled to this position because his impoverished epistemology did not allow him to say that there might be more to knowledge than having certain ideas in one's head, ideas that were certain sorts of property like yellow and red. But viewing good in this way obscured two important features of good. The first was that this account made it difficult, if not impossible, to see how good could have any necessary connection with desire and action; and this was what Stevenson emphasised. The second was that it obscured the point that good is somehow attached to the facts or properties of a thing, or that a thing's goodness is not a separate or distinct property like yellow, but somehow just that thing with its properties; and this was what Hare emphasised.

However, both Stevenson and Hare were, no less than Moore, dominated in their own analyses of good by empiricism, whether explicit or implicit. But within empiricism, Moore's move of identifying good with some peculiar property of its own is about the only one it is plausible to make to keep good within the sphere of the knowable. Since Stevenson and Hare rejected this move for the reasons given, they were compelled to make a move out of the cognitive sphere altogether, and to say that good was not a truth or an object of knowledge, but something volitional. So they sought different ways to say good was really used to express volitional acts, not cognitive ones. This was how they endeavoured to understand the 'something more' of good, and called it the emotive or evaluative meaning of good.

All these accounts are, as has been argued, inadequate, but, using the analysis of good just given, it is possible to show how they have truth at their basis. Good is supervenient and, precisely because it is, it does not signify a property of its own; as non-supervenient or category terms do, such as yellow and red, or what is generally intended by the term 'fact'. Good just signifies the same thing or property it is said of, and not something else. Nevertheless it adds a something more. What it adds, however, is not a fact or any particular determination of being, but just the difference of a certain respect, the respect of a reference to desire or of finality, which follows any fact or being whatever just as the fact or being it is. So when pleasure, for instance, is said to be good, the only fact or thing in question is pleasure; no additional one is brought in by good, as there is by red, say, when a strawberry is said to be red.

The elements of this account of good are present, if inadequately explained, in the thought of Moore, Stevenson and Hare. For good is not a fact of any sort, as Hare and Stevenson stressed, and yet it is tied to or attached to the facts, as Hare stressed. Moreover, of whatever it is predicated it always says a something more, as Moore, in the open-question argument, stressed. This something more is, further, a reference to desire, and so it involves something volitional, as both Hare and Stevenson stressed. But this volitional element (the so-called emotive or evaluative element) is not an act of desire; it is a *reference to* desire, and that is not at all the same thing. Consequently it is possible, in this way, to preserve the point, held to by Moore, that good, despite its oddness, is a truth to be known. To say good adds to being the respect of the desirable, the respect of a reference to desire, or signifies the idea of being in its finality, is to assert a truth, not to express an act of desire.

There is another respect too in which this analysis can account for something that Moore, Stevenson and Hare insisted on, namely that facts and modern physical science are neutral. Since good indicates being, any being, under the aspect of finality or reference to desire, to consider beings without considering this aspect is to consider them without considering their goodness. It is clearly possible to do this, and it is, indeed, just what, as part of its method, modern physical science tends to do. In this respect it is like mathematics, to which its method is so much indebted, for mathematics does not consider good either (Aristotle, *Metaph:* 996a18-b1; Aquinas, *ST:* Ia, q5, a3, ad 4; *DV:* q21, a2, ad 4). Scientific facts are, in general, just the observable properties of things, considered above all in their mathematical relations, and any reference to desire and finality is eschewed because this is no part of the intention of this sort of science. Facts, even scientific facts, can, nevertheless, be considered under the aspect of good, just as any being whatever can be; hence facts too are good, insofar as they are. Facts are only neutral taken scientifically; taken in their being they are not neutral; they are all good, though not all good in the same way, or for the same things.

Most, if not all, the puzzles about good that have been so widely debated under the heading of the naturalistic fallacy (insofar as this debate has touched on metaphysical matters), spring from the fact that good is one of those peculiar terms, like one, thing and true, that are supervenient, or, to revert to the term of older writers, transcendental. That the debate about the naturalistic fallacy has thrown up such inadequate explanations is due, principally, to two things. First, the impoverished epistemology in which it has been carried on, namely empiricism, or the despair of speculative metaphysics; and second, the failure to look at good in all its scope, not just in its application to ethics, a failure one can trace back to Moore's hybrid metaethics. Perhaps one benefit of going through all this is to show the inadequacy of empiricist epistemology, as well as some of the merits of the older thinking.

CHAPTER 7

Nature and the science of nature

THE STUDY OF THE NATURAL

Ethical naturalism has, as its name implies, a lot to do with nature, and it is therefore necessary to consider what is meant by the term. The custom nowadays is to assume that the determinant of nature and the natural is modern science, especially modern physics, the paradigmatic form of modern science. This is certainly the assumption, explicit or implicit, that lies behind the thought of the authors discussed in the first chapters. But it is fairly clear that if this is how nature is to be determined, then it is going to be of no use for ethics, for as so determined it does not and cannot involve any reference to good or value. The sort of idea of nature that ethical naturalism needs is, however, going to have to be one that does involve or include such reference. Is there such an idea?

I have already said in the last chapter that there is, and have given some arguments in support of this contention. It is now necessary to argue the case more systematically and in more detail. But since within the limits of modern mathematical science such a case cannot be made, the implication of making it is that there is some other legitimate method, besides science, of investigating the natural world. This is a controversial position to adopt. To defend it one must say something about this other method, and specifically one must say something about how both it and modern science can exist together. The best way to do this is actually to engage in that other method, and give a concrete example of how it proceeds and what results it comes to. One will then be in some position to compare it with modern science and show how the two relate to each other, and how they are or are not compatible. Since I need to engage in that other method anyway in order to confirm the view about nature I put forward in the last chapter, the two tasks can go hand in hand. In what follows I will first undertake an analysis of nature and the natural world using that other method, and then I will compare it and its results with those of modern science. The method needs a name, and as what I propose to do coincides pretty largely with what I take it the older thinkers were doing when they engaged in what they called natural philosophy, that seems the only appropriate name to give it.

NATURAL PHILOSOPHY

The concern of natural philosophy is the world of immediate perception, and the things that directly confront such perception. It is concerned, that is to say, with the macroscopic things of ordinary, daily experience. One must stress, therefore, that what underlies it, as the cardinal principle on which it stands or falls, is a thoroughgoing realism, or a conviction that through the senses we are brought into direct awareness with a real world of objective, self-subsistent things, whose real structure and character is in principle accessible to us in that direct awareness. We may, and indeed often do, make mistakes about what we are thus directly aware of, but this does not mean that the way things really are must be thought of as cut off from us, inaccessible to direct perception, and only detectable (if really detectable at all) by means of some special method or process of inference. This is not required by the phenomenon of error; indeed it is excluded by it, as our experience of becoming aware of error testifies. When we discover or discern that we have made a mistake about the objects we perceive, what happens, at least in most cases, is not that we perform some transcendental deduction to a hidden world, but that we perceive the very thing itself – only more clearly, carefully and precisely. In other words what corrects mistaken perception is just more perception, not something other than perception. For instance, when we realise that what we supposed to be a rabbit in the field opposite was really a piece of wood, it is because we have perceived just what we perceived before but more accurately or more near to hand (we see the shape and texture, for example). Learning that one has perceived erroneously is only possible because perception is directly of things; only thus could further perception reveal that the thing is really other than was at first supposed.

This fundamental epistemological realism is something that I have already appealed to in the last chapter while discussing the idea of good and being, and I have no need to repeat here what I argued there. But it might be worth adding at this point, since the question of perception has been raised, that perception cannot be regarded as a mere passive reception of sense impressions. A complete perceptual act requires the joint operation of memory, imagination and judgement, as well as of the sense organs; for we have to retain, compare and arrange our various perceptions through expanses of time if we are to see whole objects and not a hazy sensory blur; and we have to judge these wholes to be wholes, and wholes of a certain sort, if we are to perceive them as determinate objects and not as unintelligible jumbles. Because of the need for this joint operation of several faculties, and because this requires effort and activity on our part, it is not surprising that error can be possible even when perception is essentially direct awareness of real things. Error is detected and removed through what is a sort of re-arranging of the parts of the perceptual act with respect to what we are immediately aware of and in response to the evidence of that awareness, as happens in the case of the rabbit and the piece of wood. It is not a matter of supposing that the real is always hidden behind the directly perceived. This is the error of Bacon and Descartes, and it is an error that has unfortunately, but not surprisingly considering the extent of their influence, often been repeated since.

Given epistemological realism in the sense indicated, the question that at once arises concerns the structure or character of the real. And here the question is to be understood as posed at a highly universal and abstract level – what is the character of this real as such, or as it is found in all particulars, not as limited to this or that specific sort? The claim that is now to be defended is that this structure is one of change, or movement and process. Or in other words, that the real is dynamic.

There should be little difficulty in accepting the truth of this claim, at least at the level of basic description, for change is something that leaps at once to the eye. One only needs to pause and reflect briefly to recognise that the whole natural world is in a state of movement, development, change. Trees swaying in the breeze, clouds forming and reforming in the sky, birds flying through the air, children playing in the park – all these manifest the phenomenon of change. The same is true of the change from day to night and night to day, or the many revolutions of the heavens – for all the physical bodies in the universe seem to be in perpetual motion (at least relative to each other).

Such examples are of course of movement in place, and fairly obvious ones at that. But there are other kinds of movement. Things do not just change place or position; they also change their appearance, their shape, their size, and even their structure and form. We find this not only in inanimate things, as when wax becomes fluid and transparent in the presence of a flame, but more significantly in animate things. All the forms of life from plants to animals go through a seemingly unending process of birth, growth, decay and death; and with some of these there are strange metamorphoses, as in the case of the butterfly and the frog. This sort of change, indeed, is (as will become evident) a more profound one when it comes to analysis than mere change of place, but it is evidently no less obvious or real than change of place. Still, however this may be, one may fairly say that there is nothing in the physical world of our experience that does not seem subject to some process of change, even if at given moments it may not in fact be changing.

This changeability of things is not just a capacity to alter in various ways. There is a pattern to a thing's changing that one can generally isolate and discern. This is true for instance of the elementary particles which have distinctive patterns of behaviour, both individually and in great masses in the stars and galaxies. It is possible to discern these patterns or these life histories, to describe them and even to state the rule or order that determines them (which is partly what is meant by a physical 'law'). And just as there are patterns in elementary particles, so there are more obviously patterns in living things as well, where similar forms of life go through the same, or nearly the same, process of birth and death. Indeed, one may say generally that all study of natural things is, in some sense, concerned with the way or pattern of motion of these things – what processes they typically go through and what governs these processes. Of course there is nothing inexorable about these patterns in the sense that they are incapable of being interrupted, or that they cannot go wrong, either from within or without. The point is that they exist nevertheless, and it is because of this that they can constitute a special subject matter for investigation.

The study of natural things is consequently a study of things that are marked in their being by a certain more or less distinctive dynamism – it is a study of dynamic things. If one is to conduct this study at its most universal and abstract level, one will have to concentrate on the question of what it is to be dynamic, or of what it is to be a thing for which to be is a sort of ordered pattern of change. The supposition of such study, of course, is that change, motion and activity are real and not mere surface appearances hiding a different reality beneath. The legitimacy of such a supposition has already been argued for above, but here it is of considerable importance for my purpose to spell out one particular approach that it specifically excludes. The approach I have in mind is that which collapses movement or change into a series of discrete moments or parts, or which denies that change is a process that is continuous. Whatever might be thought to the contrary, such a position simply denies the reality of the dynamic and puts something static in its place.

What I mean is this. To assert that motion or change is to be understood as a succession of stages, each separately describable and isolatable, is to say that these stages are discrete, and that, when taken on their own in separation, there is no longer anything one can call motion. For motion, on this theory, is not the isolated parts but the succession of them. But what is this succession? Simply the replacement of one part by another, so that whereas first there was this, now there is that. There can be no question of *process* here, of the alteration of one part *into* another, so that there is continuity between them. On the contrary each part on its own is just that part, fixed and frozen, and, as it were, for ever the same. It is not itself in motion, nor in the process of becoming something more, since to assert this could, according to this theory, only be to assert succession, that is, the cessation of this part and its replacement by another. The fault that vitiates this theory as a theory of *change* is that to take any moment in the supposed process and separate it from some other moment in it is not to grasp the process but to freeze and halt it, rather as a camera halts and freezes moments in an action. And to try then to reconstitute the motion out of these frozen parts, by placing them next to each other in a succession, is not to reconstitute it at all, but rather to posit a series of discrete elements, each of which is static, motionless, and really and logically quite independent of the part next to it. Motion consequently becomes a series of different things that replace each other, or a series of instantaneous creations and annihilations, and not the same thing undergoing some development. Thus the reality of motion is lost.

The point may be clarified and reinforced by considering more directly this idea of sameness or identity, for on this account one loses the identity of the thing that is said to be changing. For what is it for a thing to change? Evidently to become in some way different from what it was before; but not entirely different, in the sense that what was before the change no longer exists in any way at all after the change. To say this would be to say that the original thing did not change but altogether ceased to be. A thing can only change, and can only be said to change, if it somehow endures or persists through the change and is still there at the end. In other words the thing that changes must remain somehow identical or the same throughout the change. Not the same in every respect of course, for then it would not have changed, but the same at least in the sense that while it is there in one state or condition at the beginning, it is still there, though in a different state or condition, at the end. Consider the example of the heating of water – the water begins cold and ends hot, but the same water clearly endures throughout.

It is just this crucial element of identity through change that the account of change being criticised here necessarily misses out. For what one has in this case is precisely *not* a thing that is here in one condition at the beginning and is still there, but in a different condition, at the end; rather one has two quite different and independent things, that are ontologically quite discrete. If there is any connection between these things, it is not one of real identity; they are connected only in that there is some series of other independent things lying between them such that there is a sort of discernible similarity from one to the next. It may be that some thinkers have come to the conclusion that what we call the identity of things through time and change is just this fact that one can trace such a succession of different things between the stages; but if so they have not explained identity through time; rather they have denied that genuine identity in these cases is possible or conceivable (as the example of Hume makes quite clear; *Treatise:* Bk.1, pt.4, ch.6).

Perhaps there are many who are attracted by such a conclusion, but let them not suppose that they have preserved the dynamism of nature in this way, for they have not. If one is to have genuine dynamism, and if one is to be able to say that things really change, one must simply reject this theory of the succession of discrete parts. One must talk instead of genuine continuity, which is to say one must talk of genuine identity, and assert that what changes in a change is something that endures throughout the change, and is there at the end as much as it was at the beginning.

This point is important. It means at once that to cope with the reality of change and to explain it as it is, instead of explaining it away, one must have recourse to the traditional concepts of potentiality and actuality. A thing that changes is a thing that is not yet what it is becoming, but is nevertheless the same thing that will be what it is becoming when the process is complete. This means that it must have already now, before it has become, a potential for so becoming; it must have in itself, as an integral part of its present being, the capacity to be something more; otherwise it would not admit of enduring throughout the change, and could not be called the same thing at the end as at the beginning. This is to say, in effect, that the thing's capacity to be is not exhausted by what it already is, but that there is present in it an openness to something further. Its becoming that something further is precisely what is meant by its changing – just the fact of its becoming actually what it is at present only potentially, of the realisation or completion of its already existing capacity for being. Consequently, if the natural world is a world of dynamic things, of things that genuinely undergo change, development and so on, it is a world of things that are not at once all they can be. It is a world of things that are both actual in some way, insofar as they already exist, and also at the same time potential, insofar as they do not yet exist in ways in which they have the capacity to exist but in which they are (or may be) coming to exist. It is only thus that one can secure the reality of a world where there is genuine change, and where things do become and are not merely a static moment in a succession of instantaneous annihilations and creations.

There are difficulties involved in giving a clear and coherent account of the notions of identity through change, of potential and actual, and of how a thing can actually now have a potential for further actuality later (a great deal of ancient natural philosophy was taken up with explaining these points). But these difficulties cannot concern the correctness or legitimacy of the ideas; only the precise determination of them. At least this must be so if one is to maintain a position with respect to the natural world that recognises in it a real dynamism.

The implications of the reality of dynamism, and hence of the reality of things that are a mixture of potentiality and actuality and for which change is the progressive realisation of that potentiality, are far-reaching. But to uncover them it is first necessary to draw a distinction between two basic kinds of change – between a change towards being and a change away from being, or between growth and decay. It is fairly evident to reflection that both these kinds of change exist. Certainly this is so in the case of living things. The development of the embryo in the womb, the growth and development of the new animal once born to the stage of maturity where it starts the process of procreation all over again, and its gradual, or not so gradual, decline towards death, are features of the world that need only to be pointed out to be admitted. And besides the ordinary process of ageing and death, there are also various other kinds of decay that may happen at any stage of life, brought on by disease and violence from without.

The difference between these two directions of change is that one sort is towards preserving and completing the thing that changes as the thing it is, and the other is towards its destruction and diminution. Even if there may be dispute about identifying just what a given thing is (problems of classification, and of variations within classifications), there is no doubt that things are definite 'somewhats' and that the two kinds of change to which they are subject are differentiated according to what each particular thing is and whether the change serves to promote this or not.

This means that one must recognise also two sorts of potentiality in things: a potentiality to cease being what they are, and a potentiality to be more completely what they are. As the first kind of potentiality is evidently a defect in things and does not tell us what they are but only that they are perishable rather than imperishable, it is the second kind that is of particular importance if we are to understand that dynamism in things that belongs to them as the sort of things they are. Consequently, from here on the term 'potentiality' will be used only in the sense of potentiality to be, and not in the sense of potentiality to cease to be.

If natural things are really dynamic, and if to be really dynamic is to be both actual and in potential to further actuality, then understanding the nature of such a thing is necessarily understanding both what it is now and also what it is on its way still to be. For since its being is not realised or exhausted all at once, but only progressively over time, its being is a being that is coming to be; so to specify this being must be to specify how it is becoming. That means, in consequence, that to specify what the particular nature of a given thing is, it is not enough to make a list of its currently observable properties, as is typically done by contemporary thinkers when they raise the question of defining natural objects, and certainly what is done by empiricists. On the contrary, one must also say something about what it is coming to be but is not yet actually, and so not yet observably. Take, for instance, a daffodil bulb. One cannot say what daffodil bulbs are by confining oneself to a description of their observable shape, colour and so on. A daffodil bulb is essentially something that, when planted, will grow into a daffodil; that is why the term 'daffodil' already occurs in the name of the bulb, and why the name of other flowers, as tulip, occurs in the name of other bulbs. That is also why the name of the mature animal occurs in the name of the respective embryos, as monkey embryo or human embryo.

One can go further than this talk of embryos and bulbs to talk also of the fully grown animals and plants. These too must be understood dynamically, only the dynamism is now less towards further development than towards the living out of the life appropriate to such an animal or such a plant. In other words, these things are to be understood again not in terms of what may be observed in some static, frozen moment, as in a list of empiricist properties, but in terms of what they do or how they live. For the 'to be' of a living thing is to be alive, and to be alive is to move, operate and act.

Those who study living things in their living, and not frozen or cut up in laboratories, such as naturalists and field biologists, are well aware of this fact. They are certainly not concerned with mere surface features of things (such as one would find in a static, empiricist account), but rather with life-styles and life-cycles – the sort of way in which particular creatures live, that is, the unity and pattern of their activities. In such a context one understands far more what a leopard is, for instance, from its form of living than from the fact that it has a coat of spots; and likewise one understands what a fox is far more from its living than from the fact that it has a bushy tail; and the same holds in all other cases. The facts of the living of living things tell us far more about what kinds of existence or being we are dealing with than the facts of their external appearance or the enumeration of their parts. Indeed, it is in the light of the former that the latter are typically seen to make sense. This is particularly obvious in such cases as the long neck of the giraffe, the sturdy talons of the eagle, or the webbed feet of the duck.

This dynamism of living creatures, or the fact that they are things with an inherent potential for certain forms of life, and that they realise or fulfill these potentials in living through their lives, carries over just as obviously to their organic and also inorganic parts. A leg, for instance, is something that is dynamic with respect to the performance of certain operations within the life of an animal – for motion, hunting, defence and so on; a heart is dynamic with respect to the circulation of blood, an eye with respect to the operation of seeing, blood itself with respect to the conveyance of food, oxygen, and the removal of waste. In all these cases we have things that exist essentially in the performance of certain activities, or a certain more or less ordered pattern of activities; in other words things that are what they are by virtue of capacities or potentials they possess and which are realised in the relevant operations. Such things cannot be understood as the things they are except by reference to their operations, that is their capacities and the realisation of them. For they are things for which such potentials or capacities are constitutive of what they are. It is because of this fact that one can talk intelligibly of things becoming more fully or completely what they are. The phrase appears at first sight paradoxical. How can a thing *become* what it *is*? The answer, of course, is that it becomes actually what it is as yet only potentially; for what it is is a matter both of actuality and potentiality, so that its becoming more fully what it is is just its realising its own already inherent potential.

There are of course difficulties that one has to face in trying to explain what the particular potentials, and hence natures, of particular things are. One may say, though, that this has to be done in principle by working backwards from the observation of the actual to the recognition of the potential or capacity for that actuality. So, that a given bulb is a daffodil bulb is something that can only become evident if one waits for it to grow; though once one has seen several bulbs become daffodils one may be able to tell the signs of the bulb that indicate what sort of flower it will become – and even more so if one has seen the parent flower from which it came. The same also goes for birds' eggs, for instance, which are detected as the eggs that will produce such and such birds because one has seen the parent birds, or has watched the eggs hatch and the chicks grow, or both. And the same also goes for discerning the potentials of adult creatures, namely that these wings operate in flying, gliding, hovering, display, or that these talons operate in seizing, killing and carrying prey, and so on. One has to see things behaving in such and such ways to see clearly what their life-potential is.

Of course the processes of birth, growth, procreation of the same and so on, are sometimes interrupted. Apart from some eggs failing to hatch or some bulbs to sprout, there are so-called monstrous or deformed births, where the thing produced is not quite like the parent nor is able to live quite like the parent. And in addition to deformities there are all sorts of variations between parents and offspring, especially the more remote the parents, as evolution shows. What this means is that the attribution of certain potentialities to things, or the claim that certain variant features are deformities or deficiencies, is not something that can be done absolutely from parent to offspring or from offspring to parent. The continuation of precisely the same nature from one generation to the next is not infallible. In the end one has to observe how things actually work to be sure of what the potentials are.

But difficult or complex or not, the reality of such facts is not in doubt. Living things are dynamic in the way indicated; they are a combination of potentials that are realised in certain forms of activity that are more or less distinctive of them; and they do reproduce themselves more or less the same, though sometimes there are alterations, some of which may be deformities, some perhaps the opposite. Whether or not it is easy to say which is which (though manifestly it sometimes is), is not the point; for the difficulty does not invalidate at all the legitimacy of the categories and terms used.

The implications of this account of natural things, namely that they are essentially dynamic and thus constituted as both actual and potential at the same time, need to be carefully noted. At once it follows that one cannot accurately describe what a particular thing is without saying something about what it is coming to be, as well as about what it already actually is. The idea of a thing's nature breaks down into two correlative ideas – the idea of something that exists already as something determinate, and the idea that as this something it is also on its way to being something more. This in turn means that a nature is essentially something teleological. The something more it is yet to become stands to it as the goal or object of its still unrealised potential, and so as its end or *telos*.

A *telos* or goal is of course a good – the good of the thing for which that *telos* is the *telos* (as was argued in the last chapter). Consequently a correct description or definition of what a thing by nature is will be essentially a teleological description, or, to put it another way, a *normative description*. In specifying what a thing is one will specify also the norm of goodness for it, or what its goodness will be found in, namely the realisation of its potential. Such a description is both genuinely a description, in the sense that it describes what is the case, and genuinely normative in the sense that it states what the goodness is for that thing. And this is inevitable given the fact (which must be admitted if dynamism is admitted) that what a thing is is not just what it is actually but also what it is potentially. For what it is now is as much constituted by its potential, by the fact that it exists in a state of tending towards its fulfilment, as by its already realised actuality (cf. Clark, 1979: chs.II.3, III.3).

To admit dynamism is to admit that real things *exist* as dynamic, and to exist as dynamic is to exist for becoming something more. To freeze things at some given moment, to try to describe them in terms of what can be discerned in a given time-slice, is necessarily to ignore dynamism. For dynamism, or the directedness to becoming something more, is as much an empirical and observable fact about things as their already existing properties and features. The only difference is that dynamism is a fact that one can only discern by observing things over time and through time; it is a temporal property and must be discerned temporally; but it is not thereby any the less real or less observable. To suppose this and to assert that all that is empirical is what can be detected in a given observable 'now' is to suppose that motion, change and time are not observable. And that is surely false.

Once this is stated it is evident how the awareness of such dynamism and such teleology has been lost. For (as I have already argued) the static approach divides temporal sequence not into one and the same thing that is realising a potential it possesses, but into a series of discrete and ontologically different things. It lacks a genuine notion of identity through time and change, since it speaks of such identity as if it were only the sequence of quite distinct things that are progressively dissimilar to each other. But such identity is not identity at all. To have genuine identity is to have things which exist through time and are the same even though they change, because change is just the realisation of a potential that already existed in them to begin with. And to admit this is to admit teleology, and hence to admit the real ontological grounding of good in the nature of things. The good for each thing is for it to realise its potential, that is for it to realise itself as the thing it is by becoming actually what it is coming to be. That is why for each thing its good is to live according to its nature, or to grow, develop and act so as to fulfill the potential by which it is already even now constituted. To deny this is to deny the reality of genuine change.

That such facts about dynamism have come to be little regarded is due in large part to the rise of modern science. It was and is thought that to accept science is to reject dynamism, at least in the sense just analysed. This, however, must be false. What is required, therefore, is some account of science that shows its relation to the study of dynamism, and that can explain how the two are compatible, even though it may easily be thought that they are not.

The first thing that needs to be said is that modern mathematical science, whatever it is concerned with, is not concerned with explicating the idea of dynamism in nature. Indeed dynamism, in view of the teleology which it essentially entails, would have to be dismissed from modern science almost as a matter of principle. Modern science cannot therefore be said to be concerned with the analysis of change properly speaking, or in the sense of the proper being of change.

But modern science is evidently in some sense concerned with change, at least as part of its subject matter, for it does include, among its laws, laws of motion and change. The question, therefore, that needs to be asked is how it is concerned with change, and how its concern differs from the concern of natural philosophy.

Perhaps it will help to consider briefly scientific laws or theories, since these seem to be the special object of science. These laws and theories are expressed almost entirely in terms of mathematical formulae, as in Newton's law of gravity or Einstein's theory of relativity. These formulae themselves express certain correlations between measurements or possible measurements of things, as of mass and distance for instance in Newton's case. They state, in other words, what mathematical relationship or proportion generally holds between various measurements that one can take from real things. This usually also has predictive consequences; given one measure and the relevant formulae one can work out what the correlated measure must be even before one has actually measured it. These formulae are typically hypotheses – or parts of hypotheses – for it is seldom a question in science of directly finding a formula from the data; it is rather a question of constructing or postulating a formula or theory to apply to the data in order, as far as possible, to account for them, or to 'save' them. The worth of the hypothesis is then assessed in terms of its capacity to do this, as well as its capacity to predict correctly other – as yet undetected – data. But while science gives us such mathematical formulae or laws about the behaviour of things, or about their motions and changes, it does not tell us about the idea of change as such; and in fact it is clear that the idea of change cannot emerge from such laws, nor from a concern with measurements, quantifications, and the correlation of them.

The principal reason for this is that to consider change only with respect to the measurements one can make of it is to focus attention, not on the movement as such, but on moments or stages in it which one can measure or between which one can take measures. So in the case of speed, for instance, which would appear at first sight necessarily to involve reference to motion, one understands this in terms of distance covered and time taken. But to measure either of these one has to isolate in the distance and the time certain fixed points between which the measure is to be taken. The actual reality of change, which only exists in the 'between' (there is no motion that takes place in an instant), is thus subordinated to the concern with the end-points of the 'between'. Furthermore, to the extent that the 'between' is considered, it is considered just as a numerical quantity (so many measures of a given unit), not as a *process*. One should also note that all these elements are present in this analysis as things conceived of as actual. Change is only considered with respect to what in it is already actual, and not as regards its being essentially something that is becoming something more; for each point or moment in the motion is treated as actual when actually considered. Hence the dynamism of change is not focussed on at all. For instance, one measures the speed of a motion after the motion is finished, because before then one does not have an actual distance or an actual time to measure. Or if one does measure the speed of something still moving, this is either because one measures a part of the motion that has already been completed and, supposing that the speed is remaining constant, takes this to be the speed of the whole motion; or because, in the case of speedometers, one measures the revolution of the wheel, or the equivalent, that is actually happening now. At no point does one focus on something properly potential or dynamic.

There is of course no denial of the reality of change in any of this (on the contrary this reality is presupposed), but neither is there any concern with analysing its dynamism. What is the focus of attention is, as has been said, the quantitative aspects in it which make it capable of measurement. And what has been said about the relatively straightforward case of the measurement of speed, will apply also to physical laws and theories in general insofar as these too are predominately, if not exclusively, mathematical in nature.

One may say as a general comment on this that the subject matter of science, particularly modern physics, is not so much things in their ontological reality as in their quantitative, or quantifiable manifestations. Science deals with 'mathematicised phenomena' (cf. Maritain, 1959: chs.2 and 4). At least this description of science captures a fundamental element of its method. It also helps to explain several other features of it that have been the subject of remark by philosophers, scientists and others. The features I have in mind are its lack of concern with sensuous properties; its special claim to objectivity; its tendency to reduce things to their measurable parts, while ignoring the whole; its depiction of the world in a way that is peculiarly foreign to ordinary experience.

If science systematises the phenomena it investigates into mathematical laws and theories, it can only concern itself with what is mathematically quantifiable. This means that the properly sensuous qualities of things, colour, sound and so on, are omitted. A scientific account of yellow and the perception of yellow, for instance, will consist just of those aspects of the yellow and the perceiver that can be measured (Schrödinger, 1967: 166-168). This does not necessarily imply that the sensuous properties are not knowable, for manifestly they are, but just that they cannot be brought into a mathematical systematisation. Nevertheless this fact tends to generate a claim to objectivity on science's behalf. Objectivity is opposed to subjectivity and is taken to indicate a certain elimination of the subject, namely the individual scientist, from the assessment of things, as well as a greater reality or truth for the data so objectified. There is an element of truth in this because when it comes to measuring quantities it is more accurate to use an instrument of measurement than to make an estimate directly. To measure is to assess a thing according to some standard measure or rule and hence requires a comparison of it with the rule. To estimate a measurement is, in effect, to perform this comparison in imagination, and it is evidently more accurate to perform this instead with the aid of a rule directly applied. Moreover, if a refined instrument is used, one that can detect minute quantities, the result will be more accurate still. This is, in fact, what science particularly promotes, for as it is concerned with quantities, the more accurately these are measured, the more accurate will its treatment of them be. What happens, then, is that the instrument does the measuring and all that is required of the individual scientist is to read off the measure it gives. The subject, therefore, comes in at one remove and does not judge the thing measured but the instrument measuring (as Bacon had recommended). This relative exclusion of the subject results, indeed, in a more accurate measurement. But the exclusion is only relative, and the subject is not, and cannot be, wholly removed. Moreover, this sort of exclusion is only appropriate in the case of measuring quantities, and not in the case of knowing other features of the real.

The lack of concern with the sensuous is clearly one way in which science departs, and departs quite radically, from the familiar world of ordinary experience. But there are also other ways in which it does so, namely by moving from what can be directly perceived to what cannot be directly perceived, and from the macroscopic to the microscopic.

Science is concerned with measurable data, as much as possible and in as many respects as possible. Particularly is this so with the powers of things, or what effects they can cause, and their parts, or what they are made of. Powers are revealed in exercise, and ordinarily things may never be put into a position where their powers are revealed. To discover these powers it is necessary to create the conditions artificially, and in such a way that their powers can be measured. This is the purpose of experiments. Unlike experience, which is from ordinary observation, experimental knowledge comes from deliberate torturings of things (as Bacon would put it). Consequently, in its pursuit of these hidden powers, science passes over things as they are knowable in ordinary experience. This inevitably generates a tendency to view the hidden as real and the apparent as unreal. This is evident in the case of Bacon and Descartes, and of many others, both philosophers and scientists.

The same tendency, however, recurs in the case of parts. What we perceive are complex wholes, but all these wholes are divisible into the parts that make them up. This can be done at the level of ordinary perception (bodies can visibly be separated into arms, legs and so on), but it can also be continued beyond it. Wherever there is a physical thing, unless it is altogether simple, it can be divided into parts, and these again into their parts. While the simplest things are beyond the range of perception, they are not beyond the range of instruments. We can, therefore, have access to them using the measurements of them given by instruments, and we can use these measurements to characterise and describe them. Atoms, for instance, are known as combinations of particles (or wave-particles) possessed of a certain electrical charge, a certain mass or frequency, a certain speed and so on. Because of the discovery of such particles and their measurable properties and effects, there is a tendency to hold that the gross macroscopic things we directly perceive are reducible to such collections of minute particles and their ceaseless motion. So there is also a strong temptation to view this hidden, unperceived collection of particles as the real, and the gross object as somehow unreal or a subjective construct.

It was the conviction of the early propagandists of the new science that this divorce between the world as we ordinarily experience it and the world as described by science had to be explained by supposing that only the latter was the real world, and that the world of the senses was fundamentally illusory (as has already been mentioned in chapter 5). This meant that any attempt to describe the world in the terms of our ordinary awareness of it, as in the ancient tradition of natural philosophy, had to be wrong; hence the rejection of the doctrines associated with that tradition, especially teleology.

What this shows is the connection between accounts of how the world really is and accounts of the reliability or unreliability of our ordinary experience. The legitimacy of natural philosophy as a valid form of teaching about the world stands or falls by the reliability of this experience, which is why I stressed at the beginning of this chapter that it is based on a thorough-going epistemological realism. That is why those who wished to reject natural philosophy did so by attacking that realism. This is most evident in the case of Descartes, whose method of doubt is designed precisely to get that realism out of the way first, so that he will then be free to present in its place his modern scientific physical teaching as the true account of things (so *Meditations:* I; *Discourse:* part 4; *Letters:* 94). The rejection of the basic trustworthiness of the senses and therewith the rejection of natural philosophy has been an integral part of the modern tradition, and this helps to explain the perennial importance for it of scepticism.

However there was never any logical necessity for the rejection of the senses strictly speaking. It was indeed highly problematic from the start. Since the world as depicted by science is only accessible to us in the last resort through the senses, for it is they that tell us the results of experiments, using science to deny the reliability of the senses inevitably presupposes that reliability in the first place (Schrödinger, 1967: 177). It was also incoherent to argue, as Locke and others did, that perception was representative, not direct, in that what we perceived was not real things but mental images which represented, if rather imperfectly, the real world hidden beyond them. For the attempt to say something about the world as it really is, and about how our inner mental ideas do or do not reflect it, when we are supposed only ever to know one side of the comparison (namely our own ideas and not the real world), is doomed from the start. Idealism was one way of overcoming this difficulty. It simply denied that pole of the comparison called the real world, and attempted to say instead that everything was just a sort of projection of our own minds.

But there was nothing necessary about adopting idealism either. One could as well have gone back to the original direct realism (cf. Warnock, 1962: 31-32). What made this return difficult was precisely the question of how to describe the findings of science. How could these findings be about the real world if the real world was not as science depicted it? And yet surely, if one was going to speak of a real world at all, it was absurd to deny that science was about the real world. The answer to this is to say that it is about the real world, but about the real world as viewed at one remove, so to speak, or in a certain abstraction. This follows from the contention already made that the object of science is not things in their full reality, but in their measurable manifestations. For to take these manifestations on their own, or to consider things primarily if not exclusively in their quantitative phenomena, is to take them in abstraction from their ontological grounding in the real. Science is to be understood as a partial, limited investigation of things, and its depiction of what they are like as an abstract, idealised one. This at once leaves open a space for natural philosophy also as a legitimate study of things. The two studies are not rivals or in opposition, nor is it necessary to deny epistemological realism to get science going. All that is necessary is to draw a few distinctions and recognise a few requirements of method. And this is what a number of recent thinkers have already been suggesting (e.g. Maritain, 1959; Wallace, 1979; cf. also Husserl, 1965; Heidegger, 1966).

Unfortunately such a move, or such a middle way, as a solution to the problem, has only recently come into prominence and even so has not proved very popular. The old conviction that only the modern scientific is the real has been behind a lot of recent thought, for instance in the human sciences (Bernstein, 1976: part 1), and is basically what lies at the root of contemporary non-naturalism in ethics, with its heavy bias towards empiricism. Perhaps, therefore, it is worth saying a few more words about this empiricism to clarify and reinforce the present argument.

It has already been indicated how an empiricist approach to change is incapable of explaining the dynamism, and hence the reality, of change. This is because, while there is a concern with observable features, both sensuous and quantitative, there is no concern with the being of things, and hence with the terms within which this being is analysed, notably, in the present context, potentiality and actuality. The empiricist approach imitates the approach of modern science; only it goes to a greater extreme because it expressly denies the validity of other approaches, whereas science proper just uses its approach without going into the philosophical, non-scientific, question of whether there are others and how, if at all, its own relates to them.

What is thus lost to sight in empiricism as regards the analysis of things, is also lost to sight with respect to knowledge and the increase of understanding. This comes out in the analytic/synthetic distinction, and since that distinction has been used to bolster anti-naturalist arguments, it is necessary to consider it more carefully here. Once objects have been reduced to their observable features, or so-called empirical data, they can only be spoken of as unities or combinations of data; whether these unities are thought of as *a priori* with Kant, or empirically derived as with the British empiricists, makes no difference for present purposes. Thus horses and cats, for instance, can only be spoken of as the data that go to make them up, and a definition of them can only be a listing of such data (and this of course is how Moore speaks of definition). More importantly, a thing is supposed to be exhaustively defined by a complete list of such features; this means that a thing is understood in terms of what it actually is and nothing is or can be said about what it potentially is. So its existence as tending to be something more is simply ignored. Such definitions are, of course, empirically false; they are also incapable of functioning as evaluative norms.

Moreover, if these data are regarded as simple, irreducible and incapable of further analysis, such that to know them is to know them completely at once without the possibility of knowing more (and this is how they are regarded in the theory), then it is evident that if there is to be any advance in knowledge it can only be by the addition of fresh data. Hence no statement is informative unless it does this, or unless what the predicate says is an addition of something that is wholly external to the subject. Statements that, in the predicate, just state data or facts already signified by the subject do not constitute any such addition, and so are not informative, except in the limited sense of indicating how a word is being used, that is to name this set of data.

If one turns, however, from this empiricist preoccupation with data and considers things instead in terms of their being, the case is different. Here what is in question is the understanding of what we experience, so there is first our sensible awareness of things, and next the attempt to disclose their meaning to understanding by raising them from the level of sensible experience to that of intelligibility. So, for instance, some aspect of our experience is taken, say change, and this is received first of all just as to the fact of it, for our experience makes evident that there is change, or that there are changeable and changing things. But the mind's grasp is not exhausted in the recognition of this as a fact, for it can go on to uncover for itself how this fact is possible, or what is involved in the constitution of its being, namely, in this case, that it involves the actualising of a potential in the thing changed. It is thus that one comes to understand change, or to make sense of its being.

Evidently there is no question here of adding one datum to another, for, first, all the relevant data or experience must be presumed to be given (this is the subject matter to be understood and so must be present already); and, second, it is not the case that this subject matter consists of elements that are known all at once. Everything that belongs to the intelligibility of the subject is already given in the experience of it, in any and every experience of it, but it is not given in such a way as to be expressly recognised and conceived at once in the experiencing of it; just as the ideas of potentiality and actuality are present in any change whatever yet are not expressly thought in the experience of change. There is advance in knowledge in this case, not by the addition of fresh data, but by the intellectual or conceptual clarification of what is first received without such clarification. So the advance is not by the input of more of the same from without, as there is when data are added, but by an uncovering from within, an uncovering that is at the same time an ascent to a higher cognitive level. The distinction between the analytic and the synthetic, as this is usually understood, cannot therefore be applied here. And just as this must be said about the understanding of the being of change, so it must be said about the understanding of the being of anything else, whether triangles, circles, horses, or, more importantly in the present context, good.

MERITS OF EACH

The above remarks about the notion of change, and the different approaches to it of natural philosophy and modern mathematical science, have been designed to show how there can be a sense of nature that both yields norms or standards of goodness, and is yet at the same time a genuine description of what is the case. However, lest my remarks about modern mathematical science, which have been largely negative in view of the context and purpose of the present chapter, seem unduly harsh for this reason, I will conclude with some comments about the value of modern mathematical science with respect to natural philosophy.

This may be done under two heads: with respect to knowledge and with respect to technology. In the first way the value of science is both direct and indirect. Indirect because science is so committed to gathering data that it has stimulated a greater interest in, and a greater dedication to, the exploration of evidence of all kinds. Empirical investigation certainly flourished among the older thinkers (as witness Aristotle, Theophrastus and Albert the Great, to name but a few), but modern thinkers surpass them in this respect, in scope, dedication, and sheer numbers. Part of the reason for this is that ancient philosophy is concerned above all with the understanding of experience, which is a reflection on evidence not a gathering of it; and while evidence must be gathered, a lot is available at once in ordinary life without the need for gathering further afield. There was, instead, in ancient philosophy an intense concern with the details of formal analysis, as in the analysis of change, potentiality and actuality discussed above.

The emphasis of modern science is rather different, and, what is more, it is concerned with gathering evidence that is not available from observation but only from experiments.

There was little of this before, and so a whole range of evidence was left unexplored. The development of instruments required for such experiments itself increased this knowledge. This may be noted, in particular, in the case of the heavens, where our knowledge vastly exceeds what was available before, and has refuted a great deal of ancient speculation.

Directly science has increased knowledge since it is itself a special kind of knowledge, namely a knowledge of quantified data and the mathematical systematisation of their relations. This hardly existed at all before, except minimally in the case of astronomy. Since such measurable facts about things are a genuine part of what they are, even if science considers them in relative abstraction, to know them is to know the world and its beings in greater detail. Moreover this science is the only one that can penetrate certain areas of reality which are otherwise hidden to investigation. The latent powers of things, or the elementary particles, or the distant bodies of the universe, are only observable to the extent they can be detected and measured by instruments. And since our knowledge of these things is confined to their measurable data, the science of such data will be the only science that is competent to investigate them.

Perhaps more important historically, and for ordinary perceptions of science, is its technological value, its 'pay-off' in terms of practical uses for the benefit and comfort of our lives. In technology the powers and properties of natural things are turned to our use, and it is not possible to do this without knowledge of these powers and properties. Moreover, this knowledge has to be precise and cast into a mathematical form if it is going to be possible to make the necessary calculations about how much is required, in what proportion, combination and so on, to produce the required result. For example, to put a rocket into orbit it is necessary to calculate the attraction of gravity at different distances from the earth, the force to overcome this attraction, and the amount and type of fuel to produce this force. Precisely because science discovers the latent properties of things, reduces them to precise measurements, and combines them in mathematical formulae, it is rich in technological applications.

When modern science was first emerging, this practical advantage of it was the one that its early devotees, especially Bacon and Descartes, did most to emphasise and promote. They did this in pursuit of a certain goal, the conquest of nature for human benefit; and they presented science above all as the tool of this conquest. However, science itself does not treat of goals and values; for its method does not extend to being to know either goodness or nature. The good of a thing is its *telos*, and there is no knowledge of a *telos* if there is no knowledge of potentiality and actuality. One cannot look to science to determine values, either the value of itself or of other things. To determine what values are really values, to what extent, in what contexts, and which take precedence over which, one must turn to the science of value, or rather human value, namely ethics and politics. Bacon and Descartes were implicitly aware of this, because their promotion of science is based on certain prior ethical and political beliefs, beliefs about what the human good is.

The pursuit of science, and especially technology, must be subordinate to, and governed by, the science of goals; or, in other words, ethics and politics are prior and possess a certain authority over science. How far the pursuit of science is good, in what way, by whom, and for what ends, are not questions for science or scientists to decide, but for political legislators (cf. Aristotle, *EN:* 1094a27-b2).

It is worth concluding the present chapter with the following observation. As science is unable to judge of good and the good by nature, it is pointless to look to it to explain ethical naturalism. Any attempt to do so will be fallacious because it will be an attempt to explain goodness by reduction to something from which goodness is excluded, or an attempt to explain value by reference to what is not value. This is the burden of the non-naturalists' case, and as such that case is quite correct. The sort of naturalism they attack is fallacious, and fallacious for the reason they say it is. However, this non-naturalism has itself fallen into error because it has tried to make the scientific the paradigm of knowledge and the knowable, or in other words, because it has been dominated by an empiricist understanding of things and of our knowledge of them. But if one accepts that this is a limiting and impoverished position to adopt, that it is not only not warranted but is actually contrary to the empirical facts, and if one accepts also the insights of natural philosophy, then one is in a position to recapture a sense of nature that does make naturalism a real possibility.

CHAPTER 8

Willing and thinking

THE QUESTION POSED

As the question of nature is central to the question of ethical naturalism, so is the question of thinking and willing and their relations. It is a claim of non-naturalists (with the exception of Moore) that one's choice and will are not determined by objects of knowledge, for knowledge is of facts and facts, in the way meant, are evaluatively neutral. Thinking, in other words, does not move willing. Naturalism, on the contrary, does maintain that there is some dependence of the will on thought and knowledge, for it maintains that there is knowledge of good, and that the will follows the good that is known or thought.

This question, indeed, of how far, if at all, what one thinks determines what one wills, or how far the influence of thought on will is dependent on prior commitments of the will in favour of what is thought about, has arisen several times in the course of recent debates (as the previous chapters have shown). It is clearly a question that is in need of direct examination.

According to non-naturalism, thinking does not move willing unless the will is already committed, independently, to what is being thought about. In other words, in any process of reasoning that has choice or action as a result, there must already be a choice, or an evaluation or an attitude, implicit in the premises beforehand. So Hare, for instance, says that no 'ought'-conclusion can validly be deduced from pemises that do not themselves contain an 'ought', implicit or explicit. If one wants to conclude, for instance, that smoking ought not to be advertised, one must have some such premises as: what is injurious to health ought not to be advertised, and smoking is injurious to health. Here the first or major premise contains an 'ought', and only because it does so can the conclusion also contain an 'ought'.

In the same spirit Ayer and Stevenson say that no amount of agreement about the facts will lead to agreement in attitude unless there already exists some prior agreement in attitude. So, if A and B are arguing whether x is y or z, their agreeing that it is y will not make them agree in approving x unless they already agree in approving y. If this is not the case, and there is no other agreement in attitude further back to which x can be related, then the disagreement in attitude is absolute and insoluble. There is a radical breakdown in reasoning, or, as it is said, deadlock is reached.

This view about the ineffectiveness of thinking with respect to the will is based on the view that good, value and so on, are not knowable. This view is itself based on certain views about nature and knowledge. It has already been argued at length that the understandings of knowledge, good and nature involved here are deficient, so the arguments about willing and thinking based on them may be set aside without further comment. There are, however, other arguments that remain, and which do give the belief that thinking does not move willing some plausibility.

First, there is the fact that value disagreements, especially moral ones, are peculiarly intractable to reasoning in a way in which other disagreements typically are not. Second, there is the fact, which one notices even in one's own case, that the belief or thought that something is good or desirable, or ought to be done, is not sufficient to make one necessarily choose and act in accordance with it. There is, in other words, the phenomenon of weakness of will or incontinence. Third, with respect in particular to the claim that there are things naturally good, it is argued that if this were so there would be things no one could fail to choose, but it is evident that there is nothing of this kind. People can and do choose and pursue the most diverse things, including what others regard as bad, even bad by nature. If there are natural goods, there is no agreement about them, nor are they necessarily chosen, and this needs explaining if they are goods one can discover by thinking, and if what one thinks good determines how one chooses.

It is clear from these considerations that even if good is an object of knowledge, and even if thinking does move the will, this moving is by no means infallible. Willing cannot be totally subordinate to thinking; there must be some opposition, or room for opposition, between them also. Indeed, one must even admit that thought is in some way subordinate to willing. For we can think when we wish; and the length of time we think, over what subjects, in what ways, in view of what end and with what degree of care, are all, in some measure, determined by our own choices and desires. So whatever analysis one gives of will and thought, it must at any rate be such as to explain and accommodate these points.

THE IDEA OF WILL AND OF THE WILLED GOOD

To turn to the question of the analysis of willing first of all, there does seem to be an obvious sense in which willing is tied to thinking, namely with respect to the object willed. Even those who deny that good is an object of knowledge would nevertheless admit that one's attitude or choice fixes on some object, and that that object is given by thought. For, in their view, one takes up attitudes towards facts, but one could not do this if one was not aware of the fact or facts in question. Willing must, accordingly, be something conscious and rational at least in this minimal sense, that it is of something one is conscious of and can reason about.

But the consciousness in question here cannot be merely sensation; or, to put it another way, willing is not the same as what is called sensible appetite. By this is meant the inclination of one's sensitive nature, one's emotions, feelings, passions and so on, towards what one perceives or senses. The various bodily urges, to food, drink, sex, fall under this heading, for these are inclinations in one's physical being to objects present to sense or imagination. They also have bodily manifestations, as quickened heart-beat, and are themselves sensations, as pangs in the stomach, or dryness of throat and lips. Physical pain and pleasure are all of this sort, being ultimately the sensation of sensible objects, or conditions, that either agree or disagree with the senses and the body itself. Warmth is agreeable and pleasant, for it stimulates the senses and the body in a way that accords with their disposition; but extreme heat, as a flame, is painful because it destroys that disposition, just as bright light is painful to the eyes and loud noise painful to the ears. Sensible appetite is thus the inclination of a sensitive being towards what it feels or senses and, conversely, a shrinking from such objects when they are contrary; for it is characteristic of appetite both to pursue and flee – to pursue the agreeable and flee the disagreeable.

One must distinguish sensible appetite in this sense from will and choice, or rather one must recognise that not all our desires or inclinations are physical or sensitive ones. One can, for instance, readily identify a sensation that is the thirst for a drink, or the hunger for food, but one can desire to drink or eat without such a sensation. One may, for instance, choose a certain regimen for one's health which requires one to eat at fixed intervals; so one eats at those intervals even though one may not feel hungry. One may also choose against one's sensations, as when one chooses not to satisfy a thirst (as with the dropsical, whose cure requires them to resist their desire to drink), or to drink against one's revulsion to drink (as when one takes nasty tasting medicine).

This is even more true in the case of desires that, unlike thirst and hunger, do not have an object for which there is also a readily identifiable sensation. Such is the case with the desires for knowledge, or justice or liberty. Feelings may certainly be aroused over these matters, but they do not come about physically, as hunger and thirst do. Rather they arise mentally, or as a result of thoughts and judgements, for these values are only grasped mentally or by thought. Moreover these sort of feelings do not arise necessarily or always, because opposition between choices and feelings may be even more marked here than in the case of judgements about health and the sensations of hunger and thirst. So with knowledge; one's body may be weary or sick, and yet one may force oneself to continue studying. The same goes for justice, honesty, integrity, fidelity and so on, when men and women are prepared to suffer all kinds of physical pain and hardship for the sake of religion, country and friends. It is true that animals manifest something similar, when they face various threats and suffer various physical pains for the sake of something else; as males fighting each other over females; females facing their natural enemies to protect their young; animals in flight forcing themselves through thickets, careless of the tearing of flesh, to escape some predator. But there is a difference here in that the goods in question are not abstract things like justice or religion. Nor do the animals conceive them as goods, or reason about the preferability of sacrificing one to another, but seem to act on the basis of some instinct. Or if there is some reflection and ratiocination involved (as some authors argue, e.g. Barnett, 1967; Clark, 1982), this must just be construed as indicating the more or less embryonic presence in them of something more than merely sensible appetite.

It seems clear, then, that there is in humans manifestly, in animals possibly, a capacity for choosing and willing that is distinct from any physical or sensible appetites. Philosophers have, through the ages, recognised the existence of such a capacity, from the older thinkers, to Rousseau, Kant and Hare in more recent times (for the capacity for making decisions of principle, or willing the categorical imperative, or being part of the general will, is evidently such; Aristotle too speaks of an appetite that follows thought, *de An:* 433a22-b13; as does also Aquinas, *ST:* Ia, q80, a2). This capacity has attracted to itself the distinct name of *will*, and its presence in humans is tied to the presence in them of thought, since it is an inclination towards things thought as opposed to sensed. Justice, integrity, wisdom can, strictly speaking, only be conceived.

Insofar, then, as the intellect gives the will its objects, the connection between thinking and willing is close. But this is not all. It has been argued that the intellect knows good, or that good is an object of knowledge. Good is also the proper object of the will, for good is being taken under the aspect of order to desire, and as will is a species of desire, its object as such must be the good or the desirable. This, it has been said, is what answers to the will as its proper object, just as the visible answers to sight as its proper object, or as the audible answers to hearing. And as the visible makes seeing actual and the audible makes hearing actual, so the desirable, or, to be more precise, the conceived and apprehended good, makes willing actual.

It is not enough, therefore, to conceive something for it to be an object to move the will; it must be conceived under the aspect of the proper object of the will, that is, as good (just as not any object will move sight but only a visible object). So the intellect must not only think what is willed, as non-naturalists would admit, but must also think it according to the idea or sense in which it is willed, namely as good, which non-naturalists would deny.

Consequently, one must say of will that it is an inner inclination that proceeds from, or according to, an inner principle of knowledge and reason, or that it is rooted in the rational understanding of good (cf. Aquinas, *ST:* Ia IIae, q6, a4). The 'want' of will is, therefore, not like the 'want' of some sensible desire, which is, as is sometimes said, a sort of psychological state. For if will is a rational power its 'want' is bound up with determinations of reason, not sensible feelings; its 'want' is, in other words, a rational commitment to good, not a sensation. (This sense of 'want' has been noticed by contemporary writers, though the account given of it is different; Hudson, 1969: 235-239; 1970: 269-270.) The conclusion that follows from this is that the proper object of the will, which moves it as the objects of other faculties move them, is the good as conceived or apprehended by thought; hence thinking is a mover, or the mover, of the will.

Given that this is so, it further follows that not only is thinking such as to move the will, but the will must be such as to be moved by thought. As has been argued, there is in us, besides the capacity to think good, also the natural ordination on the part of the will towards good. This, indeed, is just what is meant by saying that good is its proper object. If this ordination of the will to good were lacking, no amount of thinking about the good would have any effect on it (just as no amount of visible things would affect the eye if its ordination to the visible were lacking).

Thus, in answer, to those who say thinking about something will have no effect on the will or choice unless the will is already committed in favour of that thing, one may say, first, that good is an object of knowledge and can be thought about directly just like any other object of knowledge; and, second, that there is in the very idea or nature of will an ordination to good; or, if you like, it has a 'natural commitment'. Since this commitment belongs to the structure of the will as such, it exists in it even when nothing is actually being willed (as the ordination of the eye to seeing exists in it even when nothing is being seen). But, just as importantly, since this is a commitment to good generally, not to this or that particular good, the will is not by nature engaged in favour of one possible good more than another (again as the eye is open to all visible things and is not fixed by nature to this or that particular one). The will exists not as naturally engaged to this or that good, but as naturally disposed so as to be engaged to this or that good, as these goods are presented to it in thought and reason. As a matter of its being, therefore, will is moved by thought insofar as it is moved by the apprehended good.

The idea of the apprehended good, however, needs further elaboration. First of all, what is it to apprehend good? It is, as argued in the previous chapters, to apprehend how something responds to desire, or how the being of things constitutes a fulfilment of the potential for being. Since there are many beings there must be many goods to apprehend, including perhaps also the good of the natural order as a whole. The question then arises as to whether the will is naturally disposed to follow all these varieties of goods or just some of them. Is it, for instance, just the good that perfects us that moves us to love and pursuit, or can this also be done by the goods that perfect other things and the whole, even if these were to conflict with the good for us?

One might be inclined to suggest only the first. It is true that the mind can range over the whole of being and know the goods of all things, as for instance the good of spiders, insects, fishes and the like (as that eating flies is good for spiders, or that feeding off rotting flesh is good for certain insects). But it is not these goods, or not these goods viewed as goods of other creatures, that moves our will to choice and action, but only goods viewed as goods for us. One may indeed desire to eat a fly or some rotting flesh, but if one does it is hardly because one views them as good for spiders or insects to eat; it is rather because one views them as good for oneself to eat. Accordingly it would seem that the good that moves the will must be specified as the good for humans, and that only when goods are apprehended as falling under this idea do they constitute the proper object of the will.

This, however, must be an error. It relies on an assumption that humans are necessarily self-regarding and that they are drawn only towards what they hold as perfecting or benefitting themselves. This assumption may be widespread, but it is refuted by the facts of experience. Experience points not only to selflessness on the part of humans towards their fellows (as Hume well showed), but also towards other things, as is shown by those who devote themselves to the care and protection of other creatures. It seems hardly true to say that this behaviour is self-regarding at root, because, say, of the pleasant feelings or the hope of reward that one is presumed to get out of it. This may be true in some cases but experience indicates that it is not true in all.

The possibility of such an other-regarding dimension to human choice and action is supported by the contention that human beings can conceive the goods of all things, and if they can conceive them, and if will follows what is conceived, they can choose to act for the sake of them, and not just for the sake of goods more proper to themselves.

But the question does not rest here, for given this other-regarding dimension to humanity, founded, as just suggested, on the comprehensive grasp of good, the possibility arises that humans are by nature such that their being is only complete or perfect when it is not for itself but for others, or for the whole. Or, to put it differently, perhaps human being, and its potential for being, is a *being-for* or a *being-towards* what is more or beyond itself. The facts under consideration here of the human capacity to know and so to love the goods of all things evidently suggest this. Such a capacity is certainly a capacity to transcend the confines of one's own limited and immediate existence. In such a case the human good, and the beyond-human good, would prove not just not to conflict, but in some sense to be one; human perfection, or the human good, would lie in being for the perfection of other things and for the whole, that is for the more than human good. And if so, one should perhaps go further and say that the object of the will, the apprehended good that moves it, will not be some limited good within the realm of goods, but the complete and universal good, or the most complete and universal good possible.

However this question of what the human good is, or of what human perfection is and how it relates to other perfections, is one that must be left for more detailed examination in the next chapter. Here it is necessary to consider some other implications of the claim that human will and choice are of goods as apprehended by the mind.

One may say generally that if choice and desire follow thought, because they follow thought goods, then their characteristics will tend to mirror the characteristics of thought. One of these characteristics is that thought can be false; hence human choices may also be false. That falsehood is possible in the case of good and choice may be denied by non-naturalists, who say that good is not an object of knowledge and so not something one can err about; but it has generally been admitted by naturalists and must certainly be admitted here, since it is an implication of the claim that good is an object, or a possible object, of knowledge. If what is meant by good is what perfects the natural being of things, then one will be wrong about what is good as often as one is wrong about what this natural being is – whether of oneself or of other things also. This good is therefore something objective or something determined by nature; it is not dependent on one's opinions or acts of will. For the same reason it is an object of investigation and science; it can be worked out and discovered by reflection on the being or nature of things, as these are given to us in experience.

One important result of this is that the good must be divided into the real and apparent. The real good is the good by nature, for this is the good that is good in and of itself and not just in our conception of it; while the apparent good is what is thought to be good but is not so. And since we are moved, as a matter of fact, to desire and choose what we apprehend as good, it clearly follows that we need not necessarily desire and choose the really good, but rather what, for some reason, we apprehend as good at the time; and this may or may not be the really good.

In this way one can see how it is possible to hold that everything we desire or choose we desire or choose as good, even though sometimes we desire and choose what is bad. We desire under the aspect of good, for the will's object is good, but sometimes, for various reasons – ignorance, passion, habits, stubbornness and so on – we misapprehend and so conceive as good what is in fact, or by nature, bad. It is evident, for example, that when criminals and terrorists steal, kill or maim, they do so supposing that these actions, at any rate in the particular case, are good or means to some good. This is how one can talk of bad desires or desires for bad, for they are desires for what is really bad but taken under the aspect of good.

There are some who have tried to argue that we can, in fact, choose something bad precisely insofar as it is bad, and not because we suppose it at the time to be good. But this is mistaken. One can, indeed, choose something reputed to be bad, and choose it just because it is so reputed, but in doing this one is viewing the reputed bad as good. Or it may be that one is viewing the act of opposition as good. This possibility, in fact, explains how one may choose or consider good the very opposing itself of good, for the opposite *qua* opposite of good and the opposing of good are not the same. When one chooses, just for the sake of it or out of perversity, to oppose a good, what one's attention is focussed on is not this good, but the going against it, and nothing prevents this from being considered good. Thus one may say in general that one cannot choose or desire bad *qua* bad. For to choose is to fix on something as an object to pursue and achieve, and to do this is necessarily to view it as something worth achieving, which is precisely to view it as good.

These facts, namely that the good divides into the real and the apparent, and that will and choice are always of good, though of the apprehended good, helps to explain some disputed points between Hare on the ond hand and Foot, Anscombe and others on the other. The latter want to limit the good that one can will and choose to some definite things (those which they say are connected with benefit and harm), while Hare wants to say there is no limit at all but that one can in principle will and choose absolutely anything. In this dispute both sides are in a sense right and in a sense wrong. There is indeed a limit to what can be willed and chosen, namely the limit defined by the notion of good itself; for only something viewed as good can be an object of the will and hence a particular thing cannot become such an object unless it is so viewed. Moreover there is also a limit to what can actually be good, namely the limit defined by the objective nature of things.

In this sense, then, Hare is wrong and Foot, Anscombe and others are right. But in another sense Hare is right and the others are wrong, because these limits are in a way no limits. The objective natures of things do indeed limit the really good, but they do not limit the apparent good. Since human thought is so fertile, various and ingenious in its inventions, there seems nothing at all that could not be considered good. Consequently, since will and choice are of good as conceived by the mind, which good divides, in the way indicated, into the real and the apparent, there is no more limit to what can be chosen and willed than there is to what can be thought. It is, in fact, on this limitlessness of will consequent on the limitlessness of thought that, as will be argued later, freedom of choice is founded.

The difference between the real and apparent good also enables one to give an answer to the objection levelled against the idea that there is a natural good. It is said that if some things were by nature, or as a matter of fact, good, then it would be impossible not to choose them and all of us would agree in choosing them, whereas in fact it is evident that neither of these is the case. The answer is that what we choose is the apprehended good, and we do not necessarily apprehend the natural good, so we do not necessarily choose, or agree about, the natural good. In other words, what is by nature good is not known by nature to be good, but only by reflection and thought (cf. Strauss, 1953: 9, 99). Yet even this is not the whole story, for there is a certain lack of necessity, as will be argued later, even between what we apprehend as good, whether truly or falsely, and our choice of it.

The will has for object goods apprehended by the mind, and these goods are clearly many. But since they are all presented to the will by the mind, is there a way, as many thinkers have contended, in which the mind could present or conceive all these goods as falling under the idea of a total and all-comprehensive good? Or is there such a good that would altogether exhaust the will's desire for good? The fact that the goods in question are multitudinous in their variety, and possibly even mutually incompatible, counts against this idea, but it need not decisively rule it out.

Consider first, then, the idea of human perfection. This is the idea of the most complete life one could lead, or that life and exercise of faculties which most fully realises one's potential for existence. Of course there is the question, already raised, of whether this perfection is compatible with the perfection of other things and of the whole. It has been suggested that it is compatible and even that the one is bound up with the other. But if this were not so, one would have to acknowledge a split or divorce within the structure of the whole such that at least one part was incompatible with the rest. Thus human will and choice would also be split and torn in incompatible directions, since both incompatible goods are objects of thought and hence of desire.

What might thus be true of human perfection with respect to the whole might also be true of human perfection with respect to itself, if this too proved to consist of a collection of incompatible goods, or goods that could not all be had at once. This, at any rate, appears to be the position adopted by Hobbes. His claim is that we are so constituted that we are dominated by insatiable and incompatible passions.

Such opinions seem to count against the idea of an ultimate end, but this is not entirely true. Looked at more carefully Hobbes' view does not so much amount to a rejection of the idea of an ultimate end, as to a claim that such a good, though conceivable, is unrealisable. In Hobbes' system the idea of the complete good is quite conceivable as the idea of the complete and continual satisfaction of all the passions at once; but this is of course unrealisable given Hobbes' view of the passions, that there is no limit to what they desire (as with the passion for power), and that when one passion is temporally sated another always takes its place. Still the complete good, at any rate as a formal idea, is present in Hobbes' thinking and in fact plays an important part in it. Hobbes understands human life as directed to this unattainable object of complete satisfaction, and that is why life is for him an interminable succession. Moreover his understanding of the good of peace, which is the foundation of his politics, is based on his understanding of this final end of satisfaction. For peace is good because it is the best and safest way to undertake the interminable task of satisfying insatiable passions.

If this is true of Hobbes, who expressly denied the classical idea of a supreme good, it suggests that, whether realisable or not, the idea is nevertheless a significant and legitimate one; at least in the sense in which it signifies the notion of that complete possession of all goods, or that complete perfection of one's own being and of the being of the whole, which would constitute the total object of desire (cf. Aristotle, *EE:* 1215b15-18; *MM:* 1184a8-14; Aquinas, *ST:* Ia IIae, q1, a5). No good, of course, could be excluded from this good, nor could any good be conceived apart from it. For if something were conceived of as good it would have to be conceived of as belonging to this good and so as being already part of it and not a further addition to it. Should such a good or combination of goods be impossible ever to realise, the result would be that the will would never come to a final rest in its desiring, as Hobbes, in fact, supposed. Whatever good was possessed or was being pursued, it would always be the case that one could conceive of or imagine some other good or goods that would add to it and which, by their absence, would always be a cause for sadness.

Were such a good possible, however, and not a mere notion, there is no need to suppose that every good whatever, and the satisfaction of every desire whatever, will be present in it. For some goods are only good in view of other goods, not in themselves, and are only desired in view of other desires. So when these other goods are reached, and these other desires satisfied, the previous goods and the previous desires simply disappear. Such is what happens in the case of useful goods, which are good only as means. A medicine to cure a disease is only good while the disease lasts. When one has recovered health, the medicine is no longer a good to desire. So, in the case of the final good also, there might be some goods that are part of it only in the sense that they are steps on the way towards it. Consequently, when the final good is attained these other goods will no longer be necessary. Indeed they will no longer be goods. For they are good only in view of the final good, not in themselves, and so, when the final good is reached, the reason for their being good is removed. Their absence, therefore, will neither take away from the final good, nor could their presence add to it (Aspasius, *ENC: ad loc.* 1097b17-21).

It is also worth pointing out here that there is no reason why the ultimate good may not (contrary to the Hobbesian notion) be made up of ordered parts, such that, while all are good in themselves, only one is central and supreme, and the others are secondary and subordinate to it. The ultimate good may thus essentially be this one good, and the absence or presence of the other goods, while overall adding to, or detracting from, the completeness of the being of this good, will not affect it in any substantial way. If one, therefore, possessed or was pursuing this good, but not all the lesser ones, one would find one's desire at rest and content in it, and would not consider the lack of other goods as of any great importance (Clark, 1975: 154-155). (More remarks will be made on this topic in the next chapter.)

To the ultimate end or the ultimate good as so understood was traditionally given the name 'happiness'. Now this term and its cognates have more than one application, and they are quite often used to express particular contentments or satisfactions, as when one says one is in a happy mood, or has spent a happy evening with friends (cf. Telfer, 1980: 1-2). But, despite what is sometimes said, the term 'happiness' can carry the more comprehensive meaning of the total and complete object of desire, in the possession or achievement of which one believes one will have attained all that one could want, and where one would be lacking in nothing. One can say, 'Now I am happy,' or, 'If only I had such and such I would be happy,' and mean that one is, or would be, in a state where nothing more is desired, as some people imagine they would be happy if they had lots of money, a luxurious mansion in some temperate part of the world, fast cars and so on. In fact, one may argue that even particular uses of 'happiness' are relative to this one, in that what is meant is that, at the time when one is said to be happy, there is nothing further one wants, or that one is perfectly content to carry on doing what one is doing; as one sometimes says of young children playing that they are as happy as sandboys. Here the happiness is temporary and particular, but what it is while it lasts is complete satisfaction, or at any rate absorption, of desire, in a good possessed or an activity pursued.

A distinction must, of course, be drawn between what is really happiness and what particular people may profess to find happiness in. For just as there is a real and apparent good so there is a real and apparent happiness. It is certainly not enough to say that one feels happy or content, for just as one's feelings or opinions do not determine the good – since that is in fact determined by nature – so they do not determine happiness either. If, for instance, one feels happy in what is really bad though apparently good, as, say, in the case of a hardened drunkard when drunk (if one accepts that ruining health and finances, and causing distress to friends is bad), then, at least as regards the objective state of things, one is miserable. Or if one is not strictly speaking miserable one is at any rate unfortunate, because one will be lacking the real good, however little, for subjective or other reasons, one may feel this as a genuine lack. Real happiness, like real good, is something objective, and can only be achieved, and, it might be said, only enjoyed, if one exercises some thought about it. Feelings are no sure guide, unless, of course, one says, as some do say, that human nature is such that happiness is private to the individual and is determined by what feelings one happens to have. But then this claim for the authoritativeness of subjective feelings is based on an objective claim about nature, and hence does not overthrow the ultimate authority of nature, nor does it do away with the need to think carefully about nature to see if it really is as it is claimed to be. But this is a question that must be taken up expressly in the next chapter.

GOOD AND ACTION, OR THE 'IS' AND THE 'OUGHT'

So much, then, may be said about the good and the will's orderedness to it. But since it is what moves the will, and since the will is a principle of action in us (we act as we will and choose), good must also move to action. Consequently, thought about good must have action as a result. It is necessary, therefore, to consider the nature of such thinking in greater detail.

It has been and still is fairly standard to distinguish between two types of thinking – theoretical and practical. And this seems quite reasonable if one considers the difference that is hereby intended. The first or theoretical kind of thinking is the thinking typical of the various sciences (metaphysics and natural philosophy, as well as mathematics and modern science in general), and it is distinguished by the fact that its aim is simply to know. The aim of the second or practical kind of thinking is not knowledge, or not just knowledge, but action in accordance with knowledge. In this case what is known or understood is referred beyond the mere knowing to some action or some actual pursuit of good. It differs, therefore, from theoretical thinking in its end (Aquinas, *ST:* Ia, q79, a11). But given that desire is a necessary principle of action – action is for some end or object (either the action itself or something beyond the action), and it is desire that moves one to the pursuit of ends and so to action – it follows that, if practical thinking is directed to action, desire must somehow be involved in it (Aristotle, *de An:* 433a9-26). There are, however, two ways in which thought and desire may be related. Either thought may move desire or desire may move thought.

Thought that moves desire is thought about the ends of desire, or, in other words, the apprehended good. As has been said, the will receives its objects from thought, and it is in this sense that thought moves it. But thought does not provide the will's capacity to desire, nor does it perform the act of desire. Acts of desire belong to the will and the will is a distinct faculty in us that is present by nature, not thought. Moreover thought would have no effect on it were it not already in its being such as to be moved by thought. The inherent ordination of the will to apprehended goods must, therefore, be presupposed if thought about good is to move the will.

Consequently, one must say that while thinking about the good is thinking about certain truths, the fact that this thinking has a volitional result must be explained by reference to the nature of the will rather than that of thought. At this level, indeed, thought is operating simply according to its own nature, for it studies good as it studies any other object, namely as a truth and for the sake of understanding it as a truth. Such thinking, therefore, is in its origin theoretical and its volitional result is something that follows it because of the will, not because of itself. Accordingly one cannot speak of this following as a logical inference, for it is not a following within a process of thought, but a following from thought to desire, and moreover one that has the will rather than thought as its explanation.

Desire may also, as was said, move thought, and this itself may happen in two ways. Either desire moves thought to its own act (the contemplation of truth – as in theoretical thought), or to the will's act (the pursuit of good – as in practical thought). In the first case this happens because the contemplation of truth, or the proper activity of the mind, is itself a good, and may be desired as such. Clearly we contemplate as and when we choose, and contemplation is a good for us to pursue. But this thinking, though desired as a good, is theoretical or for the sake of the act of thought itself.

It is in this sense that we are moved to the study of the particular sciences. But among these are also numbered the so-called practical sciences, ethics and politics. On the one hand, these are sciences because they are for the sake of knowing the truth about something, namely the human good, and, on the other hand, they are practical because they are ultimately for the sake of action. Practical science, therefore, has knowledge as its immediate goal, like the theoretical sciences, which is why it is a science, but its ultimate goal is action, which is why it is practical. So, to the extent that it is practical, it must be reduced to the principles of practical thinking and must be analysed within the terms of such thinking.

Practical thinking arises when thought is not only desired but is set to the service of desire, and is for studying what to do, or how to act, in order to achieve the object of desire. In this case desire does not just move to think, as it does when one chooses to theorise; it also gives the object of thought, and, more importantly, the relevant approach or orientation towards that object.

The object, of course, is good, for this is what desire desires, but as good is a truth, and may be studied as a truth, it is also an object for theoretical thought. Hence practical thought is not sufficiently explained by saying that good is its object. One must go further and say that its approach to this object is the approach of desire and not of thought, or that it approaches good as something to pursue and achieve and not just as something to know. This, indeed, is to say no more than was already said in saying practical thinking is thought moved to the will's act and not its own, or in saying practical thinking differs from theoretical in its end. For this just means that what is essential to the two kinds of thinking, or what is their specific difference, is their orientation. Consequently, if one is to set out in words what is fundamental for practical thinking, or what functions as its first principle which governs and directs all that follows, one must do so in such a way as to state or make explicit this orientation. The first principle must, in other words, express the idea of good as something to pursue. Hence it must be formulated in some such manner as, 'the good is to be pursued or done' (Aquinas, *ST:* Ia IIae, q94, a2).

What is decisive here is evidently the phrase 'is to be done', or, as otherwise put, 'ought to be done'. It is only because of the presence of this that the principle is a practical one. But this is present because of the orientation it is meant to capture, and that orientation is the orientation of desire or will. The sense, therefore, of 'is to be' or 'ought' in the practical principle must be traced to desire; this is its origin, not thought.

This is not to say that the practical principle is not a truth, or that it is really a volitional and not a cognitive act. For, first of all, it is founded on certain truths. It is only because good is being *qua* desirable, and only because the natural object of the will is good, which are both truths grasped by theory, that the will's pursuit, and hence the orientation of practical thought, is given verbal expression in terms of good. Second, the practical principle is itself a truth, a truth indeed of practice and not of theory, but a truth nevertheless. This is because what it expresses is the relation between good and action or that action is due, or is in order, in view of some good to be achieved by action. This relation is evidently something knowable, as are other purely theoretical relations. The only difference is that in this case the relation is viewed practically, or from the point of view of following it and carrying it out. To explain this difference it is certainly necessary, as has been said, to introduce desire, but it is not necessary to conclude that therefore the practical principle is not an act of thought. All one needs to say is that the act of thought is made from the point of view of desire, or that desire directs the thought, not that it replaces it (Aristotle, *EN:* 1112b11-16). This is also why action follows practical thought. For action follows desire, and practical thought is directed to reasoning out how to satisfy desire. Hence action follows it because it follows the desire that is governing and directing thought. This thought is action-guiding, therefore, because it is itself being guided by desire.

It is in the light of these remarks that one must explain how judgements of what is the case can have action as a result, or how it is possible to get from an 'is' to an 'ought'.

It is, however, first necessary to note that 'ought' is essentially relative to good. A practical 'ought' expresses that some action is to be done, but action is for an end, so the action is only to be done, or is only due, in view of the end. The end, of course, is the good, so a practical 'ought' presupposes good as its ground and justification. This, incidentally, is why giving advice about what to do involves informing the mind, for it involves relating what to do to the good to be attained by doing it, and good is an object for the mind to know.

To say that 'ought', or obligation, is relative to good is to deny that there is anything unconditional or categorical about 'oughts', moral or otherwise (in the sense in which 'categorical' means, as in Kant, not relative to good). 'Oughts' in practical matters are dependent on, and justified by, some reference to good; good is prior to 'ought' (Aquinas, *ST:* Ia IIae, q90, a2). Indeed, if desire and will are necessarily of something conceived as good, then even a supposed unconditional 'ought' or categorical imperative is only followed insofar as it is looked upon as good, or insofar as obedience to absolute commands is looked upon as good. Hence, even here, in deed if not in word, the thought of good will turn out to be prior, and to stand behind the thought of the command as what is really operative in it. It is not enough for those who wish to deny this to assert that there are absolute 'oughts' that bind absolutely; they must defend their assertion. It is not enough either to appeal to popular conceptions of morality, for it is not evident that people have the sense of such an 'ought' (even the 'ought' of the divine law amongst religious persons is relative to divine goods); or, if it is, it is not evident that they are not in error or confused in some way.

To say that 'oughts' are relative to good is, of course, not to say that all 'oughts' are relative to the goods people actually choose, or that all 'oughts' are hypothetical in Kant's sense, and only apply if one actually wants the good in question. For there are things that are good for us that we do not necessarily see or pursue, since the real good is determined by reference to nature, not by reference to the actual desires, or the common denominator in the actual desires, of all or most of us. The real good is good for us regardless of what we think or wish, and the 'ought' of it must therefore apply whether we wish it or not. So if justice is really good, then it is really good for all and ought to be pursued by all, even by the unjust who do not care for justice. In fact everyone does in some sense pursue the really good, for they pursue what they pursue under the idea that it belongs to the good even if it does not. (It is the idea that the really good is objective, or that it is independent of what we actually wish or think, that lies behind Kant's claim that morality is categorical.)

'Ought', therefore, begins with good, and good is an object of knowledge; so 'ought' begins with knowledge, or with an 'is'. This knowledge is necessarily fitted to move the will because, as was said, the will is essentially, or by nature, ordered towards such knowledge. But as has also been said, this step from knowledge of good to desire of good, since it finds its explanation in the nature of the will rather than that of thought, is not one of logical inference. The desire of good, thus brought to be by the thought of good, itself brings to be, as was said, another kind of thought, namely practical thought, or thought in the service of desire. This step too is not one of inference, for it too finds its explanation in the will. For as will is drawn of its own nature towards the good conceived, so of its own nature it stimulates thought to reason for the sake of this desire.

Thus the practical orientation is the pursuit of good, and it is this pursuit that is expressed in the practical principle, namely that the good is to be pursued or done. Practical thought, therefore, is endowed from the start with an end and its function is simply to work out how to pursue this end. It proceeds, accordingly, from the first 'ought' of the practical principle to particular 'oughts' in the here and now about how to attain the end that the will sets before it. This process, from the first to the subsidiary 'oughts', is indeed one of inference for it takes place within thought, and not from thought to desire or from desire to thought; but, it must be stressed, it is an inference from 'ought' to 'ought', and not from 'is' to 'ought'.

The result of this thinking is, in the end, action. Because

action belongs to the will this involves yet another move from one faculty to the other; in this case from thought back to desire. So it is not a move of inference either. To be more precise, there is not so much a move from thought to desire, as an application or specification of desire by thought. For since desire is presupposed in practical thinking, and the thinking is just an instrument in the service of it, there must, along with the inference in the thinking, also be an inference or a progress in the desiring. Thought proceeds from the end desired to the here and now, in order to discover the first step that can be done here and now on the way to the end; and it is by accompanying this reasoning at each stage that desire itself is brought to bear on the here and now. With respect to the end, therefore, desire precedes and directs reason, but with respect to the way to the end, reason precedes and directs desire.

Since there is this twofold progression, one in thought and one in desire, the conclusion of this reasoning may be expressed in either of two ways. If one looks at the desire, the conclusion is the action, because desire is set on the pursuit of the end. As soon as it is brought to bear on the here and now, and to the first thing that can be done in that pursuit here and now, one at once moves to act (unless there is some hindrance). That is why Aristotle can say the conclusion of a practical syllogism is an action; because he is considering it from the side of desire (*EN:* 1147a24-31).

If, however, one looks at the side of thought, then the conclusion is the particular 'ought'-judgement, namely the judgement that such and such ought to be done here and now. This judgement expresses a truth, a truth about how to attain the end, but it is a truth taken practically or as actually directive of action. Therefore, it may be expressed in as many ways as such a directive may be expressed, including the imperative 'do this'. Indeed, because practical thinking is action-directing thinking, or because it views the truth about action from the point of view of the desire to act, it may be called imperative thinking. Its conclusions may be expressed either as imperatives or as 'oughts'. And these are followed at once by desire and action, if nothing stands in the way.

This is how Hare looks at practical thinking, and hence why he calls its conclusions imperatives. He also calls these imperatives volitions, but this is a mistake. The imperative is an act of thought, but the act of volition belongs to the will. These two acts do, indeed, necessarily go together, but they are different acts and belong to different faculties. Aquinas speaks more correctly when he says that to command is an act of reason which presupposes an act of will (he also says, significantly, that an 'ought'-judgement is an indicative way of expressing a command; *ST:* Ia IIae, q17, a1).

One may summarise the steps in this explanation of the passage from 'is' to 'ought' as follows. There is first the apprehension by thought of good, and this is a truth or an 'is'. But because of the nature of the will this apprehended good moves the will to desire. Thus set on desire the will moves thought to reason out how to act to fulfill that desire. Thought is thus made practical and takes as its first principle the 'ought' relative to the good of desire, and expressed in the form of 'the good is to be, or ought to be, pursued'. From this principle thought proceeds to particular 'oughts' about action to be done here and now. The conclusion of this reasoning is a judgement, expressed either as an 'ought' or directly as a command. But since it is necessarily accompanied at the same time by the process of desire, the desire given originally in the form of the desire for the end, but applied to the particular action to be done here and now for the sake of that end, there is also a conclusion on the part of desire, namely the actual doing of the action.

In this move from 'is' to 'ought' or to action, there is a going backwards and forwards between the different faculties of mind and will, as well as, at the end, a parallel progression in acts of mind and acts of will. Only at the stage of practical thinking, and only with respect to the movement within thought, can one talk, in the strict sense, of a logical inference. For logic properly concerns relations between thoughts or judgements and their parts, not between thought and something else that is not thought, however closely it may be tied to thought. This inference, though it is an inference of judgement about certain truths, namely truths about the order of this or that action to this or that desired good, is an inference from 'ought' to 'ought', not from 'is' to 'ought'.

The transition, therefore, from the original 'is'-judgement about good, to the final 'ought'-judgment in the here and now, is not a matter of logic, but rather of what is called theory of mind, for it concerns the interconnection between thought and desire, not between different judgements within thought. It is impossible, as a consequence, to understand this transition from the point of view of logic. It is also impossible to understand this transition if one excludes good from the sphere of the 'is' or the knowable, and if one denies that 'ought' is relative to good. This is, of course, exactly what Kant did, and what all those have done who followed him, notably Hare.

Reflecting on the 'is/ought' debate in the light of all this, one can see how the different elements in it may be judged to be both true and not true. It is worth summarising how this is so. First, it is correct to say that thinking only moves willing on the supposition of a prior willing, for this is true in the sense that the orderedness to good pre-exists in the will, but not in the sense that there must be a prior act of will. Second, it is correct to say that 'ought' has imperative force, for it is a directive to action. But this directive is an act of thought, for it concerns the truth about what to do, and this truth is judged by reason. It presupposes, however, the prior act of desire that governs such practical thought and gives it its action-guiding force. Third, it is therefore also correct to say that the conclusion of this thinking may be expressed as an imperative. And it is also correct to say its conclusion is an action or an act of desire. But it is wrong to identify these two conclusions, and to say an imperative is an act of volition. For alongside the process of thought there is a process of desire, and the action is the conclusion of the latter process, while the imperative is the conclusion of the former (cf. Aquinas, *DV:* q22, a15, ad 2).

None of this, however, compels one to deny that good is an object of knowledge, or to deny that there is a good by nature. This is an error arising from a failure to pay attention to the nature of practical as opposed to theoretical thinking, and from a failure to pay attention to the difference, as well as the interrelations, between acts of thought and acts of will. Once these several elements are sorted out, the case for non-naturalist accounts of good based on the fact that it is action-guiding simply dissolves.

One may say that the various disputes that have arisen over these matters are traceable to a basic error of methodology, the metaethical methodology derived from Moore. The question of good has been approached wholly from the side of ethics, and hence from the side of practical thinking as opposed to theoretical thinking about good. What differentiates practical from theoretical thinking is volition. Hence it was more or less inevitable that all those who approached good in this way would have, in the end, to give it a volitional analysis.

THE WILL AND FREEDOM

The idea of giving directions to action to oneself or others presupposes the idea that action lies within the power of the one directed. One does, indeed, give directions to dogs, horses and other animals, and one even praises, blames and punishes them as one does with humans; but these do not carry, or are not generally considered to carry, the same implication with animals as they do with us. We are supposed to exercise control over our acts, and to be responsible for them, and to do this by understanding and knowledge of right and wrong, good and bad. We are, in other words, subject to our own self-determination, and so are free, or causes of ourselves. It is on this supposition that much of ethics and politics is based. The question must be faced, therefore, of how we can be such causes, or of how real our freedom is.

We are causes of action by will and thought, for we move to act by our will and our will is moved by the apprehended good. The will's proper object is good and so it extends over, and is open to, all the particulars that fall under the idea of good. But any particular good, or any good that does not exhaust the whole of good, is good in one way and not in another; for while it is part, or is conceived as part, of the good, it does not include other particular goods that are also part of the good. Hence it both has goodness and lacks it. Thus it is an object of the will insofar as it is good, and not an object insofar as it is not good, or is deficient in goodness; and the will can be moved or not moved by it according to these different respects.

Consequently, as far as particular goods are concerned, though they can move the will, they need not; or, in other words, they impose no necessity on it, but each one still leaves open the way to another. Of this openness and absence of necessity we have experience when faced with a selection of goods to choose between, as whether to go to the opera, or a football match, or whether to stay at home instead. Here it is evident that there is a lack of compulsion. Which one to opt for is up to us; it lies within our choice, not in any necessity in the objects.

This openness of the will, however, to different goods is openness to apprehended goods, and so it depends on the openness or freedom of thought to apprehend different things as good, and as good in this way but not in that. In other words, judgement must be free also if the will's freedom is to be real. Freedom of choice, therefore, rests on the openness of thought to apprehend every particular good, and on the openness of will to pursue every good so apprehended. "The root of freedom is the will as subject, but reason as cause, for it is because reason can have diverse conceptions of good that the will can be freely moved to diverse things" (Aquinas *ST:* Ia IIae, q17, a1, ad 2).

Choice is the determination of the will to this or that particular good, and it is a determination that takes place by reason. The will, as has been said, is ordered to good as such, and it only becomes committed to this or that good as a result of a judgement that this is preferable to that, either simply or here and now. Deliberation is the process of working this out, though not every choice need involve deliberation; some are made at once according to settled habits or immediate perceptions of the moment; for one does not always have time or need to deliberate. Choice follows the judgement of reason about the good to be done here and now, and action follows choice, unless something intervenes to prevent it (though this order is more one of nature than one of time, for they may all be immediate with each other).

It may be objected to this that however open will and reason may be to diverse goods, and however much we may be free in these powers, when it comes to the actual exercise or determination of them to some one good, necessity must intervene. Since one chooses what is viewed as preferable, wherever there is a preponderance of one good over another it will be impossible not to choose it. But in reply it may be said that one may not perceive this preponderance, or if one does the other good may be viewed as being preponderant in some other way. For every good is in some sense preferable to any other just because it is a good and a good in a way other goods are not. Besides, action takes place in the here and now, and many things may weigh more heavily just because they are present, however much they may be inferior to something that is still future.

There is, however, a more complex argument against the reality of freedom, and one that has been more important in debates about it. Where there is something such that it can both be and not be, or such that it is open to several possibilities, as in the case of the will with respect to particular goods, then it cannot be determined to one or the other except through some reason or cause. Now this reason or cause must either be sufficient to determine it or not. If it is not, it needs something further to complete it and make it sufficient; otherwise, this cause on its own will not account for the determination, and so will not be the cause, or not the whole cause. Hence one must get to a sufficient cause eventually. But from a sufficient cause the effect necessarily follows. Consequently the choice was necessitated after all and was not free.

One may object to this that, while the choice did follow necessarily from its immediate cause here and now, nevertheless this cause was, in itself, not necessitated, but could have been present or not present. But this does not solve anything because the same argument arises again. If this cause could have been present or not present, then it was open to both possibilities and hence would have required a further cause to determine it. If, for instance, the reason why one made this choice and not that was because one reflected on these things and not those, then there must have been a further cause of this, which, to be the complete cause, would have had to be sufficient, and so would likewise have necessitated its effect. And if this further cause could also have been present or not present, then it would have required another cause, sufficient and necessitating, to determine it, and so on *ad infinitum*. One must, therefore, eventually get to some first cause that is necessarily and always present and operative, and from this all other causes would follow in a necessary chain down to this particular choice that one makes in the here and now. Consequently, no choice can be free, but all must be necessitated and determined in advance.

If one wants to escape this argument, the only way to do so seems to be to deny that choice is part of such a chain of necessary causes. And the only way to do that seems to be to deny that there must be a sufficient cause of choice to determine it this way and not that. But to say this is to say, in effect, that choice has no cause, or no complete cause, and hence that, in the final analysis, it arises spontaneously, or out of nothing, as it were. In that case the choice is arbitrary and without reason or cause, and so must escape the grasp and control of thought. Thus one seems reduced to saying either that choice is determined or that it is absurd.

Of these alternatives, one may rule out the second both as not being freedom (for it would not give us control over our actions and choices), and as not being possible. Nothing potential or undetermined moves itself to act or determines itself, for nothing potential or undetermined makes itself actual or determines itself insofar as it is potential or undetermined. So even this spontaneous, arbitrary freedom will be found to have a hidden cause behind it (as was argued in chapter 3 against Hare's view of freedom).

The first alternative may be ruled out on the ground that the argument used is, after all, not sound. One must, indeed, admit the need for sufficient reasons or causes, for otherwise one must say choice is arbitrary; but one must deny, first, that these causes necessitate their effects, and, second, that they must go back in a regressive chain.

To begin with the first point. To suppose that all sufficient causes necessitate their effects, so that to posit the cause is to posit the effect, is to suppose that nothing can intervene to prevent them. But this is not true of all causes. Fire, for instance, is sufficient to burn wood, in the sense that it has this power in itself and needs nothing else to enable it to do so. Nevertheless, it can be prevented because it can be put out, or because the wood may be too wet for it, or for some other reason. The same applies in the case of choice. The consideration that something is good, and good here and now, is sufficient to move one to choose it, for nothing else is required to justify the choice. Since the will has good for its object, anything that is presented to it under this aspect is sufficient to move it (just as anything visible, or any colour, is sufficient to move the eye to see it). Yet there is no necessity in this, for some other consideration of good might intervene, and move the will in another way.

Now this is true of any choice generally. While the consideration that the thing chosen is good is sufficient to cause the choice of it, or to ground and justify the choice (so that, to this extent, the choice would be rational and not arbitrary), yet no such consideration would exclude other considerations of good that might intervene and be sufficient, in their turn, to cause a different choice. This, however, is not enough as it stands, for the fact that a sufficient cause was not prevented, or that no preventing causes intervened, itself requires a cause. For instance, in the case of fire burning wood, there must have been some reason why the fire was not put out, or why the wood was not too wet. In explaining any action, therefore, of a sufficient and non-necessitating cause, it is necessary, in order to give the full picture, to add the circumstances and conditions, to the effect that preventing causes were absent. One may, indeed, regard this as another sense of sufficient cause, where the sufficient cause in the first sense is understood along with the absence of anything to prevent it. Here, of course, the effect must necessarily be present; for by saying that the cause is not prevented, one has defined the situation precisely as one where the cause does have its effect. So, in the case of choice, some reason or cause must be given why this consideration of good was not interrupted or overridden by some other consideration before the choice was made.

This brings us, therefore, to the second point. There is no need, to explain this, to have recourse to other causes, or a regressive chain of causes, for the same consideration of good is sufficient by itself both to cause the choice and to remove other considerations that might prevent it. If one good is chosen instead of others, this must be because it is viewed not just as good but as, at the same time, a preferable good. But it is a preferable good just because it is a good, and good in a way in which other, different goods are not. Its goodness, therefore, is sufficient not only to draw the will towards it, but at the same time, and for the same reason, sufficent to draw the will away from the others and so to exclude them. It is sufficient in and of itself to do both. Consequently, it is sufficient in both senses of sufficient cause.

None of this, however, can impose any necessity on the will. For exactly the same can be said of every other good; each one is sufficient to be chosen and to exclude other choices. This good is sufficient in itself to be chosen and to exclude that, and that good is sufficient in itself to be chosen and to exclude this. In neither case does anything else need to be appealed to in explanation of the choice. Consequently, when one of them is chosen before the others, this must lie wholly within each one's mind and will. Nothing further from outside needs to be brought in to account for it.

It might be objected that though, say, this good, x, was chosen, yet that one, y, would have been chosen instead had deliberation gone on, and there must have been some reason why deliberation was stopped. But first, further deliberation might have confirmed the choice of x, for as x is preferable to y and y preferable to x, both courses would have remained just as possible. Second, x itself might have been the reason why deliberation was stopped, for it is sufficient to move choice and so sufficient to bring deliberation to an end. Third, even if there was some other reason, as say the need not to prevaricate, this is just one more good that can be opposed by another good, as the need to choose carefully, each of which can seem preferable to the other. So the same would happen here as happened with x and y themselves, and there would equally be no need to go outside to some other cause to explain the choice of one over the other. Hence even if the cause of the choice of x was the previous choice not to deliberate further (which, however, in point of fact, it was not, for, as was said, further deliberation might have led as much to keep the choice of x as to change it to y), yet this previous choice would have its reason internal to it, and there would be no need to go back further.

Accordingly, one must say of choice, or the determination of the will to this or that particular under the consideration of good by reason and thought, that it stands sufficient to itself, or that in choosing we are our own cause, and that our choice and action are under our own control, not that of something outside us. And this is what is meant by saying choice is free. Moreover, this freedom is combined with, and rooted in, reason, for it is based on reasoning about the good and the preferability of one good to another, and this reasoning is, in each case, sufficient; there is no arbitrary leap required after reasoning stops, as there is for those who equate freedom with spontaneity.

An interesting phenomenon that helps to illustrate something of the flexibility of will and reason that constitutes freedom, is the phenomenon of weakness of will or incontinence, namely the not doing what one thinks one ought to do, and the doing what one thinks one ought not to do.

It must be noted, first of all, that one is always moved to choose and do what one holds here and now to be good or to be done. There is, in other words, no opposition between will and reason in the particular case. For choice is always of some good and the good is apprehended by reason, so that when something is chosen and done, it can only be chosen and done because it is, at the time, conceived and judged by the mind as good.

However, nothing prevents choice and reason being opposed if one considers reason, not about the good in the here and now, but about what is good generally. One may believe, for instance, that alcohol is bad and should not be drunk, but in the actual here and now believe that this particular drink, which is alcoholic, is good and to be drunk, because, say, it is sweet or pleasant. Consequently one proceeds to drink it. Now here one does have the knowledge that one must not drink alcohol, but one only knows it in general terms; one does not know it, or one does not apply it, with respect to the particular alcoholic drink here and now. Hence this general knowledge is not operative and action does not follow it. The general knowledge is not actually thought on, or if it is, the particular case is not subsumed under it but under some other opinion, as that this drink is pleasant and one should taste what is pleasant. So the fact that it is alcohol, or that alcohol is not to be drunk, is pushed aside (Aristotle, *EN:* 1146b6-1147b19). Nevertheless, the knowledge that is operative here and now, and with respect to the particular facts, is followed by choice, and that is why it is true that choice and thought are always in accord in the particular case. One may say, then, that the practical knowledge about what one ought to do only issues in action when it is actually exercised and applied to the particular case, otherwise it will not (and here one may accept Hare's claim that sincere assent to an 'ought'-judgement must issue in action, for sincere assent in the here and now always does; and Hare, in fact, intended his claim about sincere assent to be taken in this way; 1963: 83).

What prevents the exercise and application of the general knowledge is that the thought and desire of some other good intervenes and moves the will instead. This happens in the incontinent because of their passions which are in opposition to the determinations of their considered reasoning. We have a sensible part to our being as well as a rational, and what appears pleasant to the senses has the aspect of good, so the sensibly pleasant may also draw the will towards it. And it does so all the more powerfully the more one is physically disposed to the sensibly pleasant in question. So one is more drawn to drink when thirsty, for then drink appears all the more desirable; and so on in general whenever some passion is aroused.

The incontinent believe, when they reflect calmly, that such and such is not to be done, but in the particular case their passions are stirred and oppose this belief. The thought of the pleasure involved in satisfying the passion dominates and absorbs their minds, and the thought that to satisfy this passion is wrong falls out of active consideration (Aquinas, *CE:* §1062). This does not mean that the passion cannot be resisted, except perhaps in the case of those who are maddened by it, but only that it cannot be resisted without considerable effort and determination of thought. This is what the incontinent lack, though the continent possess it.

Of course, there are degrees of incontinence, and one may be incontinent in one thing and not in another. Moreover one's failure to resist a particular temptation need not mean one altogether loses self-control. One may be incontinent with respect to food and take too much, yet eat it calmly (Austin, 1961: 146, and note). Also one's failure to resist may be due to a failure to appreciate just what is involved in yielding rather than to the strength of the passion alone. So some who cannot ordinarily resist the desire to drink may suddenly find they can when it is forcefully brought home to them that their health or their finances are rapidly failing. What happens here is that the consideration of the good of resisting the temptation is reinforced by other considerations of good that previously were absent, or not present in precisely the same way.

There are, in addition, others who may not feel the passion at all, or not very powerfully, and so have no difficulty in doing what they think they ought. This may be a result of natural disposition (in some people certain passions are less easily and less powerfully aroused than in others), or of conscious development of the contrary habit; the irascible, for instance, who have learnt to control their temper, can now do so more or less as a matter of course without having always to make a special effort.

Incontinence is possible because of our freedom with respect to particular goods, so that we may opt for any of them whenever they are brought to consideration. In the incontinent the consideration of what is pleasant to the passion proves to be the operative consideration in the particular case, and removes the opposite consideration; not that it does so necessarily, for resisting the passion is also a good they can consider, and consequently choose.

The phenomenon of incontinence and the power of the passions is one reason why knowledge is not all-competent in matters of choice and action, or why there is a certain opposition between willing and thinking. But there are other reasons, reasons which have greater relevance as regards explaining why disagreements about what is to be done, or what is good, especially in morality, can be so intractable. This is not because such questions, of their very nature, fall out of the sphere of reason and knowledge, as some suppose, and are a matter for arbitrary choice, personal fancy, or social and educational upbringing to determine. On the contrary, good is a possible object of knowledge, and reason can work out how far good is attainable and in what ways. But this, like any other study, requires time and learning, and it is not to be expected that everyone will be equally capable of this.

Yet, even with those who do or can possess this knowledge, it can be rendered inoperative either by passion or by the will. One's thinking is itself subject to choice, and as desire may move one to think, so it may move one not to think, or not to think about this or that particular. So one can refuse to undertake a certain study, or refuse to listen, or to pay attention, to reason and argument. One may, indeed, be so committed to a certain good (because one has got so used to it, or because it is closely bound up with goods one holds dear, as one's reputation, or one's job, or one's life-work), that one simply refuses to consider giving it up. So one refuses to accept any reason or argument, however valid, for giving it up. One may, instead, have recourse to all kinds of specious objections or special pleading, or, in the last resort, simply refuse to listen at all, and attack one's opponent with abuse or violence. As this perversity is called into operation by a strong commitment to some good, or something apprehended as good, it is more likely to occur where good and commitments to good are especially involved, as is the case in moral matters, but not in purely theoretical ones.

The difficulties of persuasion in matters of good and morality are also increased by the existence in us of habits which may themselves accord or not accord with nature. Habits contrary to nature may severely hinder the perception of certain moral truths. To perceive something as bad, at least with respect to oneself, it is necessary to perceive it as somehow contrary to one's being; but those who have developed certain bad habits find the objects of those habits agreeable because they accord with the habit, however contrary to nature they and the habit may be. Here it will be hard, even perhaps impossible, to convince such people by reason alone that what they find so agreeable is really bad, for it is not faulty reasoning, but corrupt habits that stand in the way of their understanding, and reason by itself is not always, and certainly not always immediately, effective against opposed habits. It may, therefore, be necessary for them first to suffer some restraint or discipline so as to remove these habits, or lessen their hold, before reason can operate freely (Aristotle, *EN:* 1179a33-1180a14; Aquinas, *CE:* §§2137-2152).

It is unreasonable, in cases where one or more of the above factors is present, to expect people to be amenable to persuasion and the force of argument; and as these factors may prevail to a greater or lesser extent in most, if not all, moral contexts, it is hardly surprising that disagreements in moral matters should be frequent and intractable. Reason is insufficient here not because the questions are not decidable by reason, but because people are not amenable to persuasion by reason. There is a barrier in the hearer to the acceptance of what reason decides. To suppose that in questions where reason is competent, there all or most of us must be responsive to reason (as those do who appeal to intractable moral disagreements to show that moral or value questions are beyond reason) is to fail to notice the facts of human nature, and the interrelations between willing and thinking.

CHAPTER 9

Virtue and wisdom

THE NEED TO ASK ABOUT THE GOOD LIFE

So far the discussion of good, including the human good, has been confined to the consideration of the sense of the term 'good', or how it is to be understood. But for ethics this is, at most, a beginning, for its goal and primary object is the determination of what in fact is good and what life is really worth living. This, indeed, for each of us would seem to be what is the most important and most urgent thing, for it is of intimate concern to all to know what the good is. It is, besides, impossible to avoid having opinions here because one cannot avoid acting and making choices, and these are always made in view of something one holds to be good and worthwhile. But if one's opinions about the good are false, one will end up with something that is, overall and in fact, bad and worthless. That is why opinions about the good are both common and of the greatest seriousness, which is not the case, intrinsically, with other opinions, as about the square on the hypotenuse or the physical composition of the stars.

Most of us do, in fact, have an intuitive recognition of the importance of ethical questions. We are sensitive to accusations that we lack knowledge or good sense in these matters, or that we have spent our lives doing or pursuing something worthless. Thus we manifest our conviction that it is a major mistake to go wrong about the good life. Here, however, a certain inconsistency sets in, for the implication of this is that we should make a special effort to avoid such a mistake, and hence that we should devote time and energy to investigating the question; but this is not always done.

The reasons for this seem to be various. First of all there is the attraction of the things we already, by nature or habit, enjoy, and which we therefore hold to be obviously good, for it is indeed true that the good is enjoyable. So we do not want to give them up or to consider giving them up, despite the fact, which does not entirely escape anyone's notice, that not everything enjoyable is good. Second, there are the pressures and necessities of daily living which limit, and sometimes remove, the opportunity for reflection. Third, there is the difficulty of reflection itself, which requires care and attention, and even more so where there are so many differing views. Fourth, there is the pressure of prevailing opinions, which everyone in some measure feels, for it is hard to believe that opinions so widely held can be wrong; and this quite apart from the difficulty, and even danger, involved in resisting or opposing what the majority accept. Fifth, there is the belief that the truth is obvious and does not need searching out, for many suppose, especially in matters of such importance, that the truth must somehow be ready at hand, either to intuition or at any rate in the existing traditions. As evidence of the widespread character of this belief there is the fact that such traditions have often been traced to divine or quasi-divine sources.

Finally one may add the impediments of age. When one is young and most open to influence and change, then one is less disposed to sober reflection, being impelled rather by one's passions or one's impetuosity and eagerness to act, born of the natural exultation of youth. Conversely, when one is older and a certain calmness has settled on the soul, then one is less disposed to change and so less disposed to think it necessary to ask whether one should change, as one must if one asks seriously what it is good to do. Increasing age also brings increasing commitments and less leisure for thought.

We seem, therefore, to suffer many impediments to reflection which counter-balance the need, and the appreciation of the need, to reflect. In fact, if one ignores the natural desire to know and the effects of good education and laws, it often seems to be various external stimuli that induce us to think seriously about our lives, as public or private disasters and sorrows, exile, failure and so on. Perhaps this is the meaning of the oft-repeated dictum that learning comes through suffering. Chance too sometimes plays an important part. One wonders if Xenophon would have taken to study about virtue if he had not chanced upon Socrates in the way Diogenes Laertius relates.

There are some, however, who argue that the question of the good life is not as serious as it appears because there is no such thing, or rather because the good is what each finds to be so. Thus the answer is easy and immediate, not requiring much thought but only that ordinary experience of oneself which each possesses. This ignores, however, that what we find or feel to be good does not prove always to be so. Probably all of us have, from time to time, reflected that if we had known such and such beforehand we would not have acted as we did. Moreover, even if the good is personal to each, one might be wrong about this personal good if one lacks knowledge of oneself and of other things. It is evident, then, that some knowledge is required and that one cannot safely rely on what one feels. One must note also that to assert that the good is what each finds to be so is to assert, or claim to assert, something true. But how is it known to be true? Not just because it is asserted, for one could as well assert the opposite; nor because it is felt, for feeling does not reveal truth, or not always; nor, lastly, because it is commonly believed, for common beliefs can be false (as was the case previously over the movement of the earth). It is evident, then, that one cannot escape the need for some study, thought and reflection about the good life.

There are others who try to resist this conclusion by arguing that the question of the good life is meaningless, or at any rate misleading, because the term 'good' does not function in the way it is here made to function. But this does not help; it complicates the study of that question rather than makes it less urgent. Besides it has been argued in the previous chapters that good does function in the way required; so the question about the good life is legitimate, and so urgent and important as well.

If the question of the good life is as important as has just been argued, it becomes pressingly urgent to find out how to answer it. The claim that will be advanced here is that the answer can be found from an investigation of nature. This is because, as argued in chapter 7, the good is the *telos* or perfection of a thing's being and what this is is determined by nature. Nevertheless there are two difficulties about this claim that need to be faced: whether a common human nature is what matters, and, if it is, whether it is sufficiently definite to provide anything specific about a good life. As regards the first some argue that an appeal to a common nature could not be relevant since it is particular individuals one is dealing with. Human beings are first and foremost such individuals, and what suits or is best for the individual must be relative and private to each.

This question is not as difficult as it at first appears because in the end its truth is an empirical matter, to be decided by examination of given particulars. To say that several individuals share or may share a common nature is just to say that their particular being and potential for being are, despite individual differences, sufficiently alike for it to make sense to regard them as common. So one is not saying that each individual is altogether the same as the others, nor is one trying to ignore their differences; one is merely trying to locate them in context with each other. For if one happens to find a number of individuals whose being and potentiality for being are markedly alike, one is entitled to apply to all what is true with respect to this likeness – provided, of course, one makes allowances for, or leaves room for, the operation of particular differences in particular cases. And this, in fact, is all that will be attempted here in the discussion of human nature. What will be said about this nature must be understood as applying only to those particulars that do, as a matter of fact, share the sort of being in question.

As regards the second question, whether human nature is sufficiently determinate to specify a good life, it would seem not. Human acts and operations are of an almost limitless variety. Human beings display no uniformity in the way they live, but habits, customs and practices of the most diverse kinds seem to proliferate, according to diversity of times and places. In human life custom is king (Herodotus, *History:* III.38), and custom, unlike nature, is not uniform. What is more, the many things that belong, or may belong, to human nature are not only completely disparate from each other, but even contrary. It has, for instance, been pointed out that the following appear to be distinctive of human beings: making fire, having sexual intercourse without regard to season, despoiling the environment, upsetting the course of nature and killing things for fun (Williams, 1972: 73). It is hardly reasonable to appeal to any of these as a basis for determining the natural good; or, if it is reasonable to appeal to one, it is reasonable to appeal to all of them equally. Moreover, some of the things seemingly distinctive of humans, as the capacity for indiscriminate destruction, malicious cruelty, or excessive sexual activity, may reasonably be held to be bad. They are, in addition, opposed by contrary qualities, as the capacity to preserve and create, to be selflessly kind and loyal, to abstain totally from sexual pleasure, even in the face of extreme temptation. It appears by this, therefore, that it is distinctive of human beings to do bad and contradictory things, and hence that by nature they are no more directed to one thing than another. Nature, one may say, permits everything, or by nature everything is good.

One can reply briefly to this by saying that variety does not in itself prove anything, for humans act according to their thought and opinions and these may be erroneous, so that their acts and lives may be erroneous also. Hence there may be a naturally good life but humans fail of it because of ignorance or careless thinking, and there is no limit to the variety of forms that ignorance may take. Besides diversity itself may be naturally right, for different circumstances may make different things necessary or desirable, even when one and the same overall good is in view. But this reply is not altogether sufficient for, even granted that within the variety there is an erroneous and a true, this still leaves unanswered the question of how to separate out one from the other.

There is an answer to this, and it is one that, paradoxically, can be found precisely in that perplexing diversity of human actions itself. The clue here is too easily missed, for the diversity stands out so forcibly; yet it is a clue that is obvious enough; indeed perhaps that very obviousness is what serves to obscure it. The clue is simply that all this wide diversity is found to belong to one and the same thing, or that it is the one being of humanity that embraces all this multitude of diverse concrete formations. The being of human beings is a sort of universal being. This being would appear, indeed, of all being, to be the least limited and determined and the most open to all possibilities, present and future. Human beings are, one might say, the peculiarly universal animals. And to see this all one needs to do is to stand back and, instead of being caught up in the multiplicity of particulars, see that it is one being, the being of humanity, that is open to them all.

The universal openness of human nature is especially evident with respect to physical or bodily characteristics. Whereas all other animals are endowed by nature with determinate means of covering, defence and attack, and with determinate patterns of life in determinate habitats and climates, human beings are not. Other animals are covered with fur or hide or feathers, and they have claws, tusks or horns, or have swift speed, sharp eyes or a keen sense of smell. Humans lack such additions. They are born naked and defenceless. It might appear from this that while nature has been lavish in its care of other creatures, and given them a being fitted for a particular way of living in a particular environment, in the human case it has been mean and niggardly and left them fitted for nowhere.

This, however, would be a superficial judgement. Humans are not naturally fitted for nowhere, nor are they deprived of all specific determinations; rather they are naturally fitted for everywhere and they have a specific determination for this purpose, but, like that purpose itself, this determination is a universal one. It is the hands. These are the natural human protection and defence because they are the universal tool; the tool of tools, by which human beings are able to provide themselves with an infinite variety of coverings and weapons to meet an infinite variety of needs according to the infinite variations of time and place (cf. Aristotle, *PA:* 687a2-b25). It is because of physical nakedness, which allows human beings to receive an infinite variety of additions, putting on and taking off at need, and the possession of the universal tool of the hands, that they can be found, unlike the other animals, in all the corners of the earth, and indeed beyond the earth, in space and on the moon. Human activities are accordingly as diverse as they possibly could be.

In view of this it comes as no surprise that human beings are capable of sex at all times and in all seasons. In fact it would be more surprising if they lacked this capacity, for it would be a serious limitation to their universality. If they could not adapt in procreation to the varying needs of time and place, as they can adapt in other things, then while they could penetrate to all regions and climates of the earth, they would not survive there, having no offspring to follow them. One must conclude, therefore, that nature has been as lavish in providing for humans as in providing for the other animals. As the latter are marvellously adapted to their particular lives, so the former are marvellously adapted to their universal life.

But what is true of human physical characteristics is even more true of mental or spiritual characteristics. As has been discussed at length in previous chapters, human thought and desires have a universality to them that frees them also from any particular determination to this or that. It is here, in fact, rather than in any physical features, that human universality finds its source and, ultimately, its peak.

The universality that is manifest in human existence would be a mere potential universality and not an actually realised one if the capacity to realise it were lacking. But this capacity lies primarily and ultimately in the mind. Take, for instance, the universality of human physical existence, the nakedness of body, the instrumentality of hands, the seasonless sex. This universality could hardly be realised, nor could these parts or faculties be directed according to need to the infinite possibilities of time and place, if human beings were not aware of these possibilities, could not judge and assess them, and could not, according to their judgement, direct themselves with respect to them. That is to say, without a universal mind able to conceive and judge all things, and able to direct freely according to its conceptions, the universality in the rest of human existence would not be realised, or only fitfully and by chance.

The same goes also for the huge variety of societies, customs and patterns of life that are found in human history. This flexibility, this lack of determinacy to this or that particular pattern or manner of life, which prompted the remark that custom is king, must all be traced back to mind. For it is from the rich diversity of the mind itself, its capacity to conceive and invent diverse ways of being, that the rich diversity in human history springs.

Of course, if human universality depends on the mind, it also depends on the will and its freedom. If desire also were not universal so that human beings could wish and love good in all things, if choice were not free so that they could pursue any course of action at will and not be impelled by instinct or external stimuli, then equally they could not actually realise for themselves the universality of which they are capable. But all this just serves to reinforce the claim that it is in the mind that the source of this universality rests. For, as was argued in the last chapter, both the openness of will to all goods and the freedom to choose them depend on the openness or universality of mind to conceive all goods. It is mind that is prior and more basic; the other things are not actually universal without mind, but mind is universal in and by itself. It is, in fact, mind that is *par excellence* the universal power. It extends over the whole of being and embraces, by knowledge, the nature and existence of all things. There is nothing that may not, in principle, fall within its reach. Mind is, in a manner, all things because it can know all things; it is most unlimited and undetermined, or rather it is determined to being, and being excludes nothing.

One may also argue that all the diverse and creative human culture in art, literature, music, philosophy, science, technology and religion derives equally from the mind. The ability to engage in all these activities and to engage in them in a whole variety of ways depends on the ability to conceive and think through the many possibilities they present. Human beings could not be as diverse and rich in their constructions and creations if they did not have minds rich and diverse in conception.

On the basis of such reflections one may conclude that it is wrong to suppose, as many do suppose, that to stress reason or mind is to be unnecessarily narrow and limiting. They say it is to rule out from human life some of those things that are proper to humanity as well as desirable, such as spontaneity, or falling helplessly in love, which do not seem to be part of a life of rational self-control (Williams, 1972: 74-75). But this is to make at least two mistakes. It is to equate mind with a narrow, technological or scientific sort of reason, and it is to suppose that a life based on mind is a life only of acts of mind and not also of other faculties in subordination to mind.

If what is meant by mind is the capacity to grasp and comprehend being, there is, in principle, nothing whose goodness it cannot appreciate and embrace, including such goods as spontaneity and falling in love. To suppose that this is not so is to deny the openness of mind to being and the goodness of being, rather after the fashion of the thinkers discussed in the earlier chapters, especially chapter 5. But their narrow, scientific and instrumental reason, which does not know good or beauty or anything to do with value, has no valid claim to be the only or true account of mind.

Besides even if mind is the authoritative and directing power (because it is the universal power supremely), it does not follow that a complete human existence must consist simply of acts of mind. Rather it will more likely consist of the acts of all one's being, though, given that it is mind that knows and discriminates good, according to the judgement of mind. This may sometimes include the judgement that in certain contexts it is better for mind to withdraw and let emotion and spontaneity have their way, for it is certainly unreasonable to put reason where it does not belong, or in a way in which it does not belong. But it is worth pointing out that it is only reason that can judge this, and see how far, when and for what purpose the retiring of reason is reasonable. Spontaneity can be bad and dangerous as well as good, and so can falling in love, as the poets and dramatists often remind us. The discrimination of mind is required here as well as elsewhere, and precisely for the sake of spontaneity and falling in love themselves, to ensure that they lead to benefit and not to harm.

If the above argument is acceptable a way is made open for indicating how, despite its variety and flexibility, or rather because of its variety and flexibility, human nature can serve as a guide to discerning the movement or *telos* of human existence, and so (following the argument of chapter 7) to discerning the structure of a good life. This movement, one may say, is towards the *telos* of the universal, and hence ultimately towards the mind and the whole realm of being. This is the peak of universality. The movement towards universality in human being is a movement towards the mind, for, as has been argued, it is only by being joined to, and ruled by, mind that the universality of human being becomes a real possibility. But the mind too has a movement. This is the movement towards being, that is towards whatever is, for this is the object of the mind. It is by being towards being that mind too, together with desire and will, realises as much as possible its own universality.

Here one will find a reaffirmation of the answer suggested in the last chapter to the question whether just human nature or also the nature of the whole is relevant to the discernment of the human *telos* and the good. Both are relevant, for the one points towards the other. Human beings are particular beings within the whole, like other particular beings such as cats and dogs, trees and fish, but more than appears to be the case with any of these other particular beings, the particular being that belongs to humans has a capacity to transcend particularity and become something universal – both because natural and physical indeterminacy and inventiveness permit human beings to go anywhere and exploit, and adapt themselves to, almost any conditions, and also because their mind is open to the whole of being. Human nature points, one may say, beyond itself and its own particularity towards the universal being of the whole, as if being for or imitating the whole were, in a sense, the furthest and most complete realisation of its possibilities. At any rate, since humanity is open to the whole, the best it could realise would be the best within the whole, so that the best for human beings and the best simply would be the same. Human nature thus points to the nature of the whole as the guide to the most complete, perfect and best human life. It is consequently not so much human nature that reveals the *telos* of human existence, as the nature of the whole which is beyond it and towards which it exists. But this argument needs to be developed more fully.

THE UNIVERSAL LIFE

Universality, as has already been suggested, exists inherently in human being in that its parts and powers are in themselves undetermined and remain essentially open to a variety of possibilities. They need not remain so, however, because through living one tends to impose a determinacy or pattern on oneself through the development of habits. So people can become habituated to the performance of certain actions as to smoking, drug-taking, eating and drinking to excess, to stealing and other injustices, or to their opposites as honest-dealing, giving to the needy and so on. In the same way, and as a result of the same actions, people develop or become habituated to certain personal qualities, as generosity or meanness, courage or cowardice, envy or benevolence and so on. The original indeterminacy in human existence evidently admits of various superadded determinations to this or that, perhaps as many such determinations as are conceivable.

Doubtless it is possible to drift into such habits more or less without thought (as some people at any rate drift into habitual smoking and drinking), but it is not possible to do this sensibly. If it is, or can be, up to us to determine what habits or patterns of living to develop – and it is, for it is up to us generally to determine our lives by our own choices – then it is necessary to consider what habits to try to develop. Obviously one should try to develop habits that promote and preserve one's being, that help to bring it to its full actuality, for this is the good or the *telos*, rather than those that serve only to diminish and lessen it. But this needs elaborating.

It might have been possible for someone to have supposed, from the argument about universality and the mind's place in this, that nothing was implied in that argument to rule out the possibility that mind might exist, or at any rate be used, as an instrument for the universal or unlimited exercise of other parts of one's being. So one might suppose that universal mind could be, say, for universal or unlimited sex, or universal and unlimited drink, or universal and unlimited wealth and so on. But it seems evident that a life devoted to one of these things – which of course is a possible choice one can make – will, contrary to the words used to describe it, not be a universal life at all. Sex is just one among many possibilities or aspects to human existence, as are food, drink and wealth; so a life devoted primarily to just one of these, however extensive an amount it may have of the thing in question, will be a limited, narrow and particular life, because it will have no room, or too little room, for anything else.

If human nature is naturally universal and open to many possibilities and activities, then, as so open, it cannot become complete in its existence or realise its being to the full, if it becomes narrowed or limited to just one or a few of them. The most complete human life will be the least limited human life, and that means, in the context, the life that does not become absorbed or exclusively caught up in some limited activity or object. The most complete human life will be the life that, so to say, does not lose its balance. The one who can keep balance will be the fully actual and complete individual, the individual who has a well-rounded existence, who lives life to the full, and is not partial or one-sided in this way or in that (cf. Strauss, 1953: 127). It is the balanced individual who will be the truly universal individual.

The notion of balance in one's life and actions is the same as the traditional notion of virtue. To keep one's balance is to keep to the virtuous mean and to avoid falling over into the vicious extremes of the too much and the too little. The good individual will thus be the traditionally virtuous individual, if such an individual is the universal individual and the universal individual is the most complete and perfect individual. What is distinctive of virtuous individuals is not that they do not enjoy or engage in what vicious individuals enjoy, but that they do not enjoy or engage in them in the way vicious individuals do. They take or do each thing as, when, for what purpose, with whom etc. they ought, and not as, when, for what purpose, with whom etc. they ought not (Aristotle, *EN:* 1104b18-26, 1109a20-30; Aquinas, *ST:* Ia IIae, q64, a1, ad 2; q7). What is bad in human existence is not so much the things or the actions themselves as the 'how' of them. The many actions one is naturally open to are in principle good, for they serve to perfect and complete one's being; they are bad because they are pursued in the wrong way. And the wrong way can only be the way that has the effect of limiting, lessening and narrowing one's being, rather than of expanding and opening it up, for this will lead away from full actuality, and so away from the good and the *telos*.

But what is the right way, or what is the way that serves to preserve and extend one's being rather than the reverse? This is not something for which one can lay down any rules. It is experience itself, of ourselves as well as others, that reveals whether and in what respect our actions and desires are serving to limit our existence. One can nevertheless present oneself with certain images of what different sorts of character or life will look like, in order to get in this way something concrete by which to help form one's own judgement about where the right balance is likely to lie.

Take, for instance, the image of the miser, the person we say is excessively in love with hording money. What misers desire, of course, is not wrong or bad. Material possessions, including money, are necessary for human existence for they provide what is necessary for the health and preservation of the body. But what is wrong about misers is the excessive way they approach money and its acquisition. Doubtless they accumulate much more money than most of us, but consider how much they lose at the same time: friends, for instance, because they will not be generous nor devote time and attention to them, for they would rather spend that on getting money; decent clothes, housing, food and so on, because that requires them to spend money, not to horde it – and when they are forced by sheer necessity to buy something they do so grudgingly and meanly; finally peace of mind, because they are forever anxious that someone may discover their darling horde and come and steal it. Their miserliness thus makes them unbalanced and hence, quite literally, smaller – it deprives them of so much else they could also be and love.

This sketch of the miser could be repeated in an analogous way for the glutton, the lecher, or the person hungry for power. In every case, I think, what one would find would be various ways in which a certain kind or pattern of living is lacking in balance, and closes one off from one's potential for being instead of opening one up more fully to it. The virtuous, on the contrary, will not be limited in these sort of ways. They are the universal individuals, those who are for all seasons, who are ready and disposed to appreciate and acknowledge each thing or aspect of their being in its place and in its time, and are not blinded by any excessive preoccupation with, or even disgust for, some one sort of thing.

The condition for this state is, as perhaps will not be surprising in view of the previous argument, subjection of one's desires and one's passions to the discernment and discrimination of mind. For it is not one's desires themselves that can recognize or impose on themselves any limit or moderation; the miser's desire for money or the glutton's desire for food know no measure or limit, but are set on their object more or less infinitely (cf. Aristotle, *Pol:* 1257b23-1258a14). It is mind that will discern and so impose the limit, because it is mind, with its capacity to know all things, that will be able to know when things have gone so far that they threaten that balance which is the precondition of universality. Thus, the virtuous individuals, as the balanced individuals, will also be the rational individuals because they will have reduced the various parts of their being to subjection to mind. They will, so to speak, be on top of themselves, because they will naturally follow the movement of their mind and not be dragged about, even against their better judgement, by their passions (cf. Clark, 1982: 113-114).

Virtue is thus, in the most general sense, a disposition or habit that one has formed in oneself to follow the balance of reason. The different virtues arise because there are different ways and different desires in which this disposition to follow reason has to be realised (cf. Aquinas, *ST:* Ia IIae, q60). But there is no need to try and specify or catalogue these, because what matters here principally is the basic idea of a balanced life, not the details.

It is worth, nevertheless, saying a little more about the discernment of reason that creates and preserves balance. As already suggested, it is not rules that will be most relevant here. The balance itself is going to vary according to times, places and persons, for while the goal may be the same, there is no reason to suppose, given the variety of circumstances – both external and internal – in which one has to act, that the manner of realising it will be the same. The situation here is rather like the situation as regards health or dress. No one seriously doubts that what diet, exercise and habits of life in general will best conduce to health varies from individual to individual, and according to variations of climate, place, age and so on. Nor does anyone seriously doubt that a well-fitting dress or suit will vary according to the person, the materials, the purpose, and the state of fashion. The goal of course is the same in each case – health or a well-fitting garment – but the manner of realising it, and the precise form it will take in the given case, will vary enormously. Doubtless there are some rules to follow, but not slavishly, and anyway these rules themselves are typically generalisations drawn from experience. Besides, in the end, what really counts is the discernment of the relevant particulars in the here and now by the experienced eye of the doctor or the tailor.

When it comes to realising the balance of virtue, just this sort of experienced eye is required of the virtuous person also. The name traditionally given to this faculty is prudence (to be distinguished, therefore, rather sharply from what has typically been called prudence since Kant, which is a mere cleverness in discerning how to satisfy selfish passions). It has been well said that prudence is a sort of perception (Aristotle, *EN:* 1109b20-23, 1142a23-30). For the point of prudence is to determine in the here and now where the balance lies, and this requires especially discernment of the here and now and of how it admits of balance, which is a sort of perception. The best aid here will, again as already suggested, not so much be rules as images or patterns of characters and the typical acts of typical characters. Having an image or several images of what such and such a character is like and would tend to do (which must, by the nature of the case be concrete and particularised), will generally give one a better idea of how to imitate or avoid behaving like that sort of character in the here and now – though rules may also have a role to play (as indeed they do in medicine and dress-making; cf. Aristotle, *EN:* 1143b11-14). In this respect, in fact, one may compare the role played by the character and life of Socrates in the philosophy of Plato, or the role played by the character and life of Christ, Mohammed or the Buddha in the great religions. Prudence, one may say, thrives on characters rather than rules. That is why it would be a valuable thing to catalogue and consider lists of characters, such as one already finds in Theophrastus and La Bruyère. They used to play more of a part in moral philosophy and moral education, and perhaps they should do so again.

The balance of virtue is also, one may say, how one brings order and justice into one's being. Things are ordered when they are where they ought to be, and justice is observed when each thing is acknowledged in its place and given its due. Virtuous and balanced individuals are therefore just towards themselves and their own being, because through their balance they give a place to everything that they are (cf. Aristotle, *EN:* 1138b5-13), and so bring to fullness, as far as they can, that natural universality which is their own.

In fact, in this way the virtuous create themselves according to the image of the whole. For there is an order and justice in the nature of things that preserves their manifold variety and harmonises them into a unity. We generally call this by another name, the name of ecology or the ecological balance of nature. There is a more or less regular cycle of seasons in the natural world, and in each season different things have their time and place, coming to be and ceasing to be in order; and among the many creatures that inhabit the world, nature has generally struck a balance such that none entirely overwhelms or displaces another, even as regards predator and prey, but each gives way to each in turn. The balance and order of the natural world is observed too above us in the cycles of the heavenly bodies, which appear indeed to be more solid and stable than the cycles we observe below. Of course the balance, both above and below, can be disrupted; it is fragile. And perhaps we moderns – because of our own excesses, our own lack of balance in the treatment of nature and its forces – are, more than any others, in a position to know how fragile it is. But the balance exists, despite the behaviour of unbalanced people, and it is a sort of pattern of the balance of virtue. Thus the virtuous are a sort of imitators of the order and justice of the whole, who observe in themselves something of the geometry of the whole (Plato, *Gorgias:* 507e7-508a9), and so, in a way, complete that geometry by completing it in themselves.

Indeed, one is given, in this, another indication of the supremacy in human nature of mind. The order or balance that other things observe seems to exist in them by a sort of instinct and external constraint; they follow their appointed paths without knowing why or how. The reason that is in them is an unknowing reason. But in human beings at least this is not so. The order and balance of our life must be realised by our own efforts, by our own thinking out and our own choices. This, indeed, would appear to be our peculiar excellence, that we share in making the order of reason and are not driven, without knowledge, by the reason pre-existing in things. Other things, it appears, are realised, or brought to the actuality that perfects them, without knowledge, or by instinct and necessity, but we realise and perfect ourselves by reason and our own free choice. We govern, while all else seems to be governed.

The rule or the law that the virtuous thus impose on themselves in imitation of the whole and according to the balance of universality, is sometimes called natural law. This is a fair enough description insofar as it is nature that gives the virtuous their guide. Nature, however, only becomes in fact a law insofar as it is mediated through reason, or only insofar as reason, in judging what is naturally right, sets this up as the standard and measure of action. So it is not so much nature as nature mediated by reason that constitutes natural law. Natural law, therefore, requires the work of reason to become actual, and it is not actual, and certainly not known, without this work of reason. That is why if there is no or little cultivation of reason, then there will be no or little knowledge of natural law.

But one must not suppose from the term 'law' that this is something rigid and excludes variations; on the contrary variation must be an integral part of natural law. As has been argued, what is right varies according to circumstances. Consequently, if one is to speak of natural law, one cannot speak of it as if it were so absolute as not to require modification in particular instances, or as if it could be applied immediately without particular judgements about particular instances. Such a natural law will not be natural law, for it will not be in accord with the balance of prudence and virtue. There can be no natural law against this balance, and likewise there can be no natural right against it; for this balance is itself the natural law and the natural right. No one can have a right, least of all a right by nature, to behave unreasonably or to make unreasonable demands of others. The only right or law by nature that is absolutely right and admits of no exception or modification is to live according to the balance of reason. But this is so unspecific, and meant to be so unspecific, that it accommodates in advance all the exceptions and shifts that will need to be made in particular cases, for it is reason, as prudence, that judges exceptions.

The balanced and virtuous may thus be just towards themselves, but they will be yet more so towards their fellows. Justice is peculiarly the virtue of communal living since it gives each their due within the community; and the fact that communal life is a good is evident from the fact that it must be one of the objects of the natural movement of humanity. This can be seen at several levels.

First of all there is the level of physical existence. The needs of the body must be supplied otherwise life will altogether cease, but what provides these needs is one's own labour and above all the various arts. The cultivation of the arts which supply the needs of the body, as agriculture, fishing, house-building and so on, requires concentration, time and much practice and learning. As it is impossible for everyone to be skilled in everything, there naturally arises a need for division of labour and communication and exchange in the fruits of such labour. This is all the more necessary if one considers the needs not just of one individual but of the family. For where there is increase of numbers so there is increase of wants and need for greater cultivation of the arts. And that the family, or the union of males and females and the getting of offspring, is part of the human natural movement seems evident. Male and female have a natural attraction to each other in all creatures where the sexual difference is found. In the first place this appears to be for procreation, but in the human case, and even in that of other creatures, sheer friendship itself is as much, if not more of a motivating factor. The truth of this appears so evident it hardly needs further argument; daily observation furnishes all the evidence one could require.

To recognise friendship as a factor behind community, in opposition to mere physical need, is already to expand the scope of one's view. Friendship is a love of the other for the other's sake, whereas existence with others for the supply of physical needs is more for the sake of oneself. To see and love the other for the other's own sake is to appreciate and value for itself the good that one finds that other to be, and so it is to be drawn out of oneself, and the concern with one's own good, to a disinterested love of goods one finds to exist and flourish independently of oneself. This expansion of oneself out of oneself is evidently a part of that movement towards the universal that marks human nature. No one, indeed, is in themselves a universe, however versatile and flexible they may be. Many goods exist, because many things exist, apart from oneself, and to exist towards these goods, as would appear to be necessary if one is to exist towards the universal and the universe of goods, is to exist in one's appreciation and love of what is other than oneself. Such a love can doubtless exist from oneself towards all things, but it exists perhaps especially and most enjoyably towards one's fellows. For here there is, or can be, a mutual sharing of the good that each possesses, so that in one's friend one possesses goods that one cannot possess in oneself. One's friend becomes, in a sense, another self, and hence one's own self becomes more than oneself, because one becomes one's friend too.

This, one may say, is the ultimate point of political community and the art of politics, namely to create an association of friends where everyone lives not in and for themselves, but in and for the community which is both greater and better than themselves, and where they also, in their turn, become greater and better than themselves (Aristotle, *EN:* 1155a22-26). For a community of many is more universal in its realisation of a diversity of goods than a single individual. Humanity is capable of a whole world of skills, qualities, activities and achievements, but no one is capable of them all. Some are skilled as musicians, others as painters or sculptors; others again as carpenters, ship-builders or plumbers; yet others are skilled in the sciences and philosophy. Even within a given art, science or skill where one is oneself proficient, the proficiency of others enhances one's own because it advances the state of the art. Such things as the arts are better and more quickly developed by many working together than by one alone. A single person might advance an art or science in some way, but slowly and with mistakes and omissions, while with others to share with many of these hindrances are removed (Aristotle, *EN:* 1155a3-31; *SE:* 183b15-184b8). To be a part of a larger community is to be more of a world than one could ever be on one's own.

This communal dimension to human existence is manifested nowhere more clearly than in that gift which we possess more or less uniquely as our own – speech. Common speech makes common living possible because it is the medium by which we are most able to communicate ourselves to one another. It is not the only medium of course, but it is perhaps the most communal. It is moreover the medium through which we communicate in mind, for speech is the external expression of mind, and it is mind that is most distinctive of us and most fits us for universal life.

Because of the especial importance of community in the realisation of that universal existence which is the *telos* of human nature, the virtues of justice and friendship are among the finest and the best. These are the virtues that are most especially other-regarding and so most especially expansive of one's being, for they concern the task of giving each their due, of respecting and honouring the other's good, in possessions, in body, in reputation, in family, in friends, in mind; and in doing so just for that other's sake. Thus the balanced individual, the universal individual, the individual fully rounded in existence, is the just individual, the politically prudent and responsible individual; in a word, the complete friend (cf. Aristotle, *EN:* 1168a28-1169b2).

Neither justice nor friendship need to be defended in the way some writers do (as Hobbes, *Leviathan:* ch.15), who say justice is necessary or cannot be dispensed with because of private self-interest, in that, while it would be better in theory to be unjust, or to exploit others for one's own advantage, in practice it is better not to because one will not be able to get away with it. To suppose that self-interest is what is relevant here, is not only false, it is to fail to have any appreciation at all of what justice is and of its place in the perfection of human existence – to say nothing of friendship.

Since the topic of politics has arisen, and since it has appeared as a more complete advancement of human universality, it deserves some longer consideration.

Politics is about life in community, so the goal of politics must be the goal of common life. But the goal of common life, as of each separately, is the pursuit of the *telos*, the fullness and perfection of one's being. Hence political society must be ordered and arranged with a view to this end. The primary and central question in politics would appear, therefore, to be the question about how this may be done, or in what form of government perfection may best be realised. This question is identical with the question of the best regime (so much debated by ancient writers). That is why politics is above all the search for the best regime.

This search is not principally an empirical one, that is to say, it is not principally an investigation into the kinds and varieties of regime that actually exist in the world (though such a study will not be irrelevant), for there is no necessity that the best regime should actually exist anywhere in fact. The search for the best regime is rather a search within the mind itself. It is a matter of rational construction. This is not to say that politics is a matter of building castles in the air, as it were, for the best regime is not the result of any sort of construction, but of a construction according to the facts about human nature. It is founded and rooted in the idea of perfection (since it begins with this and reasons from it), and as this is founded and rooted in nature itself, it is far more rooted and founded in truth and reality than any other construction. Hobbes' desire for realist politics, therefore, is really a desire for politics that pays no attention to the truth of human nature, but only to the contingent facts about particular individuals and their particular passions at particular times and places, without any attempt to assess the goodness and badness, or the virtue and vice, of them. Hobbes' politics is, in other words, superficial.

The search for the best regime may thus be the principal task of politics, but it cannot be the whole of it. This is because politics, like ethics, is a practical study and must return, as far as possible, to the particular and reach judgements about how to attain the best here and now. The simply best, however, can seldom be realised, for what can be realised is determined by what the conditions are, particularly the condition of the people, and not every condition of the people allows the best to be realised. The people are, as it were, the materials for the political art to fashion towards the *telos* and the good. But just as any artist is limited by the materials (poor stone or clay limits the quality of the statue the sculptor can make out of it), so is the political artist. For instance, government requires consent, but what degree of the demands of reason and prudence the citizens can be got to consent to depends on the degree of reasonableness and prudence of the citizens, and that manifestly varies according to time and place. It is necessary, therefore, to moderate or qualify what is simply best towards the best possible.

That is why politics is not just a matter of finding the best regime but also of finding the kinds of acceptable regime. An acceptable regime is not the best but a good regime, because it is a regime that has the right end, or is directed to the perfection of all the citizens and not, say, to the pleasure or wealth of the ruler, or the dominant group. The acceptable is distinguished from the unacceptable precisely in that the unacceptable is directed to a bad end. Nevertheless it is evident that what is principal and determinative in all this is the best simply; the acceptable and the best possible are that degree of the best simply that can be realised in the here and now.

The task of deciding what is the best possible in any particular case, and of deciding how to set about attaining it, will clearly be an involved and complex one. It will be an exercise of prudence of the most difficult and most excellent sort. It is most difficult because it is harder to realise the order of reason where many are concerned than where few or one are. It is most excellent because it is better to realise perfection in many than in one alone. So it is especially for this reason that political prudence is a peculiarly important and elevated kind of virtue. Great political leaders, in fact, are distinguished by their possession of it. It is not present equally in everyone, and in some people it is perhaps not present at all. Human beings are differently disposed both with respect to potential, and, above all, with respect to the actualisation of their potential. Not everyone cultivates, or cares to cultivate, mind, nor does everyone cultivate it in the same way; for some do so in the arts, others in prudence, and others in the sciences and philosophy. For this reason there is found inequality among people, and inequality in the politically vital respect, namely in the cultivation of mind. If people are perfect insofar as they realise in themselves the *telos* of their being through mind and the rule of mind, and if they realise this differently and in different degrees, then all will not be equally perfect. There is, therefore, a place for subordination and division among the members of a political community according to the perfection and skills of each.

That people vary with respect to realisation of perfection and virtue is due, one may suggest, in large measure, to the fact that they are physical creatures. They are born of particular parents at a particular time and place, and are, therefore, subject to the conditions of birth and time and place, or, in other words, to what are called the accidents of fortune. Chance and accident, therefore, must not be supposed irrelevant to the understanding of human good, and the fact of one's being conditioned by what lies outside one's control, as well as by one's own choice and reason, must be included among those things that determine what is naturally right. The degree to which one may attain perfection, or realise in oneself the order of mind, depends on one's existing disposition to mind. But one of the things that most varies this is the state of the passions. These seem to be connected with the state of the body, so that as bodies vary so do the passions; hence some are naturally aggressive or impulsive or lustful, and others not so. Where there is less resistance to reason on the part of the passions, there it is possible to reach a greater degree of perfection, and to reach it more easily. And just as the state of the passions varies according to the state of the body, so it varies according to education and upbringing. One's tendency to anger or laziness, for example, may be lessened or increased by the training one receives, especially in youth when one is most impressionable. Thus good birth and good upbringing are of considerable importance in determining how far one can or will attain perfection (Aristotle, *EN:* 1103a14-b25).

Still, however this may be, the fact remains that, according to the argument traced above, it is the balanced and the virtuous individuals who are, or will be, the most universal and the most perfect examples of humanity. And if they chance also to live in a political community that is devoted to the best, and to have like-minded friends with whom to share the pursuit and possession of the universal good, one may count them to be truly fortunate. Or is it possible to be more fortunate yet?

THE ASCENT TOWARDS THE HIGHEST

One of the things one begins to learn through the goods of justice and friendship (and perhaps this is one of the principle concerns of education to citizenship) is the importance of the noble things, or those goods that are good in and for themselves, and not just, or even at all, relatively to oneself and the advantage or benefit they bring to oneself. The noble things, being selfless things, induce a certain self-forgetting – they take one out of oneself and one's concern with one's own subjective contentment. To love and serve one's fellows, one's country, and one's friends is already to live beyond oneself for the sake of what is other and higher than oneself.

One must not suppose that this appreciation of the selfless and the noble, of what is good independently of one's interest, is in any way rare, or hard to learn. The actions of courageous men and women in battle and adventure, who run great personal risk to save their country or their fellows, excite our admiration even from childhood. The heroes and heroines celebrated in poetry and song, or more recently in films and comic-books, have always fascinated, delighted and awed. Yet it is not the case that we admire or love these noble deeds because of any thought of our own selfish interest. Such deeds seldom have even the remotest connection with our own concerns here and now, and sometimes are directly contrary, for we admire a courageous enemy, not a cowardly one, even though the former does more to damage us (Hume, *Enquiry:* §174-5).

The selflessness of the noble is also evident from the fact that self-sacrificing actions are often the most admirable and most praised. The giving of one's life for country or friends, endurance of pain and torture to preserve faith and honour, are notable examples. They manifest a special triumph of reason, where the commitment to a higher good makes one scorn lesser ones. Particularly is this so where the noble deed exceeds what could normally be expected. So a supreme act of self-sacrifice, where one faces certain death, but which is necessary to save one's country or friends, extorts especial praise, even if it proves unsuccessful (Hume, *ibid., passim*, where one will find a rich and fertile list of examples to establish the same point; cf. also Strauss, 1953: 128-129).

What of course we admire here, even if we do not state it to ourselves, is the way in which these or those individuals are careless about their personal good for the sake of another and greater good, who live, in other words, beyond themselves. This love of the noble, which exists in us almost at once and with hardly any effort, even if we have not always the courage to imitate it ourselves, is just a further sign of one of the main contentions of the present chapter, namely that human nature is naturally not for itself but for the more and the other than itself. In this living beyond oneself one is most in accord with the natural order and *telos* of one's being.

It is this that many philosophers have come to forget. Who now among contemporary writers on morals speaks much, if at all, of the noble? But this is perhaps not surprising given the way the idea of the noble has been treated in that tradition of realism which, as argued in chapter 5, has done so much to form the content and context of contemporary moral philosophy.

The original writers in this tradition, especially Hobbes, wrote as if the noble did not exist at all. They confined themselves almost as a matter of principle (for it was not a matter of experience) to the conviction that only the selfish, the pursuit of private pleasure and advantage, was of any significance in human affairs; and they proceded to construct their political theories on this basis. They did this, of course, in order to be realistic, in order to make no demands that would require any prior moral reformation, any expansion of one's horizon or any education of one's desires from concern with self to concern with the greater than self and the noble. In this way they hoped to meet more surely with 'success'. But one can hardly call success what they meant by success. How can the attainment of anything but the really good and the best – or at any rate the striving for it – be called success? But if they abandonned the noble, and the expansion of human being towards the noble, they abandonned the really good and the best.

The sort of noble that has so far been most in question is the noble that one finds within the human world, the noble that exists particularly in selfless political action. But one must ask if there is a sort of living beyond oneself, towards goods better and more than oneself, that is a living beyond the context of human things altogether. For if the goal or *telos* of human existence is the universal, and this is ultimately the whole of being, one must not suppose, without argument, that this goal is discoverable within the human world. This would be arbitrarily to limit the scope of one's vision, and so one's openness to the truth of what is.

There is evidently more in existence than the human and the world of the human; we see this everywhere around us. There is a beauty and goodness and order in things that we can but contemplate and admire. For these things are beings, and beings other than ourselves; and each being is in its way a good because it is a being and so a realisation of a certain potential for being. To consider and contemplate these beings is to be made aware of a world that is larger than any human world may be, and so to be made aware of a goodness and reality that is larger than the goodness and reality of human existence. The mysterious order and beauty of the cosmos is fit to ravish any mind that has the leisure and the wit to contemplate it.

If humans are most fully themselves when they live towards the universal, it would appear that they are most fully themselves when they live beyond even the universe of the human, towards the universe of the whole cosmos. The *telos* of humanity would then be nothing other than the fullness of being itself.

Of course no one can become this fullness in themselves. One's own being is a limited and confined one, even if it has the capacity to be for what is beyond itself. But one can perhaps get as close to it as one can, and the only or best way to do this would seem to be by the contemplative activity of mind. The being of the whole and of the cosmos exists independently of our acting and our making; we do not bring it into being as we bring cities into being and the goods associated with moral and political life. So it is in contemplating the being of the whole just as it is, and in thus loving it just as it is, rather than in doing anything with it, that we will come nearest to it and exist most towards it. Besides, in practical activity and practical thinking our scope is limited and confined – there are many things we cannot affect at all. But to theoretical contemplation there is no limit other than the limit of things and being themselves. So if to exist towards the fullness of being is best, and one can exist towards being more fully in theoretical than in practical activity, then this existing towards will be found most of all in a contemplation, and a contemplative loving, of being.

This conclusion would seem to be appropriate also from the point of view of human nature itself. If mind is the highest human element, then the highest human activity would seem to be the highest activity of mind, the activity that extends it to its furthest, and this, as has just been argued, is found in contemplative rather than practical thinking. Besides, practical thinking is for an end beyond the thinking, namely the performance by us of some action, so it is subservient to that end; but theoretical thinking is not for anything beyond the thinking (except insofar as it is for the object of the thinking) so it is more of an end in itself and more of a good.

Accordingly in this sort of contemplative knowing and loving, which is what is meant by wisdom, one would seem to find the furthest reach of human existence, the way in which it attains its greatest degree of universality, and its greatest good. It will certainly have as object the highest and most complete good. For if being and goodness are one, that would appear to be most good which most is, and this in turn would appear to be no other than the cosmos of the world, namely that whole which contains in itself all that is through its seemingly endless cycles. Consequently if humanity is open to the whole and to all goods, so that its best is the best simply, then existing towards this fullness of being through loving contemplation, which is wisdom, would seem to be the best.

But is the cosmos the best thing there is? Is there nothing higher or beyond it? Although this is a question that does not properly belong to the study of ethics, it is a question that ethics cannot avoid. For if the human best, which is the object of ethics, is the best simply or the utmost limit of being, one cannot regard ethics as complete until one has pushed one's search for being to its limit. Ethics forces one into metaphysics.

The cosmos is just a name for all things together in their order, mutual relations and coexistence. Some of these things evidently come to be and perish, and perhaps, given time, this is true of all of them. Everything at any rate appears to have evolved over time, from stars and galaxies to animals and plants. And perhaps one day the whole will cease to be as it is supposed once, with the Big Bang, to have started to be. Or perhaps again it is eternal in that it oscillates backwards and forwards from one Big Bang to the next, in a never-ending series. At all events the cosmos and everything in it appears to be contingent and subject to change. What is in a process of becoming is not complete but can still be something more, though it might some time reach the fullness of its becoming. But in the becoming of the cosmos there seems never to be a time when everything that could be, or was, exists together. How many creatures may yet evolve, and how many that have evolved have already become extinct, never to return? The fullness of being that is possible in the cosmos is realised serially, as it were, and so is always, at any given time, incomplete. If the cosmos, then, is not actually all that it can be and is moreover contingent so that it is able not to be, does this point to some being that contains in itself the fullness of being all at once, and can never cease to be?

Since all that exists around us need not have existed, or since its existence is contingent, it remains a question why it does exist. Contingent things evidently exist because of something else, for if they existed by themselves, or were sufficient for their own existence, they would always and necessarily exist, which, however, they do not. And generally, since to exist is to be actual, contingent things, which need not exist, are related to their existence as what is potential to what is actual. But nothing potential reduces itself to actuality; nothing that is not in some way can make itself to be in that way. Therefore there must be something else actual that is the cause of the existence of contingent things. This something must be actual or have existence by itself, otherwise there would need to be something else beyond it to make it actual, and so on *ad infinitum*. But there can be no infinite regress here, for in a sequence of dependence the removal of a first entails the removal of all that comes after it, and in an infinite regress there is no first. Therefore there must be a first being which is its own existence and depends on nothing for its existence, while all other things depend on it.

If this is so, then such a supreme and first being will be the cause and source and model of all things, containing within itself the principles of all that is, or was, or could be, or will be. Since, of all the things we know, only mind is able to be all things or to contain in itself the principles of all things, this first being must be mind; or if not mind then something better than mind. At any rate, if anything deserves to be called god, this does. It will be the best and noblest being because it will, in a sense, *be* being, and so it will be the altogether, complete and inexhaustible good. Consequently if the aim here is to trace the beyond oneself towards which the movement of human nature is directed, the *telos* of human existence, and if this *telos* must be the same as whatever is best altogether and simply, then the god is this *telos*. The perfect individual, the most universal individual, and therefore the most fully human individual, will be the individual who exists for the god.

To exist for the god can, of course, only be, at least at its most complete, to exist in contemplating and loving the god, and not in some properly practical activity (how could the complete good be made good or better by any actions of ours?). But since the god is being and the fullness of being which gives being to every other being, to contemplate and love the god is, by implication, to contemplate and love all being everywhere and in everything. But this can hardly be if one does not have regard and respect for being. This may throw a different and perhaps clearer light on other elements in the structure of the perfect life discussed earlier. For the perfect individual will have respect for being everywhere, in the god first, but also afterwards in all else, as being so many images and reflections of the being of the god. So the balance that is virtue may be seen as the way one respects one's own being, and justice and friendship the way one respects the being of others. These others are first and obviously one's fellow humans and one's fellow citizens, but there is no reason, certainly no *a priori* reason, to deny this respect also to the other things in our world, especially living things.

Doubtless we need to use these things, or some of them, to preserve and make comfortable our own physical existence, and doubtless this is part of the order of being itself; but our gratuitous exploitation of them, to satisfy our whims and our insatiable passions for more, is not just to be unbalanced in oneself and so to fail to respect one's own being, it is also to fail to respect the being of those other things. It is also to fail to respect the being of the god. For they too are in their way divine, since, like everything else, they are, and to be is to be in some way a manifestation or an image of that fullness of being which is the god.

One may say that the perfect life, because it exists for the god or the perfect being, will be a life that honours and respects being everywhere, or gives each thing, as far as possible, its due in its place and in its time. And this perhaps is the ultimate meaning behind the traditional notions of natural right and natural law, namely that they are the expression of how it is the natures of things that give guidance to the just and good life. For to live respecting each thing as it truly is, observing in oneself and out of oneself the order of each thing's being, is to live respecting the nature of things.

But this is another and longer story. Nevertheless one may say that here one finds the especial glory of being human, namely that human being is the being for which to be is to contemplate and love and respect, in all its parts, the being of the whole and of each thing in the whole. Thus we will indeed be truly universal beings, if we mirror and preserve in our own mind and our own being the being of all other things. For this reason we are perhaps, of all beings, the most able to be, in our own being, an imitation of the god – the lesser god that mirrors the greater god. And this is the choice that is set before us, to become best ourselves by being most like that which is best of all, using this as the standard for all other choices also.

> What choice and possession, therefore, of the natural goods, either those of the body, or wealth, or friends, or the other goods, will most produce the contemplation of god, this is the best choice, and this standard the best. But

> the choice that through excess or deficiency hinders the worship and contemplation of god is bad (Aristotle, *EE*: 1249b16-21).

Of course there is no compulsion to make this choice. Our actions and our lives are our own to make or fashion as we will, and there is no one, and no thing, to force us to make the best choice if we ourselves do not wish it. But if we are wise, that is if (following the question Socrates put to Xenophon) we care to find out and pursue what is the best and most worthwhile life open to us, then this is the choice we will make and this the life we will most strive to realise for ourselves, and, as far as possible, for others. And if to be truly happy is to possess and enjoy true goods, then we may be sure that if any life is going to be truly happy, it will be this one. Or, if there is a life even beyond this one, that exists at a level more intimate to the divine and more caught up in the existence of the god, then this will be the happiest. At all events, whichever it is, those who are wise will live as far as they can with this life as their goal.

> One should not follow those who counsel humans to think of human things, and mortals to think of mortal things, but rather should one, as much as possible, make oneself immortal and do everything to live according to that in one which is best (Aristotle, *EN*: 1177b31-34).

Postscript

SOME CONCLUDING REMARKS

With this discussion of the human good the substance of my presentation and defence of ethical naturalism is more or less at an end. There may be more to say in elaboration of the details, or in reply to objections, but nothing more needs to be said to explain the theory itself. Enough has been presented to permit a judgement of it to be made. Still it may be well if a brief summary is given of the course of reasoning that led to it.

The first task was to understand the non-naturalist case against naturalism in its several forms and in its foundations. This was the function of the first part of the book. The result was that not only did naturalism turn out not to have been refuted, but that also none of the various forms of non-naturalism were themselves able to withstand examination. Moreover, none of the contemporary critics of non-naturalism had themselves done any better. Their own criticisms and their own alternative theories could as little stand up under scrutiny. Perhaps the main reason for this was that these critics differed much less from their non-naturalist opponents than they thought they did. In several crucial areas their leading ideas were the same, namely that thinking and willing are radically separate, that nature is non-teleological or value-free, that good is tied to actual desires or interests, and that there is no highest human good.

This posed a puzzle. Why such uniformity even between professed opponents? Why is substantially the same vision of the world shared by all? For it was not as if they spent much time defending that vision, since, on the contrary, they usually assumed it. The vision seemed to be somehow obvious. It is the privilege, and perhaps also the nemesis, of philosophy to question the obvious. The questioning in this case proved to require going back in history. This was because these thinkers themselves pointed in that direction. All, or nearly all, referred back with approval to certain authors of the past, attributing to them the origination of their own views. An examination of those authors, or the principal ones among them, in the historical progression of their thinking, helped to reveal the place of scepticism about knowledge and being and the sense of the noble in the generation of non-naturalist convictions.

This research, together with the discussion of contemporary authors, significantly clarified the problem of non-naturalism and exposed to view those areas that were most in need of examination if any headway was to be made in satisfactorily solving it. The areas were: being, knowledge, nature, willing and thinking, and the noble. The resulting discussion of these areas has filled the second part of this book. What has been argued for in the several cases is a non-sceptical account of knowledge and being, a cognitive account of good, a teleological account of nature, an interactionist account of willing and thinking, and a perfectionist account of the noble. It is thus that I have endeavoured to state, or restate, a defensible account of naturalism, an account that has, I contend, the merit both of answering the genuine questions raised, and points made, by non-naturalists and naturalists alike, and yet of not falling into the faults of either.

That account, as is clearly evident and as was pointed out in the Introduction, has been significantly informed by the thought of certain ancient authors, notably Aristotle and Aquinas. This is because they seemed to me to have provided the necessary elements from which a true account could be constructed. Of course, I did not merely repeat what they said. I presented the account in my own terms and as mediated through my own understanding. Direct quotations have been few. The answers in philosophy, like the questions, may ultimately change little, but the task of stating and defending them is always new. That is because each generation has to think things through again for itself. A truth may get handed down from philosophers who have already died, but it has to be appropriated by the living for themselves. Moreover the circumstances in which that appropriation goes on are usually different, sometimes radically so from the circumstances in which the truths appropriated were originally presented. That is certainly the case between us and Aristotle and Aquinas, as it was between Aristotle and Aquinas themselves.

Some will doubtless say that I have followed the wrong tradition. But enough has been argued about the merits and insights of that tradition to show whether or not they are right. Others will accept the tradition but say I have misunderstood or misappropriated it. There are, in fact, several such thinkers who will want to say something like this, in particular A. MacIntyre (1984), J. Finnis (1980, 1983), and G. Grisez (1965, 1983). Since I have already argued at length against those who do not accept the tradition, it is perhaps fitting that I should not end without also saying something about these other opponents who do not accept my interpretation of it.

MACINTYRE ON ARISTOTLE

While MacIntyre does refer approvingly to Aquinas, his principal inspiration and mentor is Aristotle, for it is Aristotle's notion of virtue that he is concerned to develop and defend. His strategy is to show that the restoration of such a notion is necessary because of the contemporary crisis in moral philosophy. He discusses the historical roots of this crisis in some detail, which he then follows with an account and defence of the notion of virtue.

In his historical account of the emergence of non-naturalism in ethics, MacIntyre expresses his debt to Anscombe (1984: 53). It was she who first inspired him and gave him the clue to understanding. She did this, it appears, in two ways: first, by indicating the nature of the contemporary crisis, and second by indicating how it came about. Contemporary moral thought, he says, is in a crisis of incoherence and disorder, for it is trying to make sense out of pieces that one cannot make sense out of (chapters 1-3). The reason for this is that all the pieces are not there, and the ones we have cannot be made to fit together without the others. We only have some of the pieces and not all because we are the heirs of a fractured tradition, a tradition that has not come down to us whole. MacIntyre endeavours to demonstrate the truth of these claims by an analysis of contemporary moral discourse, and by an analysis of the tradition and how it came to be fractured (chapters 4-6).

While I can agree with some of what MacIntyre says about some of the historical figures he examines, I disagree with his overall thesis. This is mainly because of his dependence on Anscombe. He repeats, for instance, her claim that the non-naturalist 'ought' arises from a lost theory of divine law (111, also 53, 60). As I argued in chapters 4 and 5 above, this is false. Non-naturalism arose in another way and for other reasons. Moreover it is not an incoherent collection of fragmented survivals from the past. On the contrary, it is a clear, and intelligible theory about the nature of goodness and moral reasoning. Of course, even though intelligible and clear, the theory may still be false and, in places, incoherent (as I have argued). But so may other theories without its thereby being the case that some fragmented tradition underlies them.

Part of the trouble with MacIntyre's book is his heavy slant towards history and his consequent tendency to explain philosophical positions in historical terms. This is something for which he has already been criticised by Frankena (1983). He has, it is true, endeavoured to reply to this criticism, but not successfully. Philosophical arguments and positions, he says, cannot be examined in abstraction from their social and historical contexts because they do not exist in abstraction from these contexts. So in order to describe, assess, support or refute a philosophical position one must engage in historical enquiry. But while it is true that philosophers only exist and philosophise in particular times and places, it by no means follows that therefore they cannot escape the bounds and limitations of time and place in their thinking and reasoning. For nothing has yet been said to show that thought and reason are not precisely those features of human beings whereby they can and do escape such limitations. Indeed, that thought and reason are such features is what it means to say that they are universal powers, for the universal is distinguished from the particular precisely in not being bound to the here and now. Most pre-modern philosophers accepted the universality of reason (as MacIntyre himself admits in the case of Aristotle; 146-147), although they could not have been ignorant of the fact that human beings only live, speak and write in time.

MacIntyre, however, expressly rules out this universality of reason. He says that "there are no general timeless standards", that "there are *no* grounds for belief in universal necessary principles ... except relative to some set of assumptions", and that the theory he adopts is "a kind of historicism which excludes all claims to absolute knowledge" (266, 268, 270). But these assertions are false because they are self-refuting. MacIntyre's position is, in fact, a combination of conceptual relativism and fallibilism, and so it falls foul of the criticisms I directed against Lovibond and Lee in chapter 4 above. If absolute knowledge is impossible, if all claims to knowledge are corrigible, if the most one can say is that this is the best so far, then is the theory that asserts this likewise non-absolute, corrigible and, at most, the best so far? If so it becomes impossible to say that absolute knowledge is impossible, for we can never be sure that some absolute knowledge might not eventually turn up. So is the thesis that no knowledge is absolute and incorrigible supposed itself to be absolute and incorrigible? Then in that case some knowledge is absolute and incorrigible, namely the thesis itself. So whatever one says, MacIntyre's position is refuted.

The historical and social context of human existence is not just imported by MacIntyre into his general thesis about thinking and reasoning, it is also, not surprisingly, imported into his version of Aristotelian virtue. He is well aware of the teleological character of Aristotle's ethical teaching (the fact that human nature is to be understood functionally), and of the biological and physical basis on which this teleology rests (52-53, 58, 184), but while he accepts the teleology, he rejects the biology and the physics; he replaces both with history (146-147, 159, 162, 179, 196-197). The goals of human life, in terms of which the virtues need to be understood, are found, not in nature, but in social roles and a more or less coherent tradition of viewing a whole human life as a unity. This is why he puts so much emphasis on the idea of social and historical narrative. Human beings are what they are because of their social and historical position, and their good is determined for them accordingly. One is, indeed, not so bound by one's history (the 'social narrative' into which one is born) that one cannot move out of or beyond it, but one never moves into something non-historical or universal, some good for human beings as such, as opposed to some particular good for some particular human beings living in some particular here and now. For there is just no such universal good to move into (221-222).

Aristotle's fault in MacIntyre's eyes is that he was blind to history and could not see that his theory about virtue just reflected the limited historical situation of human beings in fourth century Greece. That is why he believed (falsely) that it was universal and founded on some unchanging human nature (159). This argument of MacIntyre's presupposes the truth of historicism, but, as has already been argued, historicism is self-refuting. If MacIntyre really wants to show Aristotle is wrong he will have to confront Aristotle's theory directly, and not indirectly through an appeal to history. The same applies also to Aristotle's doctrine of being. It is being, and not history, that constitutes for Aristotle the universe of thought and discourse. Particular beings may come and go, but their being, what it is for them to be, does not, and thought is focussed on being (Simpson, 1981, 1985). That is why the truth about things is always the same and always accessible, whatever the historical conditions may be from which one starts. If one tries to deny this one will fall into the historicist and fallibilist difficulties of MacIntyre, Lee and Lovibond.

FINNIS AND GRISEZ ON AQUINAS

The principal inspiration of Finnis and Grisez is Aquinas. However, their interpretation of him is, in large part, determined by their acceptance of the non-naturalist understanding of the 'is/ought' distinction. Both Finnis and Grisez are emphatic in asserting that no move from 'is' to 'ought' is logically possible, and their reason for this is the same as that given by Hare, that 'ought'-judgements move to action while 'is'-judgements do not (Finnis, 1981: 33-36; Grisez, 1983: 105, 108, 112 n.21). To use other terms, 'is'-judgements are theoretical and 'ought'-judgements are practical, and according to Finnis and Grisez, reason is practical of its own nature, not by any deduction or derivation from theoretical reason, so that ethics has no foundation in theory (Finnis, 1983: chapter 1; Grisez, 1983: 195-196).

These claims have generated considerable controversy (cf. Schultz, 1985). And not surprisingly, for they constitute a denial of the usual picture of Aquinas' theory according to which normative conclusions about what to do are in some way derived from factual or theoretical assertions about nature (McInerny, 1982: 55ff.; Veatch, 1985: 95-98, 102-104). But Finnis and Grisez say that this picture is false to the historical Aquinas. In their view Aquinas does not derive his normative claims from a theoretical grasp of nature, for he does not derive them at all; he regards them as self-evident (Grisez, 1965). Moreover, this is practical self-evidence, because what is established is ethical prescriptions of the form, 'Life, knowledge, health (and so on) are goods to be pursued'. These are said to be self-evident in that they are primitive, and cannot be argued for by appeal to anything prior, as for instance by appeal to some presumed facts of nature (though one can argue for them negatively in the sense of showing that any attempt to deny them overthrows itself; Finnis, 1981: chapter 3, esp. 73-75).

Such is the interpretation. What Aquinas himself says is that the first precept of law, namely that good is to be done and pursued and evil avoided, is self-evident, and that all the other precepts of natural law are founded on this one, so that all those things are to done or avoided which practical reason naturally apprehends as being good or bad. That which practical reason apprehends as good and to be pursued is everything towards which human beings have a natural inclination.

These inclinations fall into three groups according to the three grades of being: simple existence, animal existence and rational existence (*ST:* Ia IIae, q.94, a.2).

Practical reason, not theoretical reason, is clearly what is operative here, but practical reason differs from theoretical reason only in its end, in that it seeks truth with a view to action while theoretical reason just seeks truth (*ST:* Ia, q.79, a.11). Practical reason thus moves to action while theoretical reason does not. But the first origin of movement to action is the will, so it follows that practical reason only moves to action insofar as it is itself moved by the will (*ST:* Ia IIae, q.17, a.1). Reason is practical or action-guiding, then, only on the supposition of an act of will underlying it. What this must mean is that any propositions about nature will be of no consequence for practice unless and until they are taken up into some willing, or some thinking that itself presupposes some willing. But this clearly does not mean, nor does it imply, that if such propositions are interpreted theoretically, they cannot in any sense serve as the basis of any reasoning about how to act. All that is meant and implied is that, to serve as this basis, such propositions have first to be transposed into the practical sphere (as I argued above in chapter 8). One can see this already in the case of the first precept of law, for what this is, in effect, is a taking up into practical reason of the theoretical truth that the notion or idea of goodness is 'that which all things desire' (*ST:* Ia IIae, q.94, a.2).

Of course it may be that most of the time our understanding of human goods arises in a practical context, so that we understand our own natures from within instead of, as in our knowledge of other creatures, from without; and it may be that this is the best or the primary way in which we do so understand (Finnis, 1983: 12, 20-25). But this does not mean that the nature of the human good can only be expressed practically and not theoretically. Both ways are possible. Moreover the sort of experience from which we understand the human good is likewise, or can be, theoretical and practical, that is, both a matter of investigating human beings, and a matter of oneself making judgements of what it is worthwhile to do. It is not the case that the only way of doing this is through practical reason, or through theoretical reason, and not both; nor is it the case that it is impossible to move from one to the other, or that, if there is movement, it is only one way (either from theoretical to practical or from practical to theoretical but not both). However, it is the case that an account of the human good has not been sufficiently established until it has been founded back on truths of nature. This is always in the end an affair of theoretical reason, for it is always in the end an affair of saying what is in fact the case. Such truths are necessarily stated in 'is'-judgements, or theoretical judgements, not in the 'ought'-judgements of practical prescriptions. This remains so even if one's initial way into grasping some of these truths was through the exercise of practical judging. That is why Aquinas is rightly considered a naturalist, and rightly judged to have based his ethical teachings on theoretically articulated truths of nature (cf.*ST:* Ia IIae, qq.1-5).

Finnis and Grisez are driven to deny this because of their acceptance of the non-naturalist understanding of 'is' and 'ought'. And they are driven to this denial, in turn, by their failure to incorporate into their theory any discussion of the interplay between willing and thinking such as I gave above in chapter 8, and such as figures prominently in Aquinas (*ST:* Ia IIae, qq.6-17). Once this interplay is accepted, the 'is/ought' distinction, or the action-guiding force of good, ceases to be at all problematic, and one is saved from making such paradoxical assertions about Aquinas as that he was not a naturalist or did not base his ethics on nature.

Bibliography

Abbott, T.K., Edition of Kant's *Critique of Practical Reason and other works on The Theory of Ethics*. Longmans, London, 6th. ed., 1909.
Anscombe, G.E.M., 1963, *Intention*, 2nd. ed., Basil Blackwell, Oxford.
Aristotle, *Analytica Priora et Posteriora*, ed. Ross. OUP, Oxford, 1964.
   De Anima, ed. Ross. OUP, Oxford, 1956.
   Eudemian Ethics, Loeb Classical Library. William Heineman Ltd., London, 1967.
   Ethica Nicomachea, ed. Bywater. OUP, Oxford, 1894.
   Metaphysica, ed. Jaeger. OUP, Oxford, 1957.
   Magna Moralia, Loeb Classical Library. William Heineman Ltd., London, 1958.
   De Partibus Animalium, ed. Bekker (vol.5). Oxford, 1950.
   Physica, ed. Ross. OUP, Oxford, 1950.
   De Arte Poetica, ed. Bywater. OUP, Oxford, 1911.
   Politica, ed. Ross. OUP, Oxford, 1957.
   Topica et Sophistici Elenchi, ed. Ross. OUP, Oxford, 1958.
Aspasius, *In Ethica Nicomachea Commentaria*, ed. Heylbut, in *Commentaria in Aristotelem Graeca*, vol.19i. Berlin, 1889.
Austin, J.L., 1961, *Philosophical Papers*, ed. Urmson and Warnock. Clarendon Press, Oxford.
Avicenna, *Metaphysics*, trans. Morewedge. Columbia University Press, New York, 1973.
Ayer, A.J., 1946, *Language, Truth and Logic*, 2nd. ed. Victor Gollancz, London.
Bacon, F., *The Works of*, in several vols., ed. Spedding, Ellis and Heath. Longman and Co., London, 1857-1874.
Bambrough, R., 1979, *Moral Scepticism and Moral Knowledge.* RKP, London.
Barnes, J. (et al.), 1975, *Articles on Aristotle*, vol.2, ed. J. Barnes, M. Schofield, R. Sorabji. Duckworth, London.
Barnett, S.A., 1967, *'Instinct' and 'Intelligence.'* Macgibbon and Kee, London.
Bernstein, R.J., 1976, *The Restructuring of Social and Political Theory.* Basil Blackwell, Oxford.
Clark, S.R.L., 1975, *Aristotle's Man.* Clarendon Press, Oxford.
   1982, *The Nature of the Beast.* OUP, Oxford.

Crombie, I.M., 1962, *An Examination of Plato's Doctrines*, vol.I. RKP, London.
Daniels, N., 1975, *Reading Rawls*. Basil Blackwell, Oxford.
D'Entrèves, A.P., 1970, *Natural Law*. Hutchinson University Library, London.
Descartes, R., *Discours de la Méthode*, ed. Gilson. Libraire Philosophique J. Vrin, Paris, 4me. ed., 1967.
The Philosophical Letters of, ed. and trans. A. Kenny. Clarendon Press, Oxford, 1970.
Diogenes Laertius, *Vitae Philosophorum*, ed. Long. OUP, Oxford, 1964.
Euclid, *Elementa,* ed. Stamatis. Teubner, Leipzig, 1969.
Finnis, J., 1980, *Natural Law and Natural Rights*. Clarendon Press, Oxford.
1983, *Fundamentals of Ethics*. OUP, Oxford.
Foot, P., 1967, *Theories of Ethics*. OUP, Oxford.
1978, *Virtues and Vices*. Basil Blackwell, Oxford.
Frankena, W.K., 1983, 'MacIntyre and Modern Morality' in *Ethics*, vol.93, 579-587.
Grisez, G., 1965, 'The First Principle of Practical Reason' in *Natural Law Forum*, vol.10, 168-196.
1983, *The Way of the Lord Jesus*, vol.1. Fransiscan Herald Press, Chicago.
Hare, R.M., 1952, *Language of Morals*. OUP, Oxford.
1963, *Freedom and Reason*. OUP, Oxford.
1972, 'Rules of War and Moral Reasoning', in *Philosophy and Public Affairs*, vol.1, 166-181.
1975, 'Abortion and the Golden Rule', in *Philosophy and Public Affairs*, vol.4, 201-222.
1979a, 'On Terrorism', in *The Journal of Value Inquiry*, vol.13, 241-249.
1979b, 'What is Wrong with Slavery?', in *Philosophy and Public Affairs*, vol.8, 103-121.
1981, *Moral Thinking*. Clarendon Press, Oxford.
Heidegger, M., 1966, *Discourse on Thinking*, trans. Anderson and Freund. Harper and Row, New York.
Henry, D.P., 1972, *Medieval Logic and Metaphysics*. Hutchinson University Library, London.
Herodotus, *Historiae*, 2 vols., ed. Hude. OUP, Oxford, 3rd. ed., 1927.
Hobbes, T., *Leviathan*, Everyman's Library, Dent, London, 1914.
Hudson, W.D., 1969, *The Is/Ought Question*. Macmillan, London.
1970, *Modern Moral Philosophy*. Macmillan, London.
Hume, D., *A Treatise of Human Nature*, ed. Selby-Bigge. Clarendon Press, Oxford, 1888.
Enquiries, ed. Selby-Bigge. Clarendon Press, Oxford, 2nd.ed. 1902.
Husserl, E., 1965, *Phenomenology and the Crisis of Philosophy*, trans. Q. Lauer. Harper and Row, New York.

Jaffa, H.V., 1952, *Thomism and Aristotelianism.* University of Chicago Press, Chicago.

Kant, I., *Gesammelten Schriften*, in several volumes, edited by the Prussian Academy. Berlin, 1910 ff.

Lee, K., 1985, *A New Basis for Moral Philosophy.* RKP, London.

Locke, J., *An Essay Concerning Human Understanding*, ed. Yolton. Everyman's Library, Dent, London, revised ed. 1964.
Two Treatises of Government, ed. Laslett. CUP, Cambridge, 1963.

Lovibond, S., 1983, *Realism and Imagination in Ethics.* Univeristy of Minnesota Press, Minneapolis.

McDowell, J., 1978, 'Are Moral Requirements Hypothetical Imperatives?' in *Proceedings of the Aristotelian Society*, vol.52, 13-29.

Machiavelli, N., *Il Principe e Discorsi sopra la Prima Deca di Tito Livio*, ed. Bertelli. Feltrinelli, Milan, 1979.

MacIntyre, A., 1984, *After Virtue.* University of Notre Dame Press, Notre Dame, 2nd. ed.

Mackie, J.L., 1977, *Ethics: Inventing Right and Wrong.* Pelican. Penguin Books, Harmondsworth.

Maritain, J., 1959, *The Degrees of Knowledge*, trans. G.B. Phelan. Geoffrey Bles, London.

Moore, G.E., 1903, *Principia Ethica.* CUP, Cambridge.

Murdoch, I., 1970, *The Sovereignty of Good.* RKP, London.

O'Meara, D.J., 1981, *Studies in Aristotle*, ed. D.J. O'Meara. Catholic University of America Press, Washington D.C.

Plato, *Opera*, ed. Burnet. OUP, Oxford, 1901ff.

Platts, M., 1979, *Ways of Meaning: an Introduction to a Philosophy of Language.* RKP, London.

Rawls, J., 1972, *A Theory of Justice.* OUP, Oxford.

Rosen, S., 1969, *Nihilism: A Philosophical Essay.* Yale University Press. New Haven and London.

Rousseau, J-J., *Du Contrat Social.* Garnier Flammarion, Paris, 1966.
Discours sur les Sciences et les Arts, (First Discourse). *Discours sur l'Origine et les Fondements de l'Inégalité parmi les Hommes*, (Second Discourse). Garnier Flammarion, Paris, 1971.

Scheler, M., 1980, *Problems of a Sociology of Knowledge*, trans. Frings. RKP, London.

Schilpp, P.A., 1968, *The Philosophy of G.E. Moore*, ed. Schilpp. Open Court Publishing co., La Salle, Illinois.

Schrödinger, E., 1967, *What is Life?*, and *Mind and Matter.* CUP, Cambridge.

Schultz, J., 1985, 'Is-Ought: Prescribing and a Present Controversy' in *The Thomist*, vol.41, no.1, 1-23.

Simpson, P., 1981, 'Aristotle's Theory of Assertions: a Reply to William Jacobs' in *Phronesis*, vol.26, no.1, 84-87.
1985, 'The Nature and Origin of Ideas: the Controversy over Innate

Ideas Reconsidered', in *International Philosophical Quarterly*, vol.25, no.1, 15-30.
Stevenson, C.L., 1944, *Ethics and Language*. Yale University Press, New Haven.
1963, *Facts and Values*. Yale University Press, New Haven.
Strauss, L., 1953, *Natural Right and History*. University of Chicago Press, Chicago.
Telfer, E., 1980, *Happiness*. Macmillan, London.
Thomas Aquinas, *In Decem Libros Ethicorum Aristotelis ad Nicomachum Expositio*, ed. Spiazzi. Marietti, Turin, 1964.
In Duodecim Libros Metaphysicorum Aristotelis Expositio, ed. Cathala and Spiazzi. Marietti, Turin, 1950.
In Octo Libros Physicorum Aristotelis Expositio, ed. Maggiolo. Marietti, Turin, 1965.
Quaestiones Disputatae, vol.1, ed. Spiazzi; vol.2, ed. Bazzi et al. Marietti, Turin, 1964, 1965.
Opuscula Philosophica, ed. Spiazzi. Marietti, Turin, 1954.
Summa Theologiae, in 5 vols. Biblioteca de Autores Christianos, La Editorial Catolica, SA, Madrid, 1961-5.
Veatch, H.B., 1985, *Human Rights. Fact or Fancy?* Louisiana State University Press, Baton Rouge.
Wallace, W.A., 1979, *From a Realist Point of View*. University Press of America, Washington, D.C.
Warnock, G.J., 1962, Edition of Berkeley's *Principles of Human Knowledge*, with other writings. Fontana Library of Philosophy, Collins, London.
1971, *The Object of Morality*. Methuen, London.
Whately, R., 1877, *Elements of Rhetoric*. Longmans, London.
Wiggins, D., 1976, 'Truth, Invention and the Meaning of Life', *Proceedings of the British Academy*.
Williams, B., 1972, *Morality*. CUP, Cambridge.
Wilson, J., 1961, *Reason and Morals*. CUP, Cambridge.
Wittgenstein, L., 1961, *Tractatus*. ed. and trans. Anscombe and von Wright, RKP, London.
von Wright, G.H., 1963, *Varieties of Goodness*. RKP, London.

Index

action-guiding, 63, 65f., 69, 73, 82, 91f., 212, 217f., 268f.
actual, 156f., 251, 257; a. in analysis of change 173-180
actuality, 187f., 189f., 192, 239, 241, 245
admiration, 253
admire, 255
Albert the Great, 190
alcohol, 225
Allan, D.J., 43
amoralism, 80
analogy, 32, 143-146
analytic, and synthetic, 12f., 15, 21f., 25, 36f., 116, 188-190
ancient philosophy, tradition, writers etc., 1f., 116f., 129, 174, 185, 190f., 249; *see also* older
animals, 145, 198, 218, 234f., 257, 268
Anscombe, G.E.M., 83-88, 90, 98f., 102f., 204, 263f.
appetite, *see* desire, sensible a., will
Aristotle, 2, 20, 31, 71, 88, 112, 144f., 147, 165, 190, 192, 198, 206, 210, 212, 215, 218, 225, 235, 241-244, 248f., 252, 260, 262f.; A. and ambiguity of good, 32f.; A. and doctrine of being, 266; A. and MacIntyre, 263-266
Aspasius, 207
assent, with will, not mind, 74
attitudes and beliefs, in Stevenson, 40-56
audible, *see* visible
Austin, J.L., 226
autonomous, 84, 93, 97, 117, 124
autonomy, 120f.; a. of will, 130
Avicenna, 145
Ayer, Sir Alfred J., 36f., 38-40, 55, 103, 116, 195

Bacon, Sir Francis, 110, 113-115, 120f., 169, 184f., 192
bad/evil, as not choosable, 203; b. as nothing, 160f.; *see also* good
balance, the b. of virtue, 240-246, 258
balanced individual, 249, 252
Bambrough, R., 75, 76, 80, 84
Barnes, J., 43
Barnett, S.A., 198
beauty, 237, 255
becoming, a thing b. what it is, 177
begging the question, 17, 59, 62, 90, 130
being, 117, 122; idea of b., 139-148; the b. of dynamic things, 175f.; b. as universe of discourse and thought, 266; philosophic and pre-philosophic grasp of b., 142
being-for, being-towards, 201
Bernstein, R.J., 187
Big Bang, 257
Bloomsbury Group, 35
Brutus, 44
La Bruyère, 244
Buddha, 244

Caesar, 44
Cambridge professors, and car workers, 36
capitalism, 114, 118
capitalist, 119; c. lackeys, 95; c. politics, 118
castles, building c. in the air, 250
cat, 145, 188, 238
categories, ten c., 70f., 145
categories, in Kant, 121
catholic, 85
cause, sufficient c. in choice, 220-224; two sense of sufficient c., 222
change, nature of, 157, 170-180, 189f.; idea of c. not found in modern science, 181-183
characters, importance of for moral education and prudence, 244
choice, choose, etc., 74f., 136f., 196-198, 201f., 204f., 229, 236, 239, 245, 259f.; freedom of c., 218-224; c. and incontinence, 224f.; c. as always of the good, 203f.; c. in Hare, 63-81; *see also* freedom, will
Christ, 244
Christianity, 83
Christmas, 162
cities, 255
city, classical ideal of, 118, 120
Clark, S.R.L., 179, 198, 207, 242
cognition, in Stevenson, 40-56; c. in Hare, 71f.
community, necessity for and nature of, 246-248
conceptual analysis, 5f., 33, 37
contemplate, contemplating, contemplation, etc., 255f., 258-260
contemporary philosophy, authors, writers etc., 3-7, 33f., 254, 262; *see also* modern
contemporary moral crisis, 263f.

275

contingent things, as not necessarily existing, 257f.
Copernicus, 121
cosmos, 255, 256f.
country, 252f.
Crombie, I.M., 88
custom, as king, 233, 236

daffodil, 176, 178
Daniels, N., 5
deadlock, in morality, 89, 195; *see also* intractable
definition, nature of, 19-22, 27; d. of circle, 20; persuasive d. in Stevenson, 40f.; empirically false d., 188
deliberation, 219, 223
Descartes, R., 114f., 120f., 169, 185f., 192, 199
description, normative d., 179, 190
desirable, 86-88, 153f., 233; *see also* good
desirability characteristics, 86-88, 103; *see also* Anscombe, Lee
desire, 16, 65, 87f., 92, 99, 112, 123, 125-127, 129, 136f., 165f., 196, 199, 202, 205-207, 208-213, 215-217, 235f., 238, 241f., 261; d. and good, 148-155; d. and thought, two ways related, 210f.; education of d., 254, *see also* Plato; d. for bad under aspect of good, 203; natural d., 97, 156f.; *see also* will, good
despair, of speculative metaphysics etc., 115, 117, 120, 128, 139, 166; *see also* sceptical
Diogenes Laertius, 4, 230
disagreement, in attitude and belief, 41, 43
discrimination, 79
divine law ethics, 83-86
divine, everything as in some way d., 259
dogs, 218, 238
duck, 177
duty, 117; d. in Kant, 125-128
dynamism, see change

eagle, 177
ecology, as the order or justice of the whole, 244f.
education, 230, 254; e. to citizenship, 252
Einstein, 46, 181
emotivism, chapter 2, 57
empiricism, 128f., 141, 164, 166; e. and debt to science, 187-189; origin or inspiration of e., 115f.

empiricist, empiricists, 5, 21, 116, 117f., 121, 138f., 157, 176, 192f.
end, goal, etc., 96, 156, 158, 192, 209, 211, 213-216, 243, 251, 255f.; people as e., 126; ultimate e., 105f., 206f.; *see also* telos, good
D'Entrèves, A.P., 85
epistemic implication, *see* Lee
epistemology, epistemological etc., 14, 21, 26, 47, 117f., 120, 122, 130, 139, 164, 166, 169, 186f.,
essence, and mystification in Hare, 77
ethical, and legal, in Kant, 126
ethics, 13, 16, 22, 25, 29f., 49, 101, 135, 187, 192, 211, 218, 229, 250, 267; e. and metaethics, 30-34; e. and ordinary usage, 39f., 50; e. and views of nature, 109; e. as completed by metaphysics, 256; subject matter of e., 31, 58; the great task of e., 75f.
Euclid, 20
experiments, 114, 184, 190f.
expressivism, 98

fact, facts etc., 1, 5, 37, 45, 67, 74, 89, 116, 135, 137, 164-166, 193, 196; f. and values, 30, 54f., 86, 90, 98f., 109, 113; f. as neutral, 45, 82, 194f.; *see also* value, science
fallibilism, 103f., 265f.
family, the, 247
fanatic, fanaticism, 79, 128
fate, 81
fidelity, 198
final cause, finality 114, 165f.; *see also* telos
Finnis, J., 263, 266-269
fire, 222
fish, 31, 144f., 201, 238
flies, 201
Foot, P., 11, 15, 19, 39, 44, 69, 76, 82, 84, 86-98, 99f., 102-104, 106, 204
football, 219
form of life, 100f.
formulae, mathematical, 181
fortunate, 252
fortune, accidents of, 252
fox, 176
Francis of Assisi, St., 35
Frankena, W.K., 15, 19, 31, 32, 264
freedom, 74f., 78-82, 120, 123f., 128, 130, 137, 204; *see also* choice, spontaneity, will
friends, friendship, 198, 241, 247-249, 252f., 258-260
functional terms, 76, 86, 90

Galileo, 121

geometer, geometrician etc., 16, 17, 19, 26
geometry of the whole, 245
giraffe, 177
glutton, 242
goal, *see* end, telos
God, 83-85
god, 257-260
good, *see* most of all chapter 6; also: 28f., 32, 78, 89f., 135, 138; g. and action, 31f., 36, 66, 91f., 99, 155, 209-218; g. and definition in Moore, 11-27; g. and desire etc., 43, 61, 164, 116f., 148-155; g. and evil, 155f.; g. and cognition, knowledge, being etc., 2, 28-30, 35, 38, 77, 127, 130, 137, 154f., 213; g. as analysed from perspective of human g., 33f., 59, 73, 160, 218; g. by nature, as determinable by nature etc., 29, 75, 155, 167, 180, 195, 202, 204f., 208, 213f., 217, 232-239; the apprehended g., 200, 202, 205, 216, 219; complete, ideal, supreme etc. g., 35f., 111f., 129, 202, 205-208, chapter 9; formal idea and material instantiation of g., 24, 38, 61, 70; function of term g., 5, 138, 231; the human g., 3, 54, 59, 163, 192, 201f., 205, 211, 252, 261f., 268f.; nature of moral g., 160; nature, meaning of g., 12-27, 42-44, 59-66, 92; real and apparent g., 88, 154, 203f.; *see also* standard, supervenience, will
Greece, 266
Grisez, G., 263, 266-269

habit, 218, 239, 242
hands, significance of, 234f.
happiness, happy etc., 23f., 207-209, 260
Hare, R.M., chapter 3, 5, 21, 83f., 86-88, 91, 96f.,101, 103, 106f., 109, 116, 125, 135-138, 162, 163-165, 194, 198, 204, 216f., 221, 225, 267
hedonists, 25
Hegel, G.W.F., 110
Heidegger, M., 187
Heisenberg, W., 46
Herodotus, 233
heroes, 253
heroines, 253
historicism, 265f.
Hobbes, T., 105-107, 110-114, 116-119, 123, 205-207, 249f., 254
honesty, 198
honour, 253
horse, 146-148, 188, 218

Hudson, W.D., 4, 11, 21, 24f., 33, 39, 57, 59f., 68f., 83-91, 93, 97, 199
human, humans, and discerning the good everywhere, 162f.; h. and inequality, 251f.; h. as bound by history, 264-266; h. as causes of action, 218, 224; h. as governing, not governed, 245; h. being, beings, 74f., 77; h. being/nature in Hobbes and Bacon, 112f., in Kant, 122-129, in Rousseau, 119f.; h. being as a being-for or being-towards, 201, 238f., 256, 259f.; h. nature and the beyond h. nature, 238f., 254-256; h. nature as one and unchanging, 232, 266; h. perfection, 202, 205; h. right, 241-244; indeterminacy of h. nature, 106, 232f.; h. perfection, 128, 200; glory of the h., 259; *see also* god
Hume, D., 21, 47, 84, 107, 110, 116-118, 120-122, 125, 129, 139f., 157, 173, 201, 253
Husserl, E., 187
hypotheses, 181

idealism, 186
identity, 172-174, 180
Iliad, 144
immortal, 260
imperative, 64-78, 103, 125f., 137, 215-217,
incontinence, 224-227
indicative, *see* imperative
insects, 201
instruments, 191
integrity, 198
intellect, 198f.; *see also* mind
intractable moral disagreements, 227f.; *see also* deadlock
intuition, in Moore, 19, 23, 35f., 38
is and ought, *see* ought

Jaffa, H.V., 2
just, justice, 38, 42, 91f., 197f., 214, 244, 246-249, 252, 258

Kant, I., 21, 79, 84, 96, 107, 110, 116f., 120-130, 139, 157, 188, 198, 213f., 217, 243
knowledge, *see* being, fact, good, mind, thought, truth

language, *see* ordinary
language philosophers, 58
law, laws, 230; divine l., 213, 264; first precept of l., 267f.; natural l., 85, 245f., 259, 267f.; physical, scientific l., 171, 181, 183

277

learning comes through suffering, 230
lecher, 242
Lee, K., 98, 100-104, 265f.
Leif Ericsson, 41
leopard, 176
liberty, 197; see freedom
living things, as combination of potentials, 178
Locke, J., 14f., 18-22, 25f., 31f., 38, 47, 110, 114, 116-118, 139, 141, 186
logic, 42-44, 52, 58, 62, 80, 101f., 107, 130, 138, 210, 216f.; l. and limit of desire, 86-88, 204; l. and valid inferences, 64, 214, 216f.
logos, 147
love, disinterested l., 247f.; falling in l., 237f.
Lovibond, S., 39, 97-101, 265f.
Luther, M., 110

Machiavelli, N., 111
MacIntyre, A., 85, 106, 263-266
Mackie, J.L., 105
malaise, 106
Margites, 144
Maritain, J., 183, 187
McDowell, J., 97
McInerny, R., 267
meaning, 14, 21, 23, 33, 36; m. in Hare, 62f., 69f., 72, 87f., 164; m. in Stevenson, 40-42, 48-50, 57f., 164;
measurement, 191
metaethical, metaethics etc., 53f., 77, 166, 218; see also ethics
metaphysical, metaphysics etc., 33, 122, 128, 130, 166, 209; m. as the completion of ethics, 256
mind, 140f., 143, 155, 189, 202, 213, 216, 223, 242, 248, 250-252, 255; m. and truth, 149f.; m. as determined to being, 236f.; m. as supreme in humans, 245, 256; importance of m. in human universality, 235-238
miser, 241f.
moderation, 242
modern moral philosophy, philosophers, thought etc., 11, 22, 37, 107, 128f.; see also contemporary
modern philosophy etc., 21, 30
modern science, see science
modern tradition of realism, chapter 5
Mohammed, 244
monkey, 176
moon, 235
Moore, G.E., chapter 1, 35-38, 40, 44, 47, 56f., 59, 68, 82, 91f., 116, 153f., 163-166, 188, 194, 218

moral philosophy, 4-7; job of m. p. in Moore, 33
Mother Teresa of Calcutta, 35
motion, see change
Mounce, H.O., 88-90, 93, 97
movement, of human existence, 238, 246f.
Murdoch, I., 97f.

natural, non-natural in Moore, 28-30
natural perfection, 127f.
natural philosophy, 168-180, 185-187, 193, 209; n. p. compared with modern science, 190-193
natural right, 119f., 245f., 252, 259
natural world, 156f.
naturalism, 1-3, 5, 28, 38, 63f., 77, 104, 108f., 192f., 194; definition of n., 1, 5; older form of n., 82, 106, 108; ethical n., 167, 261f.; paradoxical n. in Stevenson, 54
naturalist, naturalists, 19, 60f., 66, 68, 202, 261f., 269; n. and field biologists, 176
naturalistic, as factual, 63; n. definition, 29; n. ethics, 12
naturalistic fallacy, fallacy of naturalism etc., 5-7, 11-28, 30, 37, 40, 46, 55, 59, 68f., 82, 104, 107-110, 125, 166; see also naturalism
nature, 1, 3, 29f., 35, 113f., 118, 122, 129f., 141, 195, 200, 209f., 230, 236, 245f., 267-269; n. as combination of two correlative ideas, 179; n. as lawgiver, 85; n. as non-functional in Hare, 76, 86; character of n., 105f., 233-235; torturing n., 113; vision of n., 109f., 129, see also good, science, teleology, value
neustic, 65
Newton, Sir Isaac, 121, 181
noble, nobility etc., 84, 117f., 123f., 128-130, 253, 262; nature of the n., 253f.; god as noblest being, 258
non-naturalism, 5, 91, 108, 130, 163, 187, 263f.; n-n. come of age, 125; complete form of n-n., 129
non-naturalist, non-naturalists etc., 53f., 85f., 90, 98, 99-103, 135, 192, 194, 199, 202, 218, 261f., 267, 269; n-n. and freedom, 81; n-n. and good, 86-91; n-n. and ought, 83-86
normative, see description

obligation, see duty
Odyssey, 144
older philosophers, thinkers etc., 28, 33, 43f., 49, 67, 70f., 75, 88, 96f., 106,

108f., 111f., 123, 127f., 131, 166, 198, 265; *see also* ancient
one, idea of o., 146f.
open-question argument, 22-27, 38, 60f., 116, 163-165
opera, 219
opinions, pressure of prevailing o., 230
order/hierarchy, 112
ordinary awareness, experience, 183-186, 190f.
ordinary discourse, language, speech etc., 27, 107, 136f., 141f.; appeal to o. d. etc., 23, 39f., 58, 60, 62, 67
ought, 38, 58, 93, 95-97, 107, 123, 127, 129, 194f., 225, 264; o. as subordinate to good, 213; categorical o., 123, 213; is and o., 83-86, 102f., 117, 124f., 209-218, 267, 269

peace, 111f., 206
people, the p. as matter of the political art, 250
perception, sensation, 114, 140f., 186, 168f., 185
perfect, perfection, 127f., 163, 202, 205f., 232, 249-252, 258-260,
Phillips, D.Z., 88-90, 93, 97
philosophy, answers and questions change little, 262f.; function of p., 3; impoverishment of p., 34; nemesis of p., 261f.
phrastic, *see* neustic
Plato, 2, 4, 31, 91, 96, 112, 244, 245
Platts, M., 97
please, and yes, 64f.
pleasure, pleasant etc., 14-16, 18f., 23-26, 41, 87f., 105, 116, 118, 126, 138, 165, 197, 225f., 251, 254
politics, political etc., 192, 211, 218, 248-251, 255
potential, potentiality etc., 156f., 174f., 187-190, 192, 205, 221, 232, 235, 242, 251, 255, 257; p. as not reducing itself to actuality, 80, 221, 257; p. in analysis of change, 173-180
power, person hungry for, 242; p. of things in science and technology, 184, 191
practical syllogism, 215; p. thinking, 209-218, 255f., 267-269
prescribe, prescription, prescriptivism etc., 63-65, 69, 74, 78f., 84, 125, 269; *see also* Hare
propaganda, propagandists, 55, 57f., 185
protestants, 83
prudence, 243f., 246, 250f.

rational methods, 45f.
ravish, 255
Rawls, J., 6, 106
realism, chapter 5, 168f., 187, 254; r. defined, 112; r. and transformation of good, 116-130
realist, 129f.
Reformation, 83, 85
Reformers, 111
regime, 249-251
religion, religions, religious etc., 53, 84, 87, 110, 198, 213, 236, 244
right, 37, 58, 126; *see also* natural r., rules
Rosen, S., 100
Rousseau, J-J., 117-121, 124, 130, 198
rules, in determining the human right, 241-244

satisfaction, complete, 206f.
sceptical, 84, 103f., 114f., 117, 186, 262; *see also* despair
Scheler, M., 113
Schilpp, P.A., 28, 31, 32
schools, schoolmen, 115f.
Schrödinger, E., 183, 186
Schultz, J., 267
science, modern s., 29, 36f., 44f., 67f., 89, 97, 101, 110, 113-115, 121f., 124, 130, 143, 167f., 180, 186, 209, 236, 248; s. and concern with measurement, 181-184; s. and concern with parts, not wholes, 184f.; s. and dynamism, 157; s. as abstraction from the real, 187f.; s. as compared with natural philosophy, 190-193; s. as neutral or value-free, 5, 29f., 76, 82, 99, 108, 165f., 192; s. as two-edged sword, 53; nature of s., 141f., 181-187; role of s. in rejection of naturalism, 30; role of s. in Stevenson's ethics, 40, 45-56; value of s., 190-192
scientists, and specimens, 72f.
sensation, *see* perception
sensible appetite, as distinguished from will, 196-198
sex, 233, 235, 240, 247
Sidgwick, H., 11
Simpson, P., 140, 266
social contract, in Rousseau, 120
social practices, *see* Lovibond and MacIntyre
Socrates, 4, 7, 91, 230, 244, 260
speech, significance of for human community, 248
spiders, 200f.
spontaneity, spontaneous, 80f., 93,

279

124f., 129, 221, 224, 237f.; *see also* freedom
standard, standards etc., 71, 82, 90, 265; s. by nature, 74f.; assenting to s., 61f.; good as s., 71, 162
Stevenson, C.L., chapter 2, 33, 55, 57f., 63-68, 82, 84, 90, 92f., 101, 106, 109, 113, 116, 135-137, 163-165, 195
Stoic, 29f.,
Strauss, L., 2, 84, 100, 111, 205, 240, 253
strawberry, strawberries etc., 60, 64f., 69, 138, 140, 151-153, 158, 162, 165
substantive moral questions, 4-6, 38
success, 254
supervenience, supervenient etc., 78f., 82, 138, 148, 154, 163-166; *see also* good, transcendental
synthetic, *see* analytic

teleology, teleological etc., 76f., 88, 97, 127, 179-181, 185, 190, 261f., 265
Telfer, E., 208
telos, 71, 179, 192, 232, 238f., 241, 248-251, 254-256, 258; *see also* end
terrorists, 89
Thanksgiving, 162
tradition, the t., *see* ancient
Theophrastus, 190, 244
theoretical thinking, *see* practical
theories, 181, 183
theory of mind, 217
thing, and being, 147f.
Thomas Aquinas, St., 2, 70, 75, 145, 149, 158, 160, 165, 198f., 206, 209, 212f., 216f., 219, 226, 228, 241, 243; T.A. and Finnis and Grisez, 266-269; T.A. on practical and theoretical reason, 267-269
thought, and being and sensation, 139-141, 266; t. as free, 219; *see also* will
Thrasymachus, 91, 94f.
transcendental, 70f., 166; *see also* supervenient
trees, 238
triumph of reason, 253
Trotsky, L., 95
truth, 51f., 149f.
tulip, 176

uncertainty principle, 46
universal, human being as universal, 234f., 238

universality of reason, 265
universe of goods, 247
utilitarianism, 79

value, 29f., 42, 63, 85, 195, 197, 237; v.-free, 29f., 261; science as v. requiring separation of facts and v., 54; *see also* fact, good, science
variety, 233, 238
Veatch, H.B., 267
verbal dispute about names, 18, 20
virtue, 91, 117f., 120, 123, 249f., 258, 263, 265f.; v. as balance, 240-246; v. in Kant, 126f.; definition of v. 242; job of v., 105f.
virtuous, 4, 7, 241f.; the v. as for all seasons, 242; the v. as images of the whole, 244f.
visible, 199f., 222
vision, of nature, world, among naturalists and non-naturalists, 109f., 113, 129, 261f.
volition, volitional etc., 42f., 57, 65, 127, 129f., 135, 137, 164f., 210, 212, 216-218; *see also* will

Wallace, W.A., 187
Warnock, G.J., 14, 31, 35, 66, 104-106, 186
weakness of will, *see* incontinence
Whately, R., Archbishop, 94
whole, being, nature of the w. etc., 205f., 238f., 259
Wiggins, D., 97
will, 124f., 129f., 163, 210, 268; w. and thought, 3, 43f., 71, 92, 107, 117-119, 124f., 131, 155, 218f., 227, 238, 261f., 268f.; w. and freedom, 67, 218-228, 236; w. and thought in Hare, 57, 67f., 80f., in Stevenson, 42; w. as moved by thought, 194-200; nature of w., 67, 199; w. and sensible appetite, 196-198; *see also* choice, freedom
Williams, B.A.O., 4, 106, 233, 237
Wilson, J., 4
wisdom, 198, 256
Wittgenstein, L., 21, 121
world, 248, 255; *see also* vision
worship of god, in Aristotle, 259f.

Xenophon, 4, 7, 230, 260

Yes, *see* please

MARTINUS NIJHOFF PHILOSOPHY LIBRARY

1. D. Lamb, Hegel – From Foundation to System. 1980. ISBN 90-247-2359-0
2. I.N. Bulhof, Wilhelm Dilthey: A Hermeneutic Approach to the Study of History and Culture. 1980. ISBN 90-247-2360-4
3. W.J. van der Dussen, History as a Science. The Philosophy of R.G. Collingwood. 1981. ISBN 90-247-2453-8
4. M. Chatterjee, The Language of Philosophy. 1981. ISBN 90-247-2372-8
5. E.-H.W. Kluge, The Metaphysics of Gottlob Frege. An Essay in Ontological Reconstruction. 1980. ISBN 90-247-2422-8
6. D. Dutton and M. Krausz (eds.), The Concept of Creativity in Science and Art. 1981. ISBN 90-247-2418-X
7. F.R. Ankersmit, Narrative Logic. A Semantic Analysis of the Historian's Language. 1983. ISBN 90-247-2731-6
8. T.P. Hohler, Imagination and Reflection: Intersubjectivity. Fichte's *Grundlage* of 1794. 1982. ISBN 90-247-2732-4
9. F.J. Adelmann (ed.), Contemporary Chinese Philosophy. 1982. ISBN 90-247-3057-0
10. E.N. Ostenfeld, Forms, Matter and Mind. Three Strands in Plato's Metaphysics. 1982. ISBN 90-247-3051-1
11. J.T.J. Srzednicki, The Place of Space and Other Themes. Variations on Kant's First Critique. 1983. ISBN 90-247-2844-4
12. D. Boucher, Texts in Context. Revisionist Methods for Studying the History of Ideas. 1985. ISBN 90-247-3121-6
13. Y. Yovel, Nietzsche as Affirmative Thinker. 1986. ISBN 90-247-3269-7
14. M.H. Mitias (ed.), Possibility of the Aesthetic Experience. 1986. ISBN 90-247-3278-6
15. P.E. Langford, Modern Philosophies of Human Nature. 1986. ISBN 90-247-3370-7
16. K. Galloway Young, Taleworlds and Storyrealms. 1987. ISBN 90-247-3415-0
17. W. Horosz, Search Without Idols. 1987. ISBN 90-247-3327-8
18. R. Ellis, An Ontology of Consciousness. 1986. ISBN 90-247-3349-9
19. M.C. Doeser, J.N. Kraay (eds.), Facts and Values. 1986. ISBN 90-247-3384-7
21. S.J. Bartlett and P. Suber (eds.), Self-Reference. 1987. ISBN 90-247-3474-6
22. P. Simpson, Goodness and Nature. 1987. ISBN 90-247-3477-0
23. I. Leman-Stefanovic, The Event of Death: A Phenomenological Enquiry. 1987. ISBN 90-247-3414-4
24 V. Tejera, Nietzsche and Greek Thought. 1987. ISBN 90-247-3475-4
25. S. Satris, Ethical Emotivism. 1987. ISBN 90-247-3413-4

Series ISBN 90-247-2344-2